M.S. HARKNESS

TINDERELLA

UNCIVILIZED

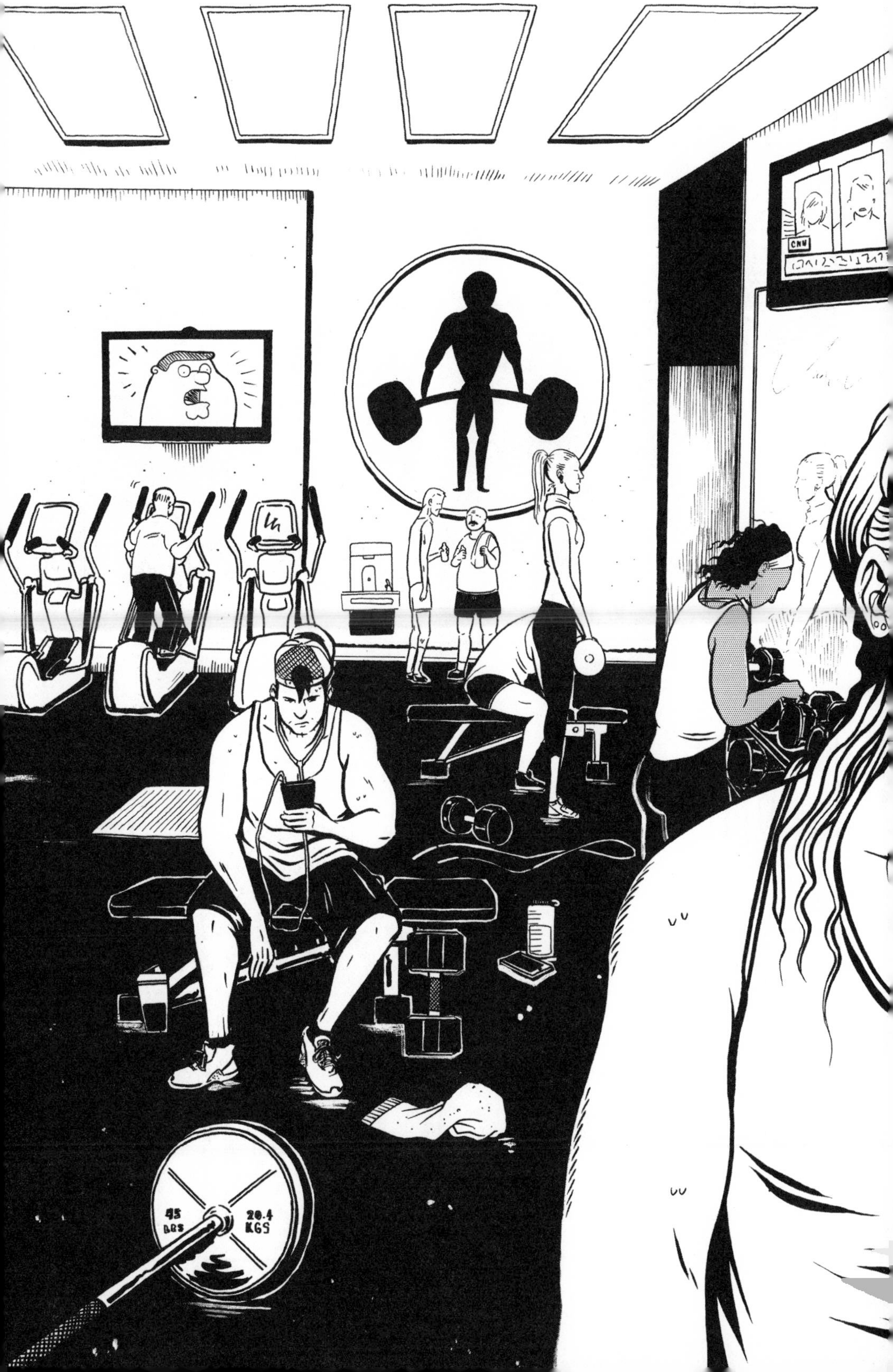
CNN
45 LBS
20.4 KGS

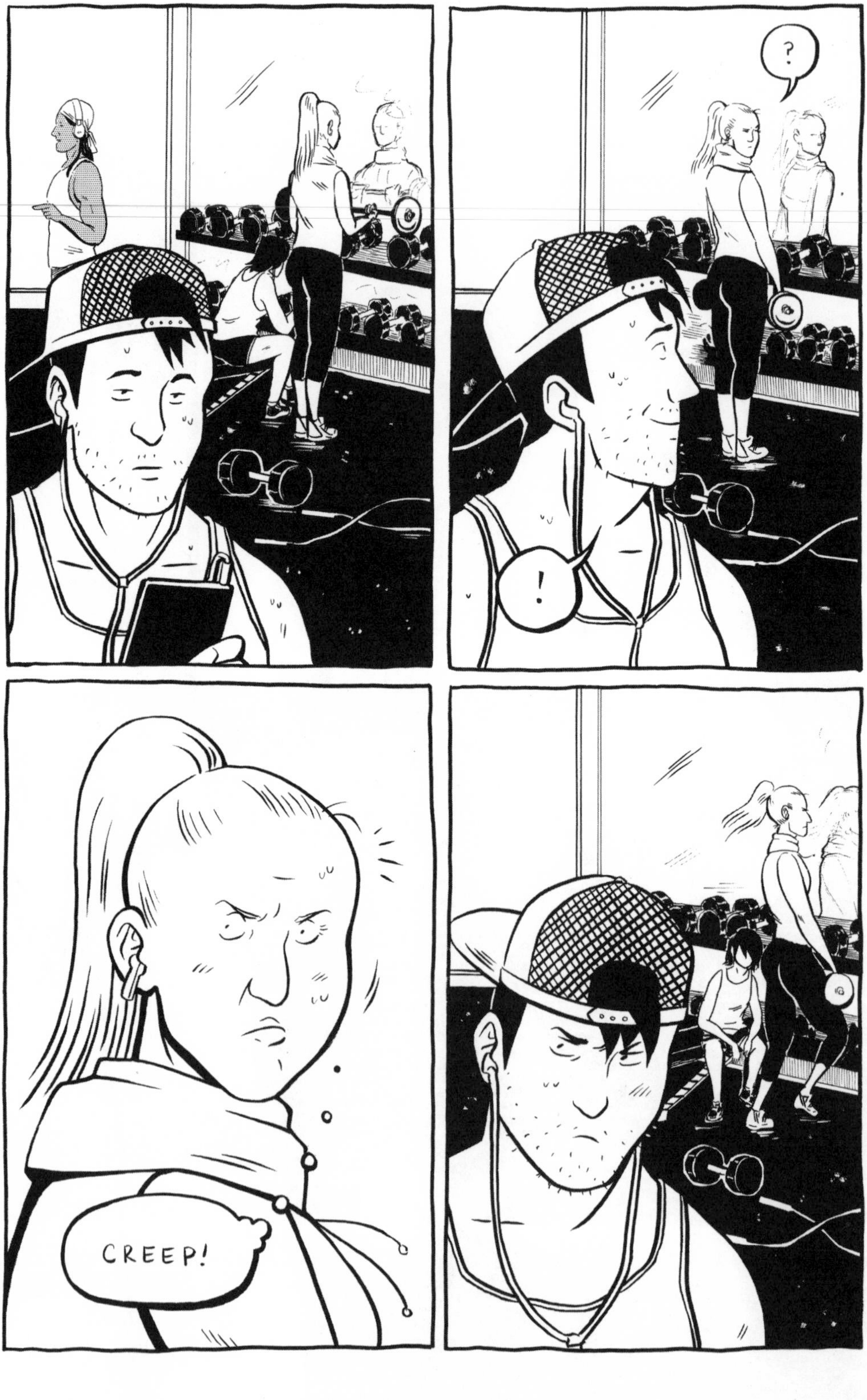
?
!
CREEP!

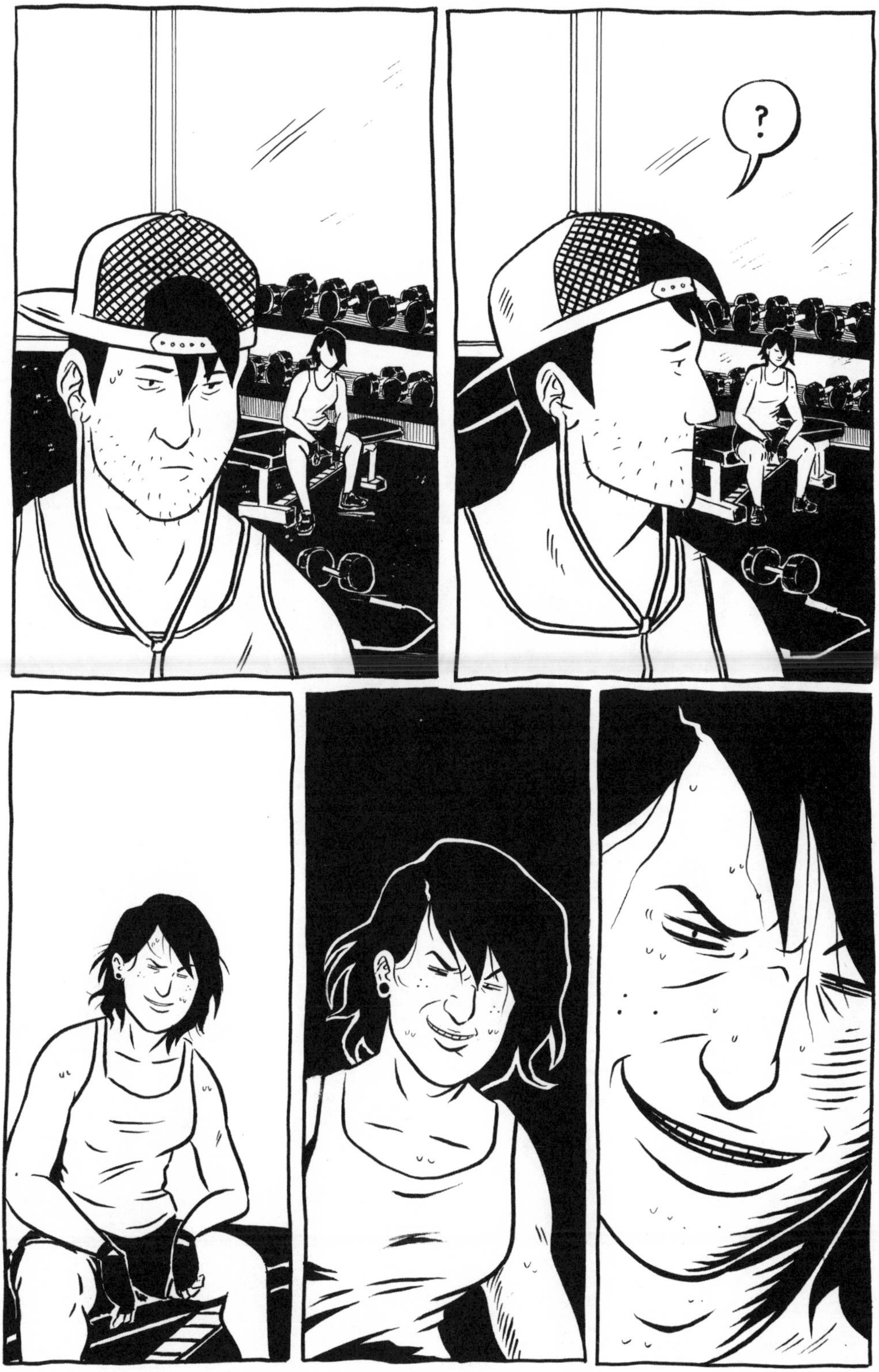
?

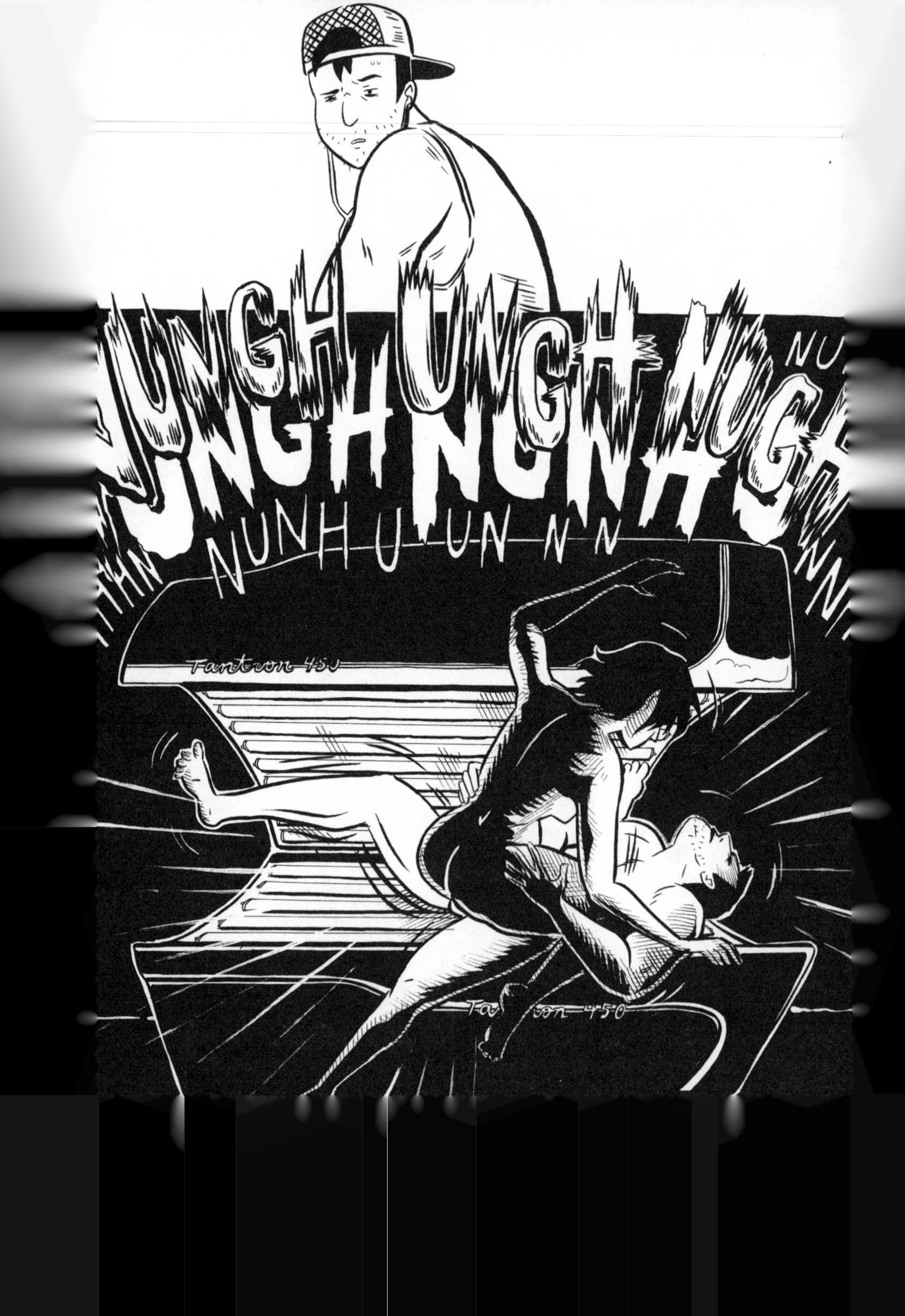
UNGH UNGH NUGH
NUNH U UN N N
Tantron 450

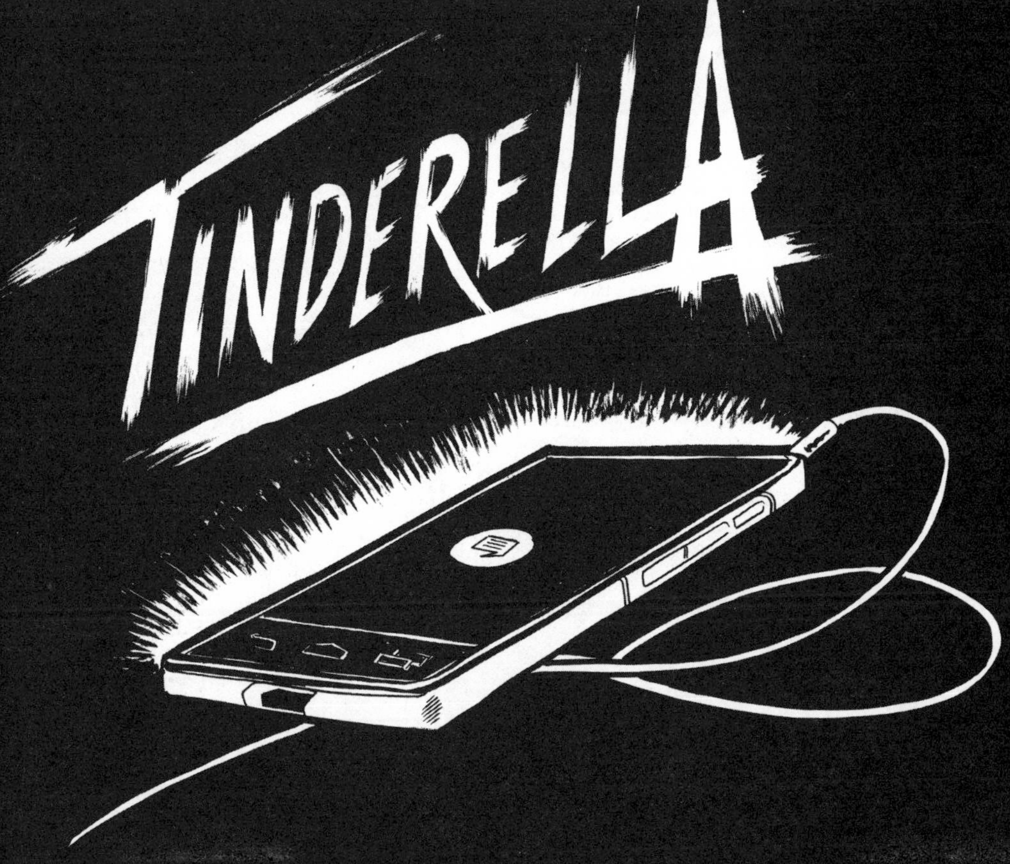
TINDERELLA

MINNEAPOLIS
MINNESOTA, LATE 2015
I'VE BEEN DOING PRETTY GOOD! SAME OL' SAME OLD!
AUDREY AND I ARE DOING GREAT. I'M STILL WORKING THE SAME KITCHEN JOBS, BUT I'M LOOKING INTO THIS LAW FIRM FOR A POSITION THAT MIGHT BE EASIER ON MY KNEES.
The NEW UPTOWN Diner
BREAKFAST COFFEE & LUNCH
OPEN LATE NIGHT
NEW EGG SAMMY
I'VE ALSO BEEN ATTENDING THIS FEMINIST BOOK CLUB- IT'S BEEN REALLY GREAT, MEETING UP WITH REAL PEOPLE AND HAVING REAL DISCUSSIONS.
OH! AND I GOT MY CREDIT CARD PAID OFF! SO NOW I CAN SAVE A LITTLE MORE MONEY.
HOW ABOUT YOU?
RYAN HARKNESS
GLOBAL CITIZEN

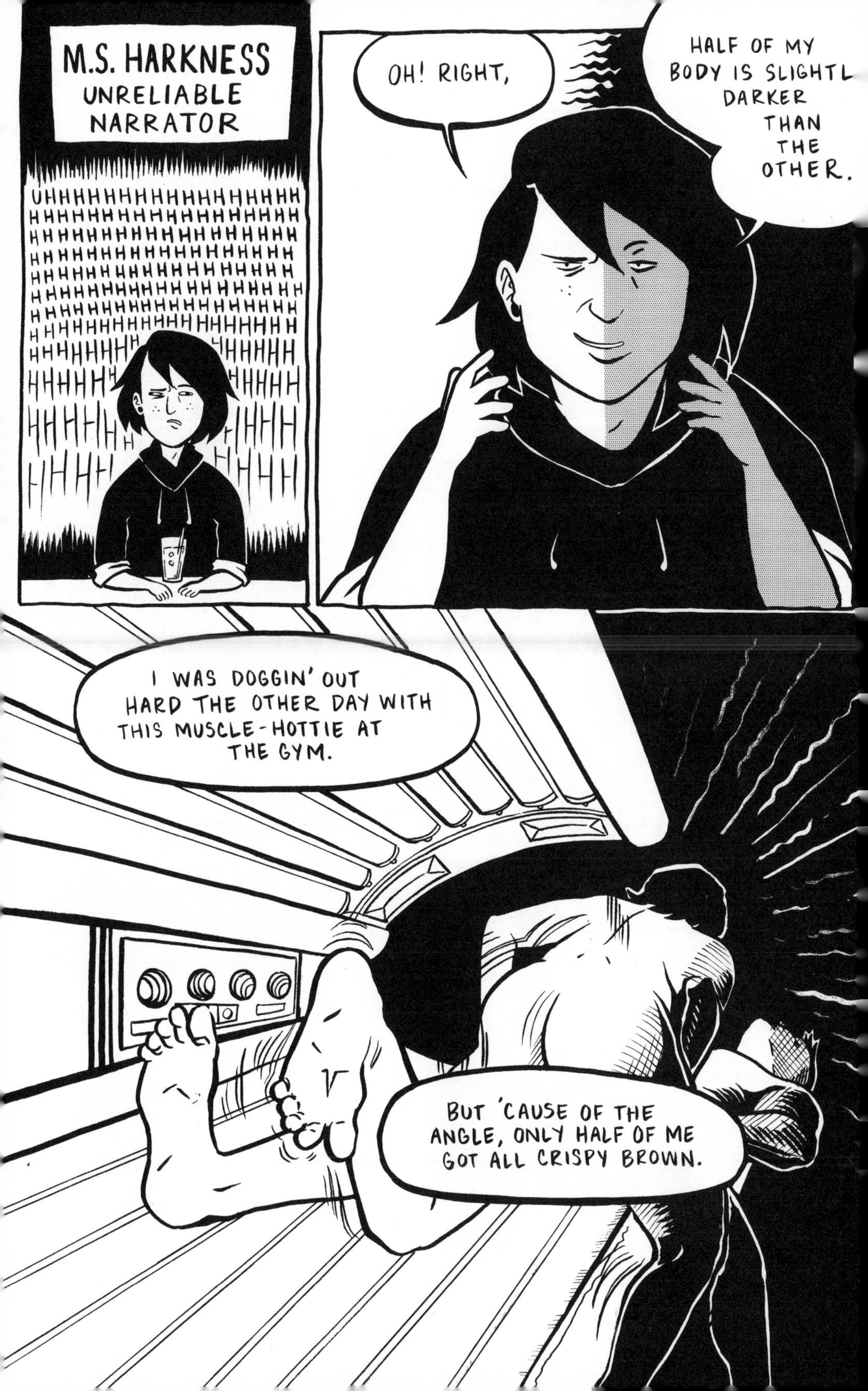
M.S. HARKNESS
UNRELIABLE NARRATOR
OH! RIGHT,
HALF OF MY BODY IS SLIGHTL DARKER THAN THE OTHER.
I WAS DOGGIN' OUT HARD THE OTHER DAY WITH THIS MUSCLE-HOTTIE AT THE GYM.
BUT 'CAUSE OF THE ANGLE, ONLY HALF OF ME GOT ALL CRISPY BROWN.

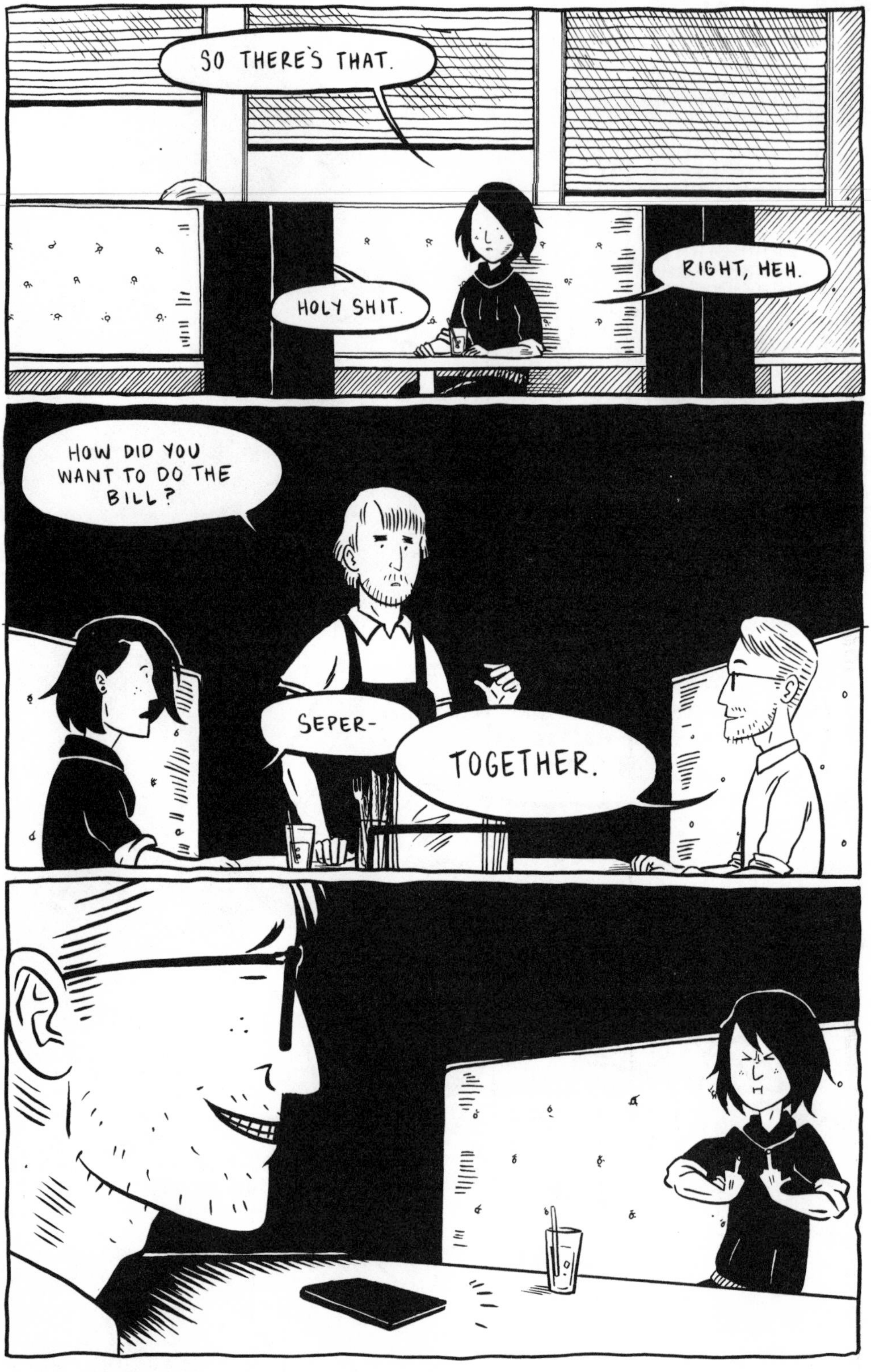
SO THERE'S THAT.
HOLY SHIT.
RIGHT, HEH.
HOW DID YOU WANT TO DO THE BILL?
SEPER-
TOGETHER.

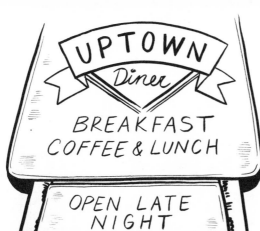

UPTOWN Diner
BREAKFAST
COFFEE & LUNCH

OPEN LATE
NIGHT

NEW EGG
SAMMY

HAVE YOU
TALKED TO
MOM IN
A WHILE?

HEH, NOT
FOR A BIT...
I SKYPED HER
A LITTLE BIT
AGO AND SHE
SEEMED OKAY.

IF YOU EVER
WANTED TO COME
OVER AND EAT
DINNER WITH ME
AND AUDREY, I'D
COOK FOR YOU!

BRING A GUY
FRIEND OR
SOMETHING.

HEH, FOR SURE,
I'LL LET YA
KNOW.

I WALKED HERE...

ME TOO...

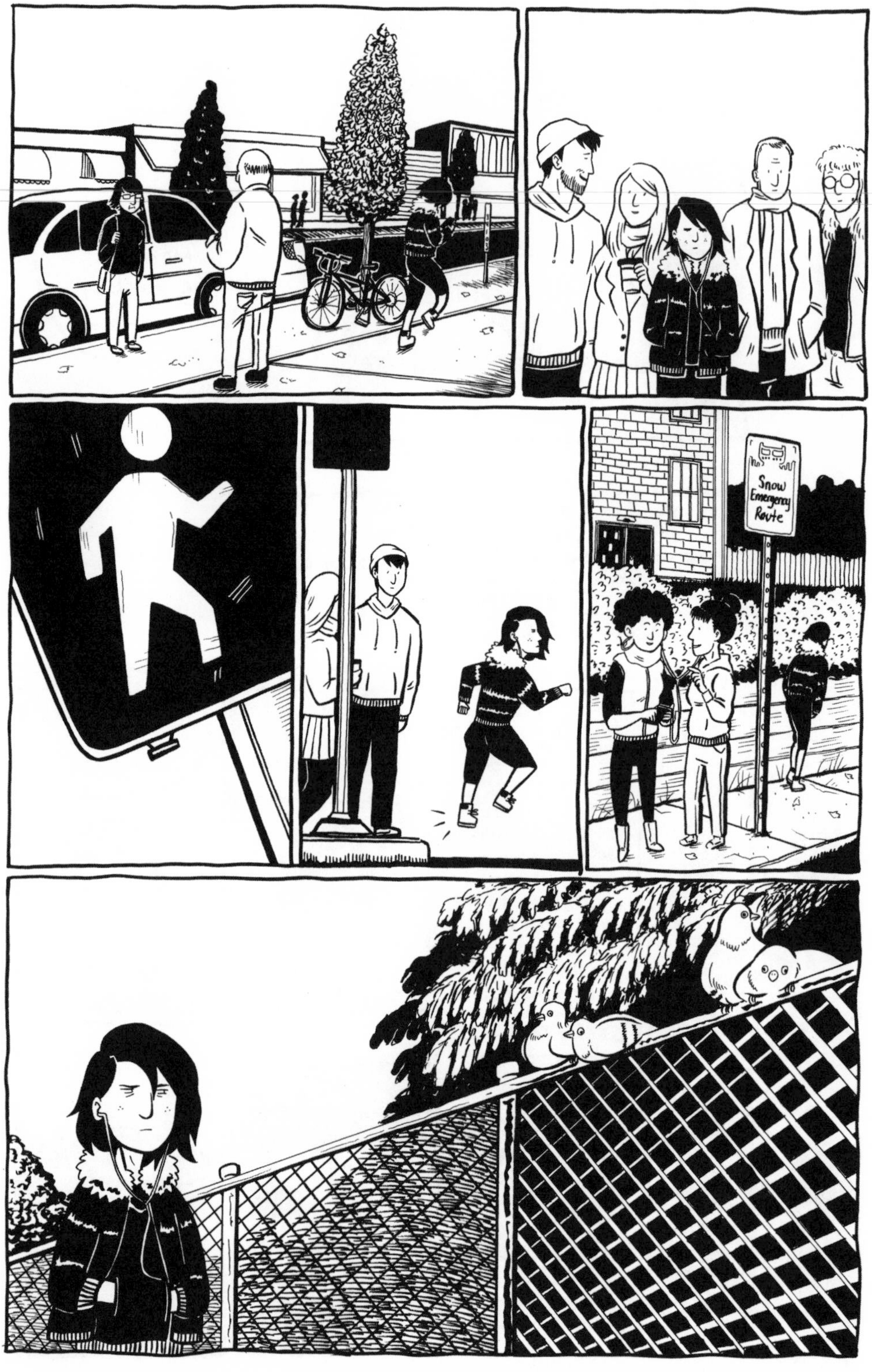
Snow
Emergency
Route

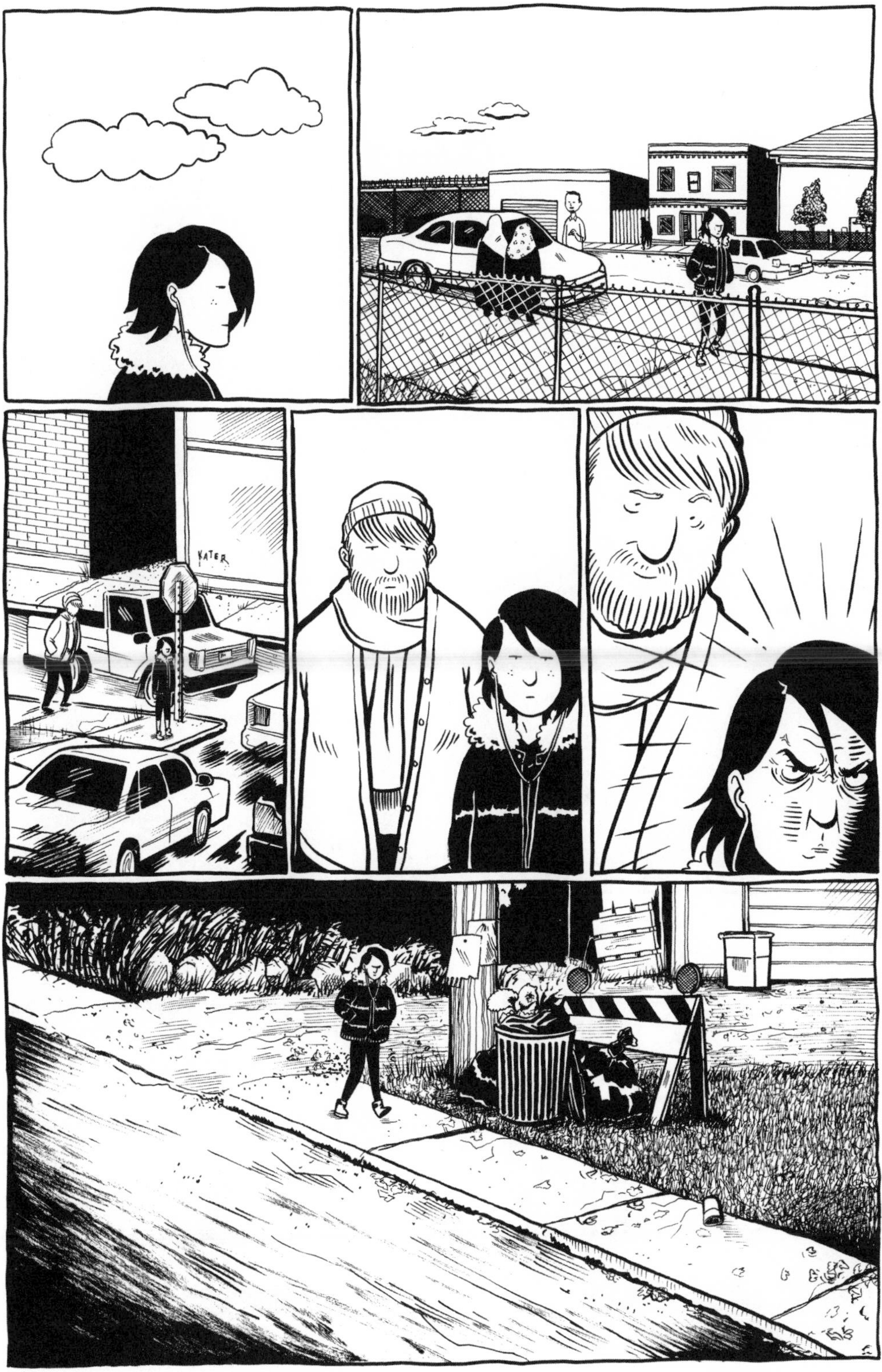
KATER

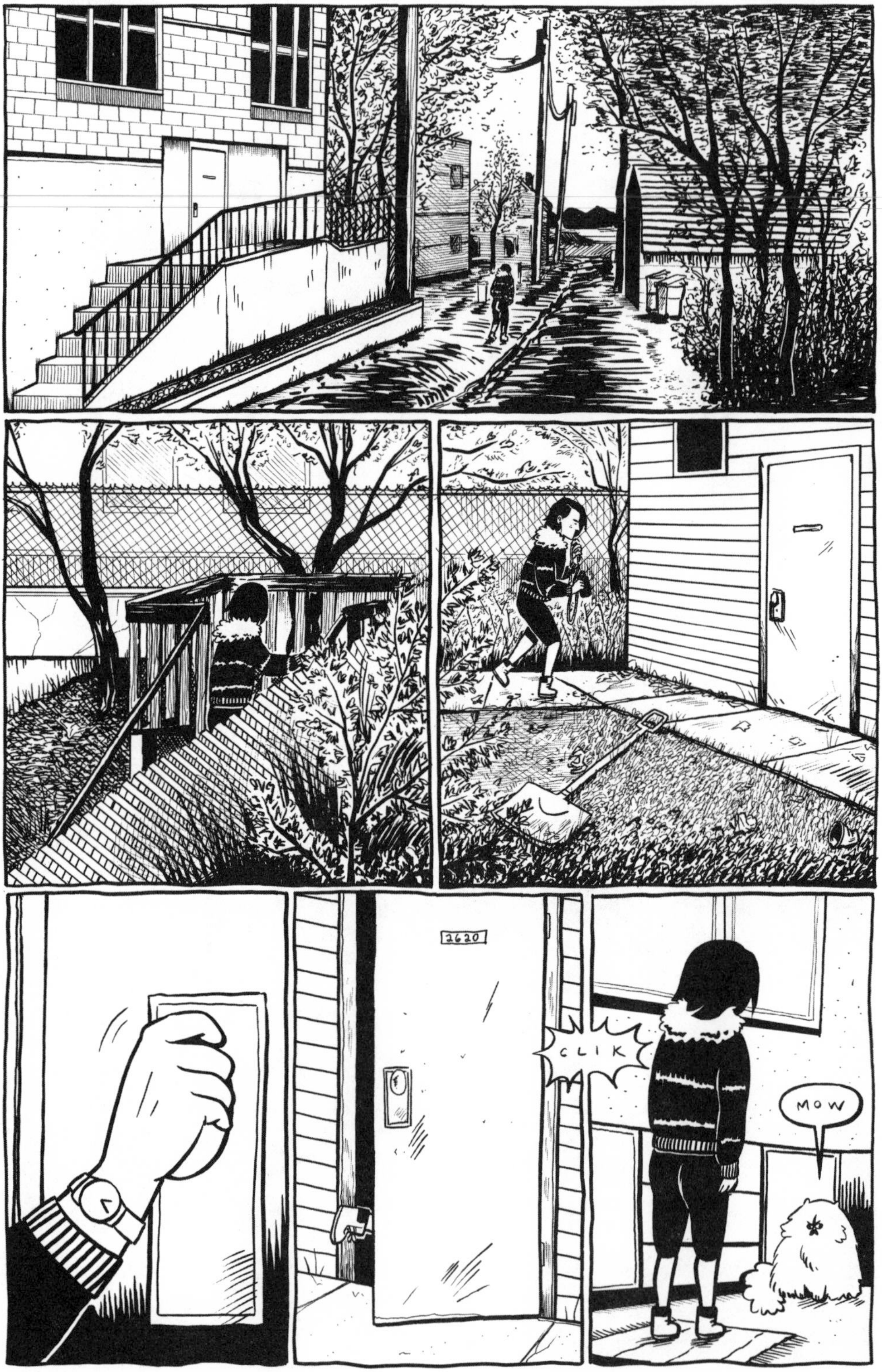
2620
CLIK
MOW

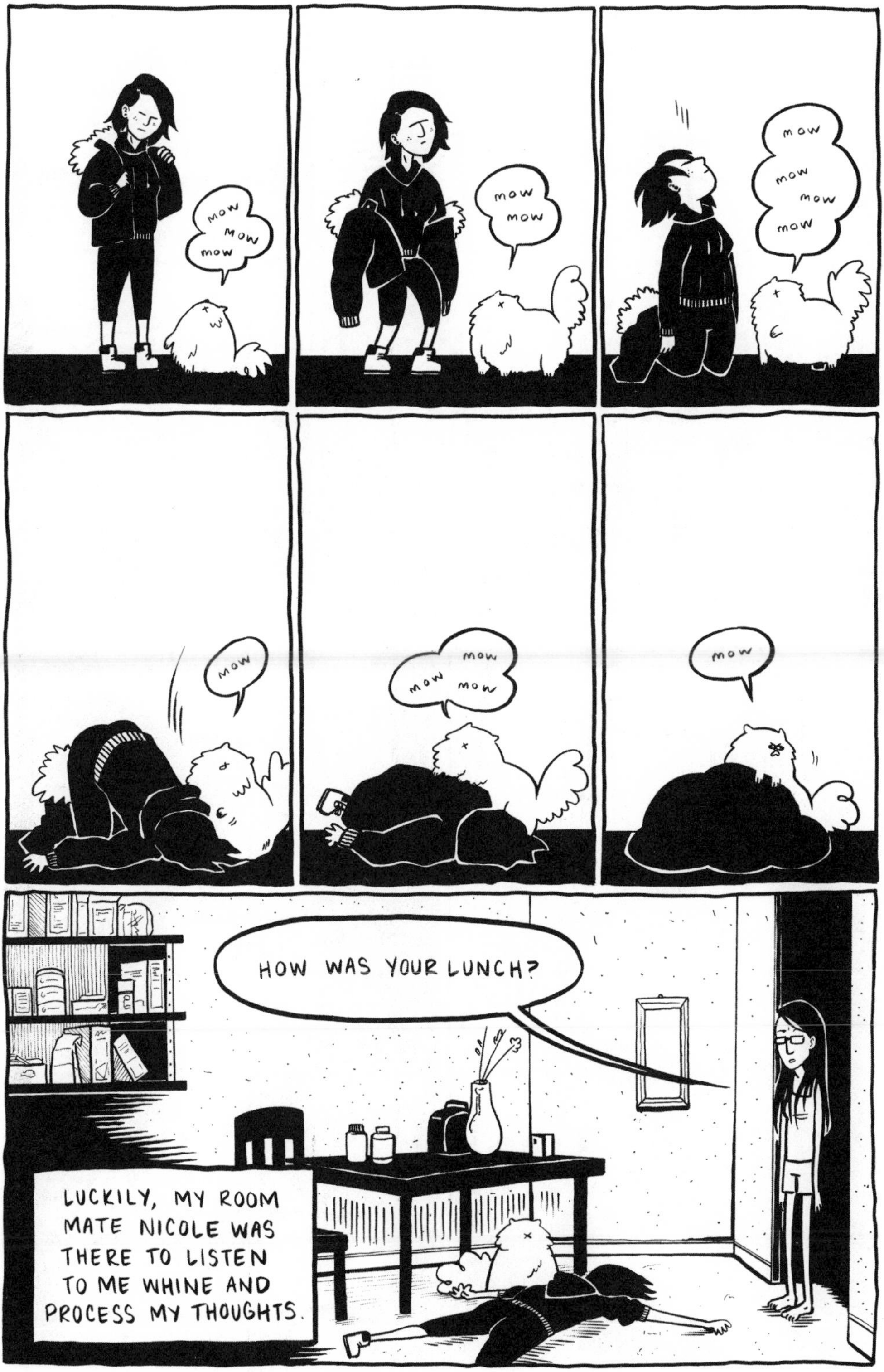

mow mow mow
mow mow
mow mow mow mow
mow
mow mow mow
mow
HOW WAS YOUR LUNCH?
LUCKILY, MY ROOM MATE NICOLE WAS THERE TO LISTEN TO ME WHINE AND PROCESS MY THOUGHTS.

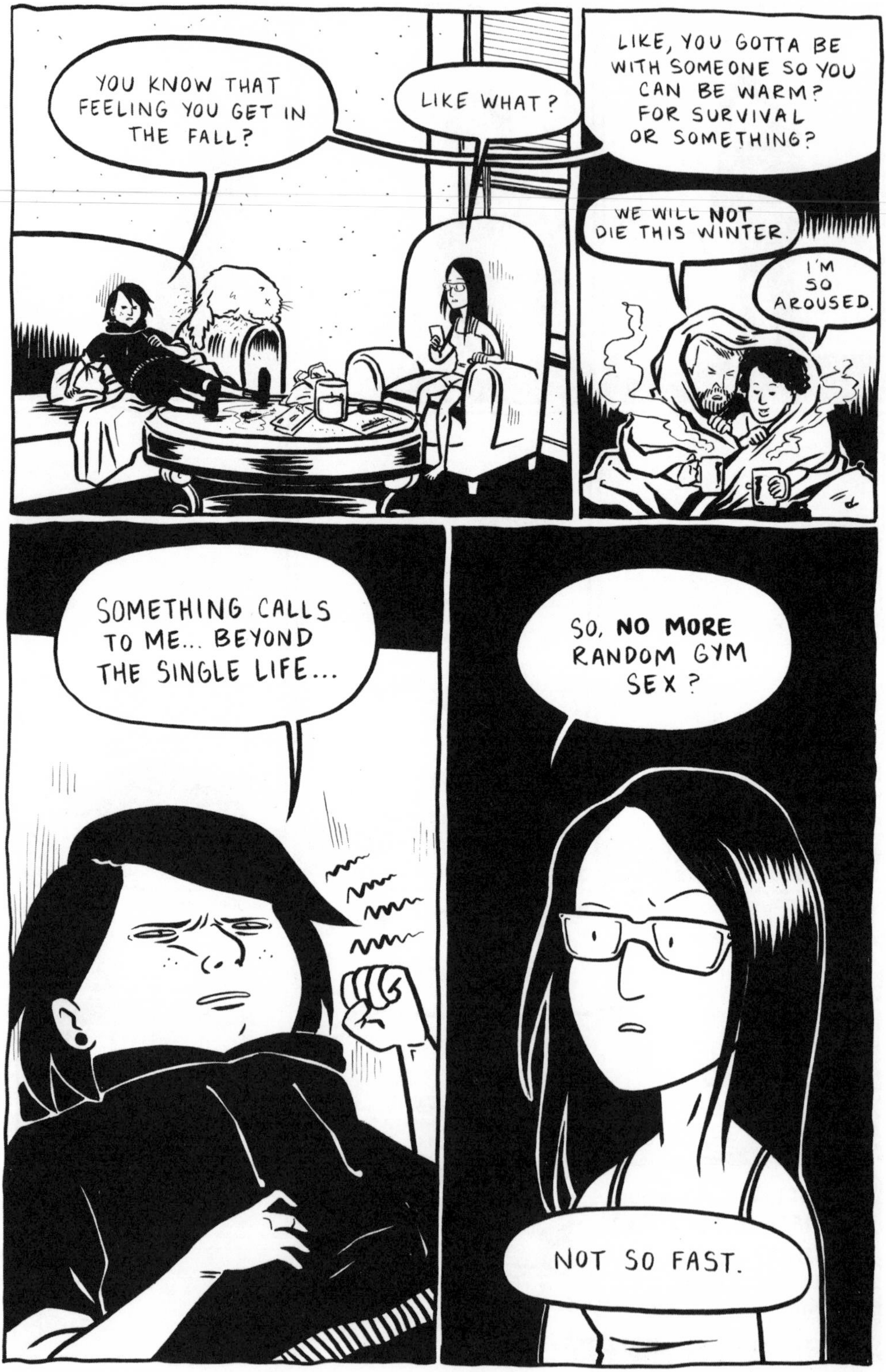
YOU KNOW THAT FEELING YOU GET IN THE FALL?
LIKE WHAT?
LIKE, YOU GOTTA BE WITH SOMEONE SO YOU CAN BE WARM? FOR SURVIVAL OR SOMETHING?
WE WILL **NOT** DIE THIS WINTER.
I'M SO AROUSED.
SOMETHING CALLS TO ME... BEYOND THE SINGLE LIFE...
SO, **NO MORE** RANDOM GYM SEX?
NOT SO FAST.

THE OBSTACLES IN MODERN DATING

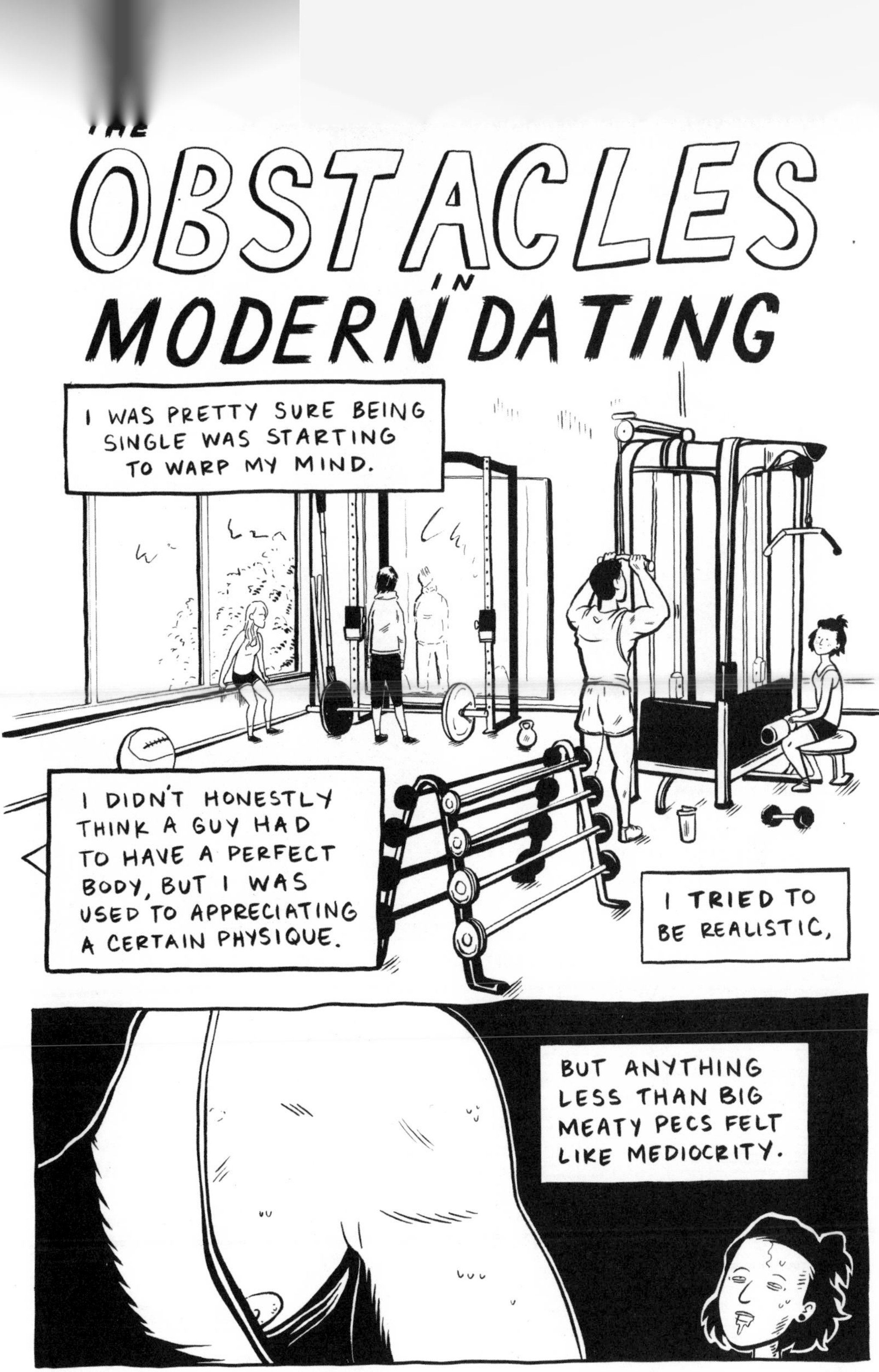
I WAS PRETTY SURE BEING SINGLE WAS STARTING TO WARP MY MIND.
I DIDN'T HONESTLY THINK A GUY HAD TO HAVE A PERFECT BODY, BUT I WAS USED TO APPRECIATING A CERTAIN PHYSIQUE.
I TRIED TO BE REALISTIC,
BUT ANYTHING LESS THAN BIG MEATY PECS FELT LIKE MEDIOCRITY.

IF I COULDN'T FIND A COMPANION AT THE GYM, MY OPTIONS WERE PRETTY MUCH LIMITED TO THE **FLANNEL-BEARDS** THAT HAD INFESTED MY NEIGHBORHOOD.

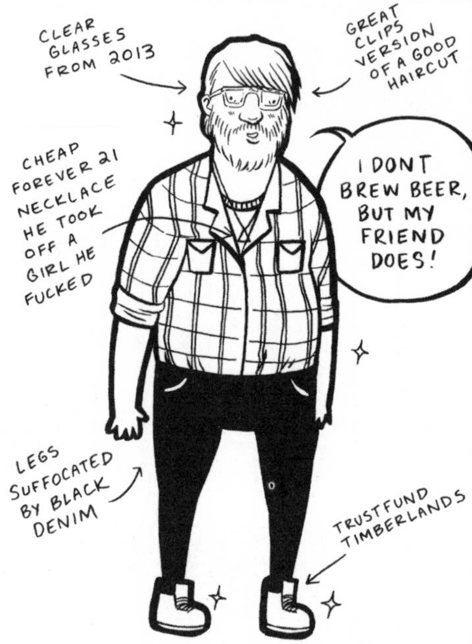
CLEAR GLASSES FROM 2013
GREAT CLIPS VERSION OF A GOOD HAIRCUT
CHEAP FOREVER 21 NECKLACE HE TOOK OFF A GIRL HE FUCKED
I DONT BREW BEER, BUT MY FRIEND DOES!
LEGS SUFFOCATED BY BLACK DENIM
TRUSTFUND TIMBERLANDS

I THINK IF YOU'RE A WHITE CHICK FROM THE MIDWEST, YOU'RE JUST EXPECTED TO ACCEPT THIS, BUT I DIDN'T WANT TO.

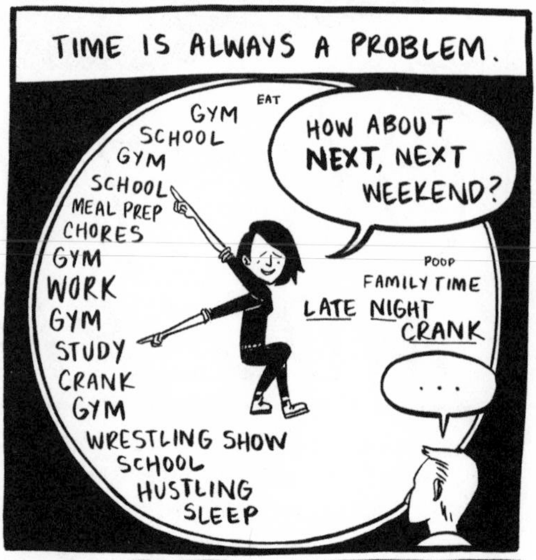
TIME IS ALWAYS A PROBLEM.
EAT
GYM
SCHOOL
GYM
SCHOOL
MEAL PREP
CHORES
GYM
WORK
GYM
STUDY
CRANK
GYM
WRESTLING SHOW
SCHOOL
HUSTLING
SLEEP
HOW ABOUT NEXT, NEXT WEEKEND?
POOP
FAMILY TIME
LATE NIGHT CRANK
. . .

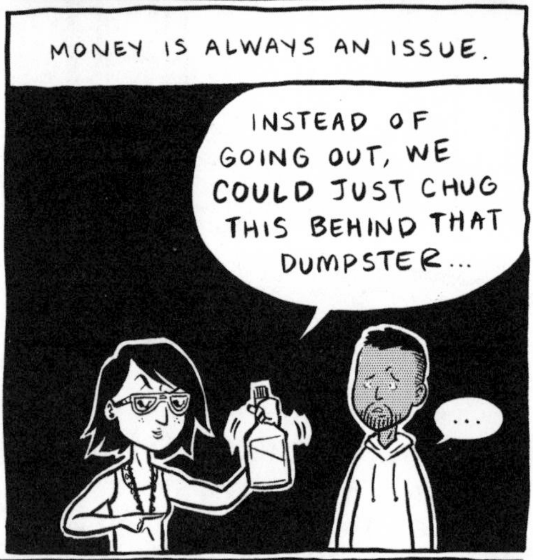
MONEY IS ALWAYS AN ISSUE.
INSTEAD OF GOING OUT, WE COULD JUST CHUG THIS BEHIND THAT DUMPSTER...
. . .

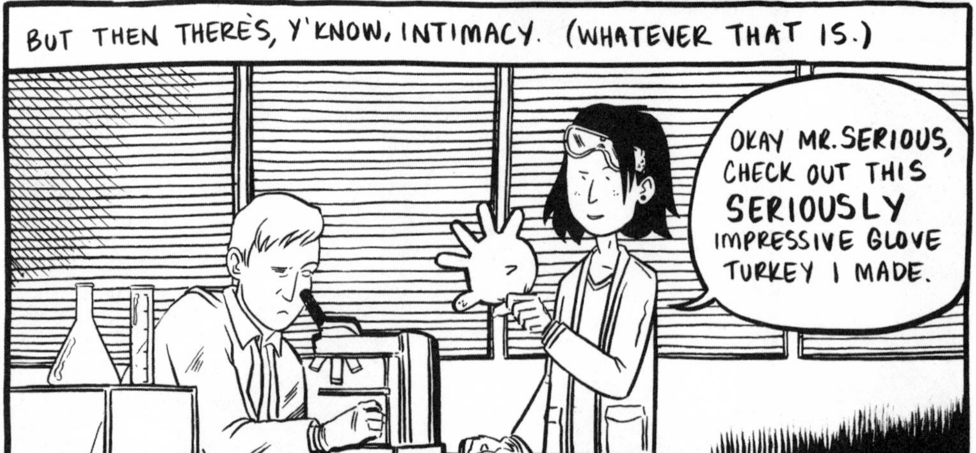
BUT THEN THERE'S, Y'KNOW, INTIMACY. (WHATEVER THAT IS.)
OKAY MR. SERIOUS, CHECK OUT THIS SERIOUSLY IMPRESSIVE GLOVE TURKEY I MADE.

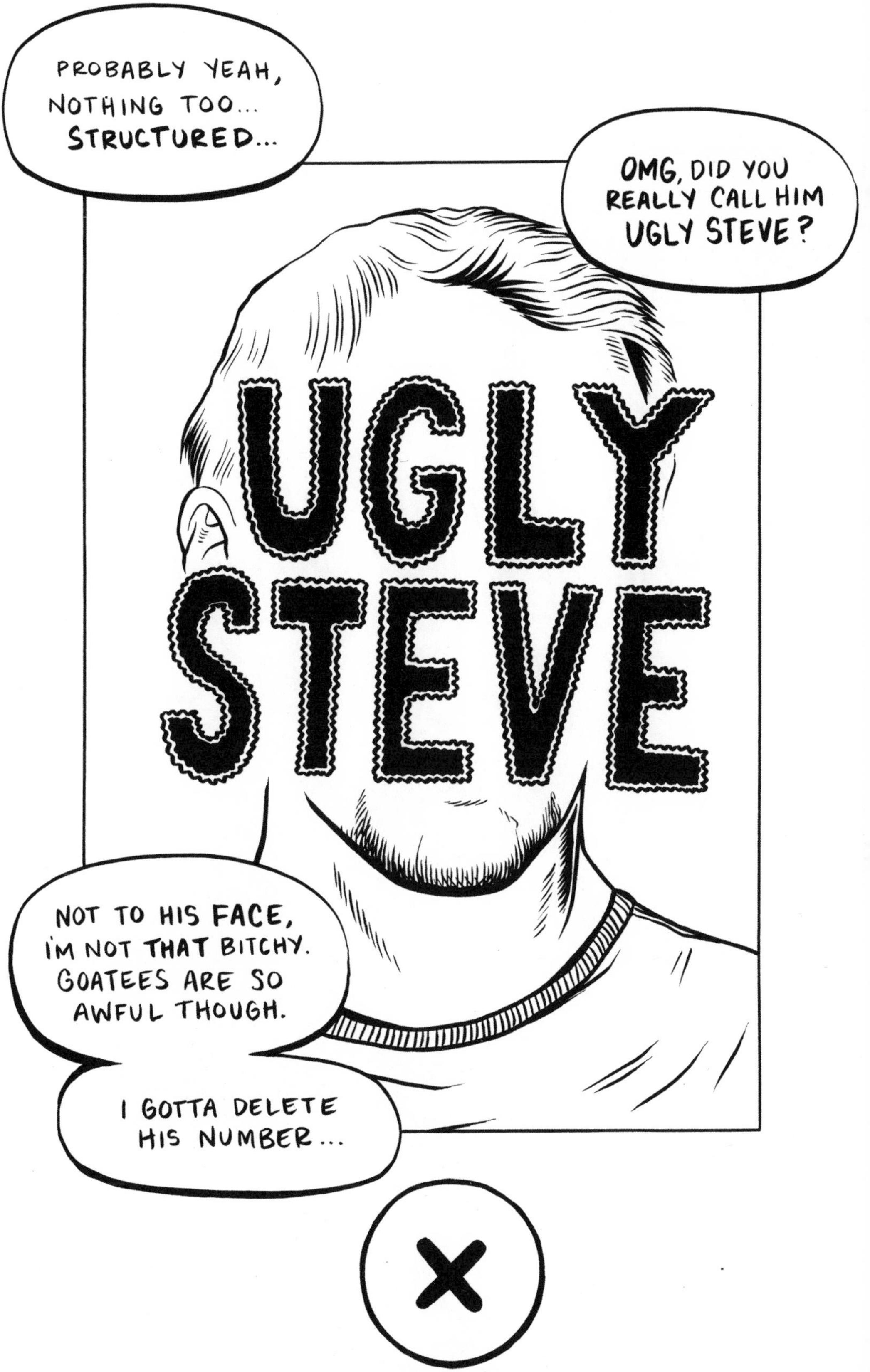
PROBABLY YEAH, NOTHING TOO... STRUCTURED...
OMG, DID YOU REALLY CALL HIM UGLY STEVE?
UGLY STEVE
NOT TO HIS FACE, I'M NOT THAT BITCHY. GOATEES ARE SO AWFUL THOUGH.
I GOTTA DELETE HIS NUMBER...

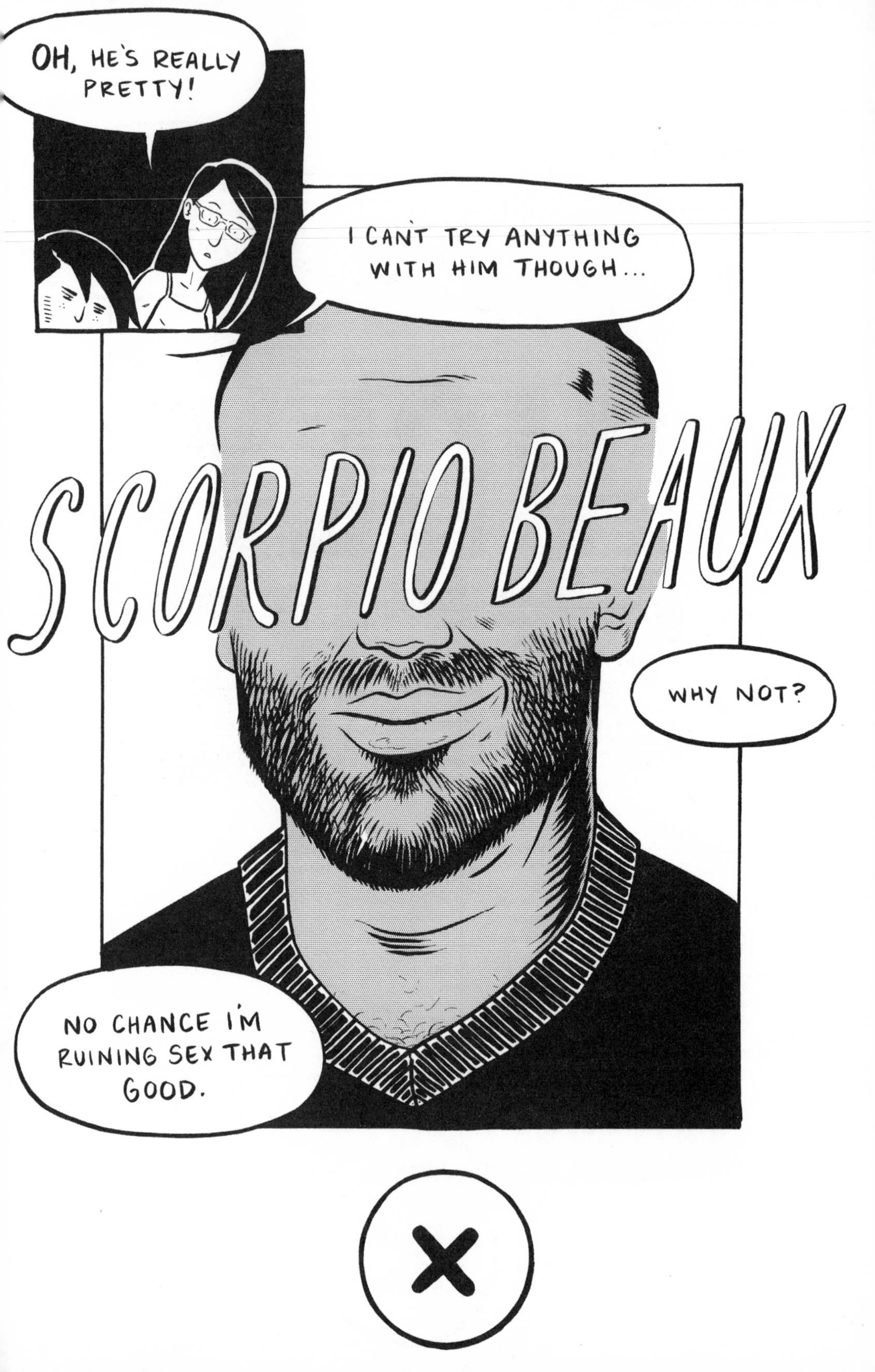

OH, HE'S REALLY PRETTY!
I CAN'T TRY ANYTHING WITH HIM THOUGH...
SCORPIO BEAUX
WHY NOT?
NO CHANCE I'M RUINING SEX THAT GOOD.

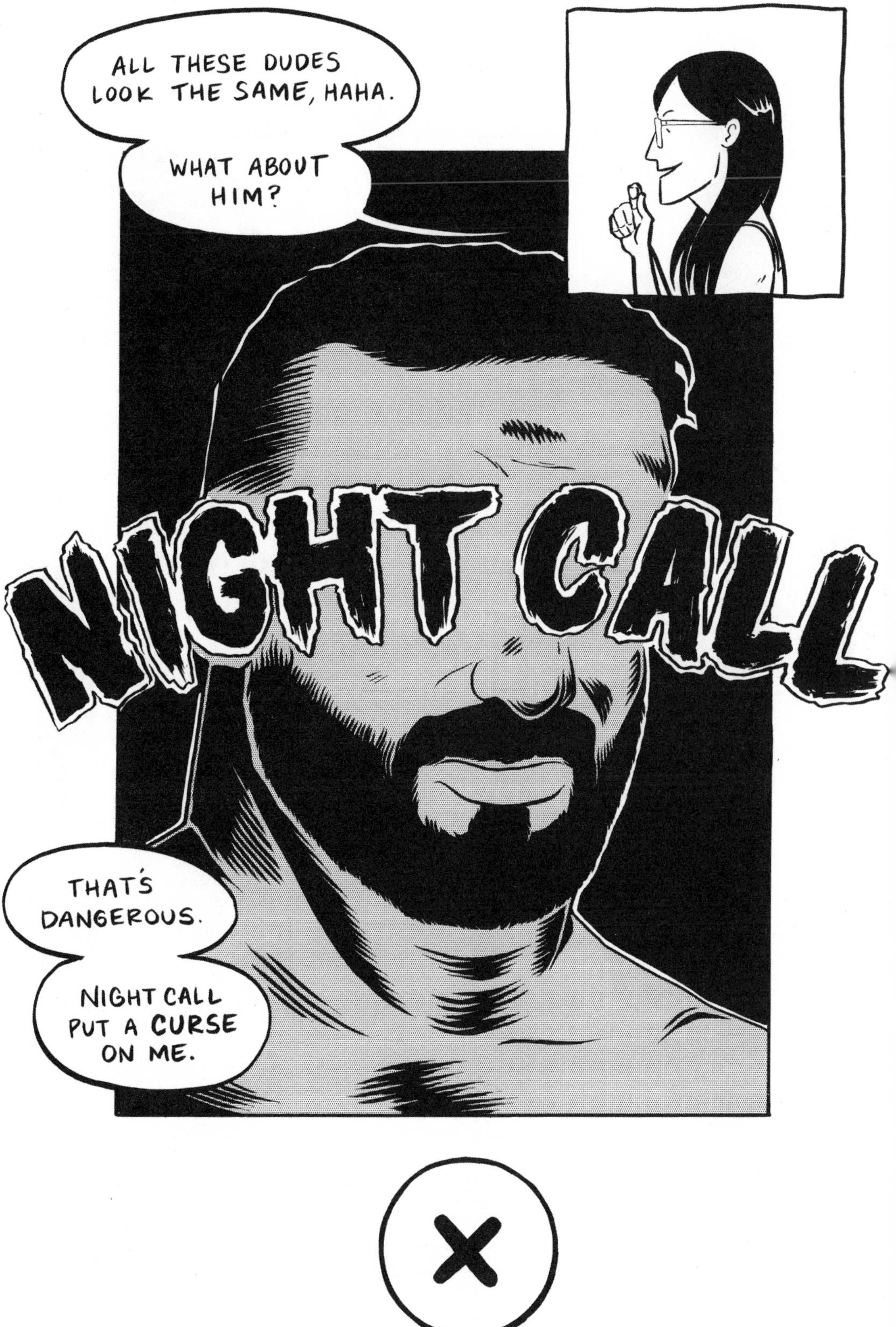
ALL THESE DUDES LOOK THE SAME, HAHA.
WHAT ABOUT HIM?
NIGHT CALL
THAT'S DANGEROUS.
NIGHT CALL PUT A CURSE ON ME.

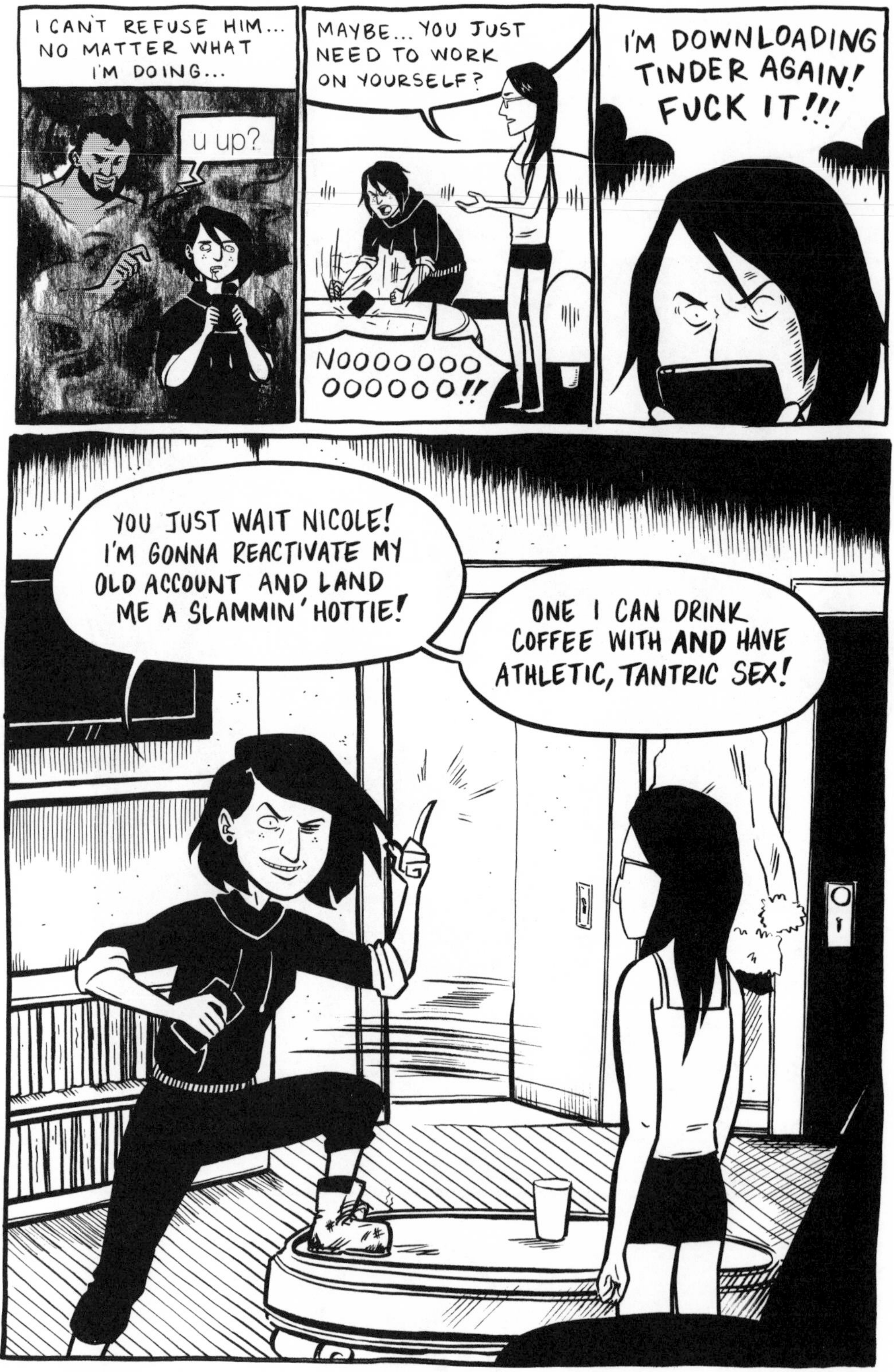
I CAN'T REFUSE HIM... NO MATTER WHAT I'M DOING...
u up?
MAYBE... YOU JUST NEED TO WORK ON YOURSELF?
NOOOOOOOOOOOOOO!!
I'M DOWNLOADING TINDER AGAIN! FUCK IT!!!
YOU JUST WAIT NICOLE! I'M GONNA REACTIVATE MY OLD ACCOUNT AND LAND ME A SLAMMIN' HOTTIE!
ONE I CAN DRINK COFFEE WITH AND HAVE ATHLETIC, TANTRIC SEX!

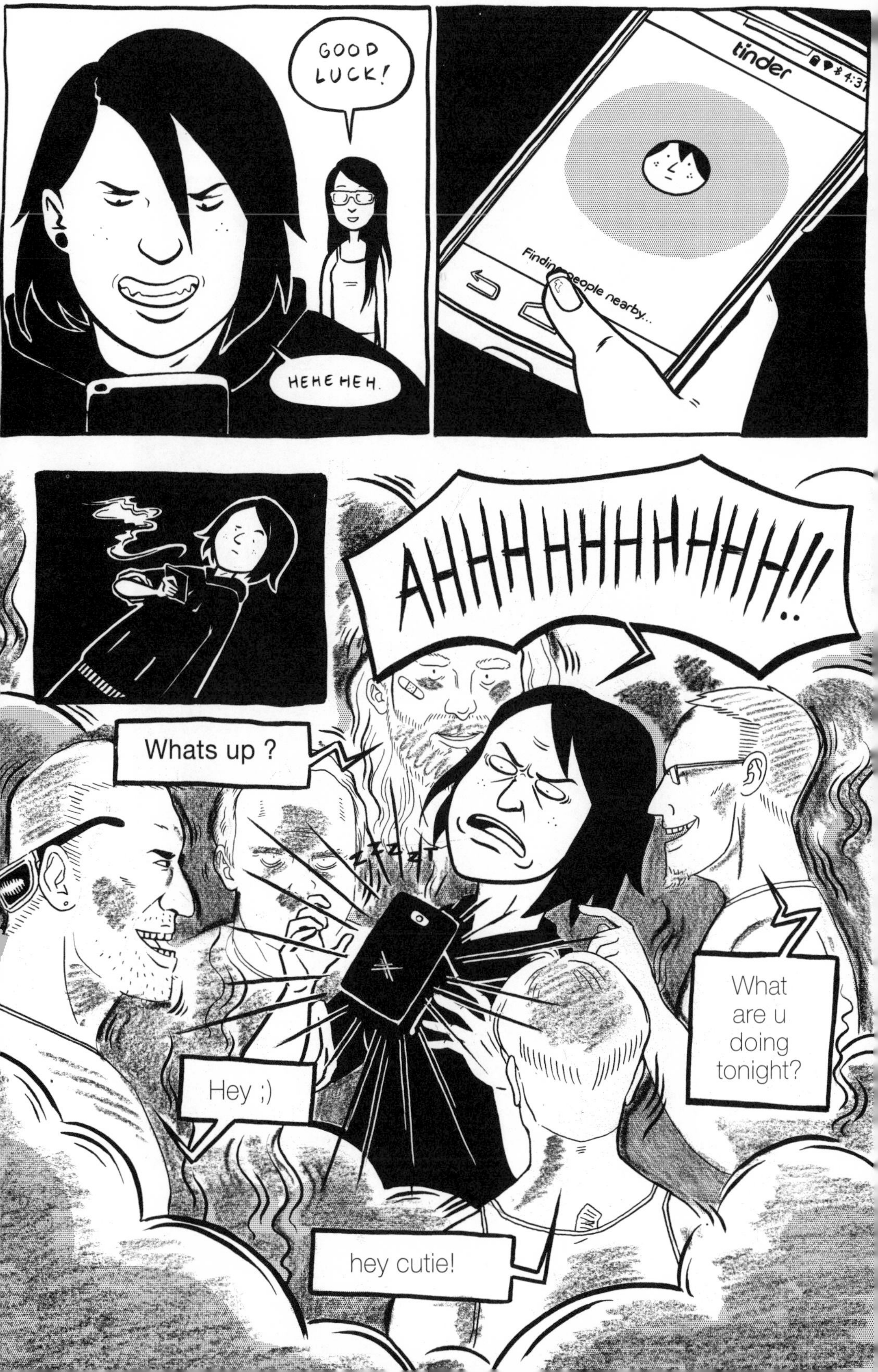
GOOD LUCK!
HEHEHEH.
tinder
4:37
Finding people nearby...
AHHHHHHHHHHH!!
Whats up ?
What are u doing tonight?
Hey ;)
hey cutie!

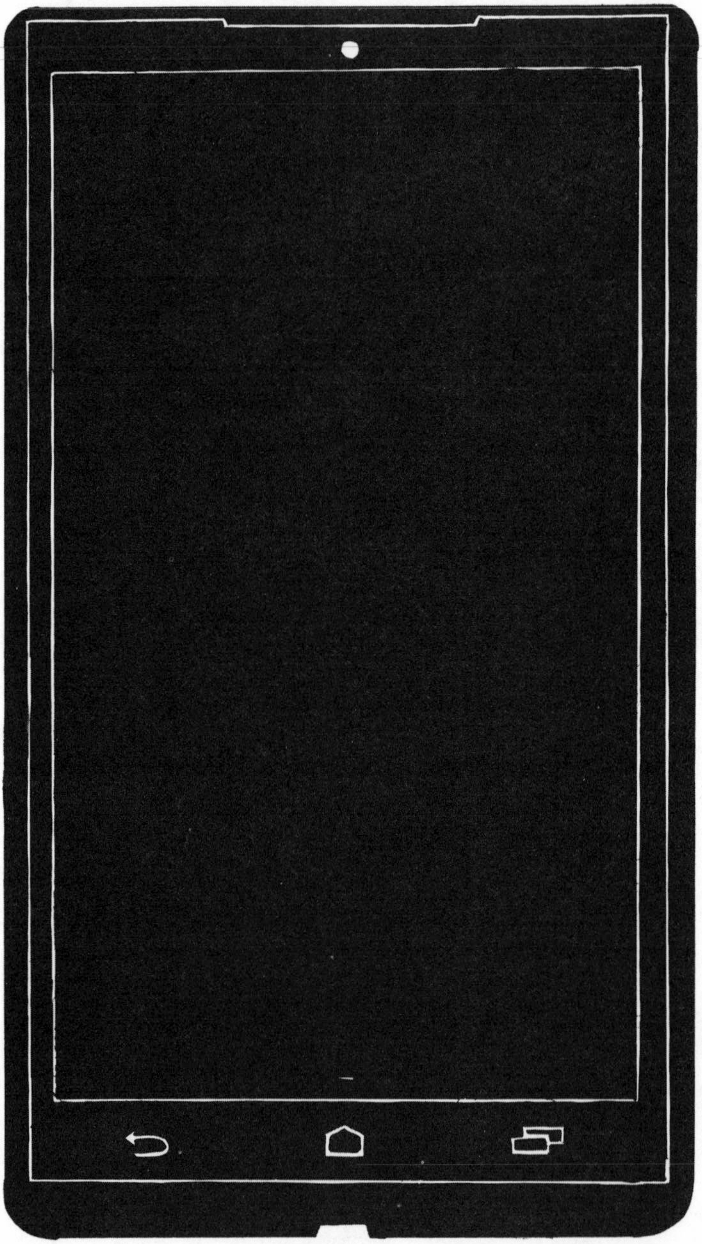

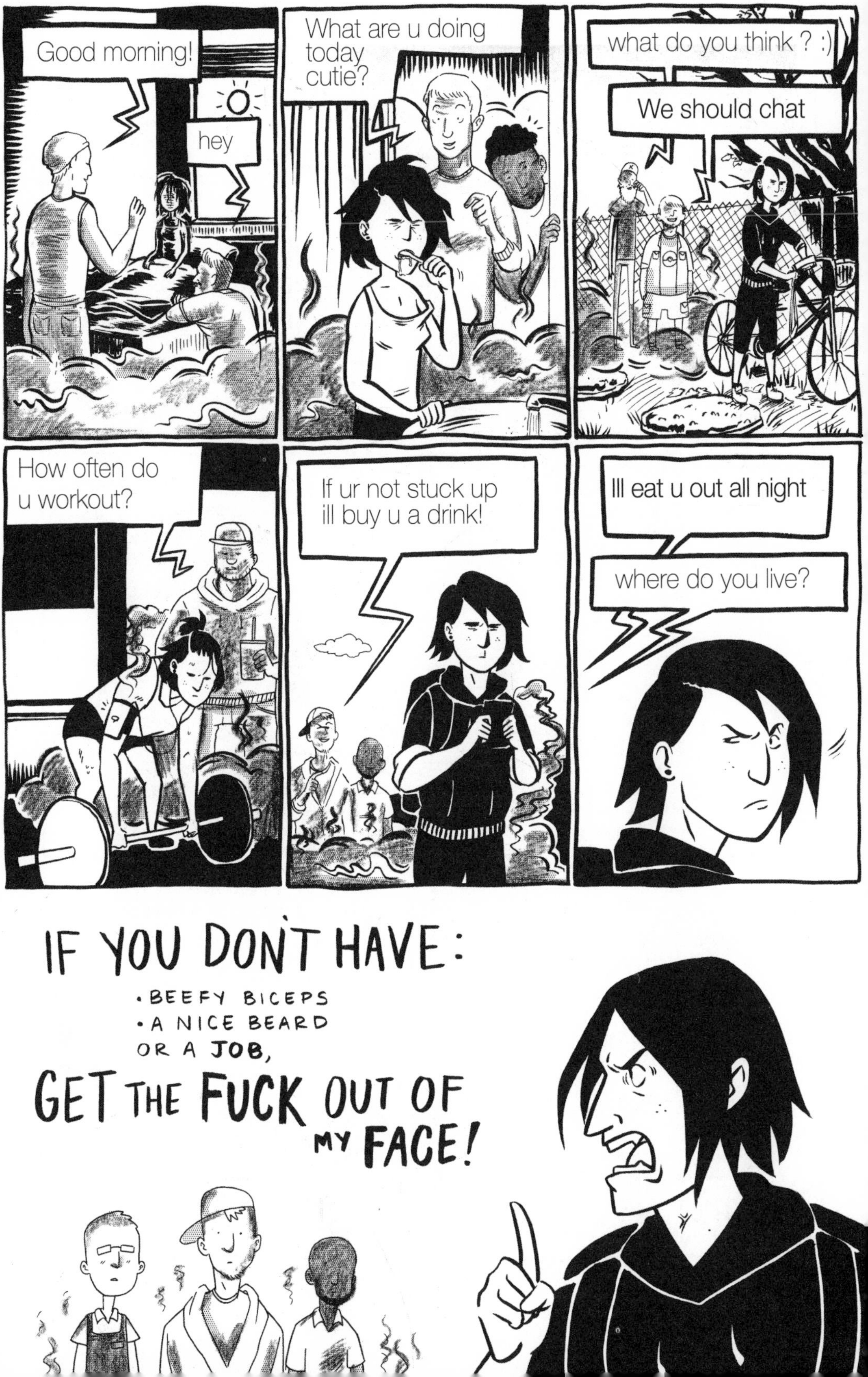
Good morning!
hey
What are u doing today cutie?
what do you think ? :)
We should chat
How often do u workout?
If ur not stuck up ill buy u a drink!
Ill eat u out all night
where do you live?
IF YOU DON'T HAVE:
• BEEFY BICEPS
• A NICE BEARD
OR A JOB,
GET THE FUCK OUT OF MY FACE!

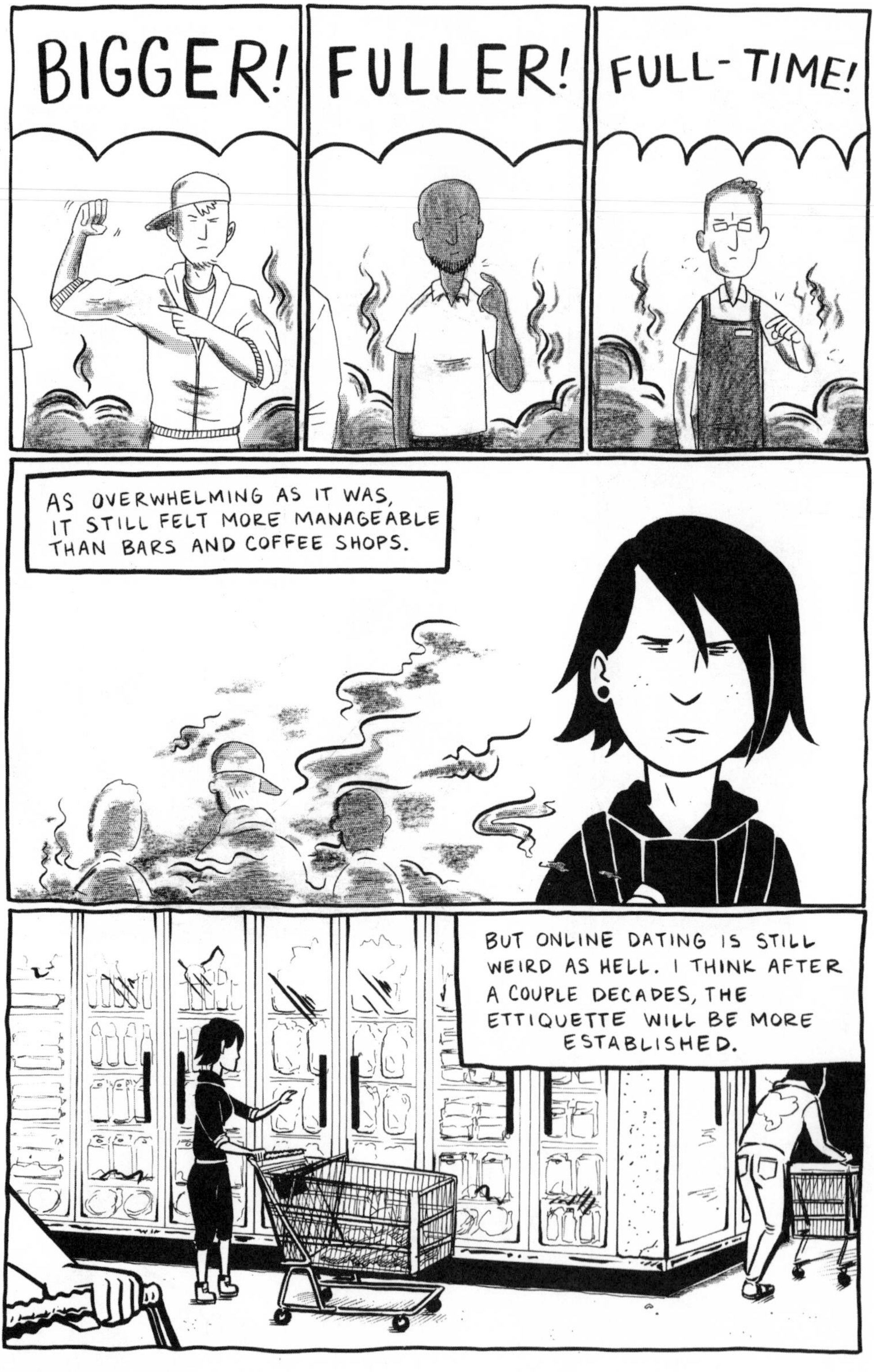
BIGGER!
FULLER!
FULL-TIME!
AS OVERWHELMING AS IT WAS, IT STILL FELT MORE MANAGEABLE THAN BARS AND COFFEE SHOPS.
BUT ONLINE DATING IS STILL WEIRD AS HELL. I THINK AFTER A COUPLE DECADES, THE ETTIQUETTE WILL BE MORE ESTABLISHED.

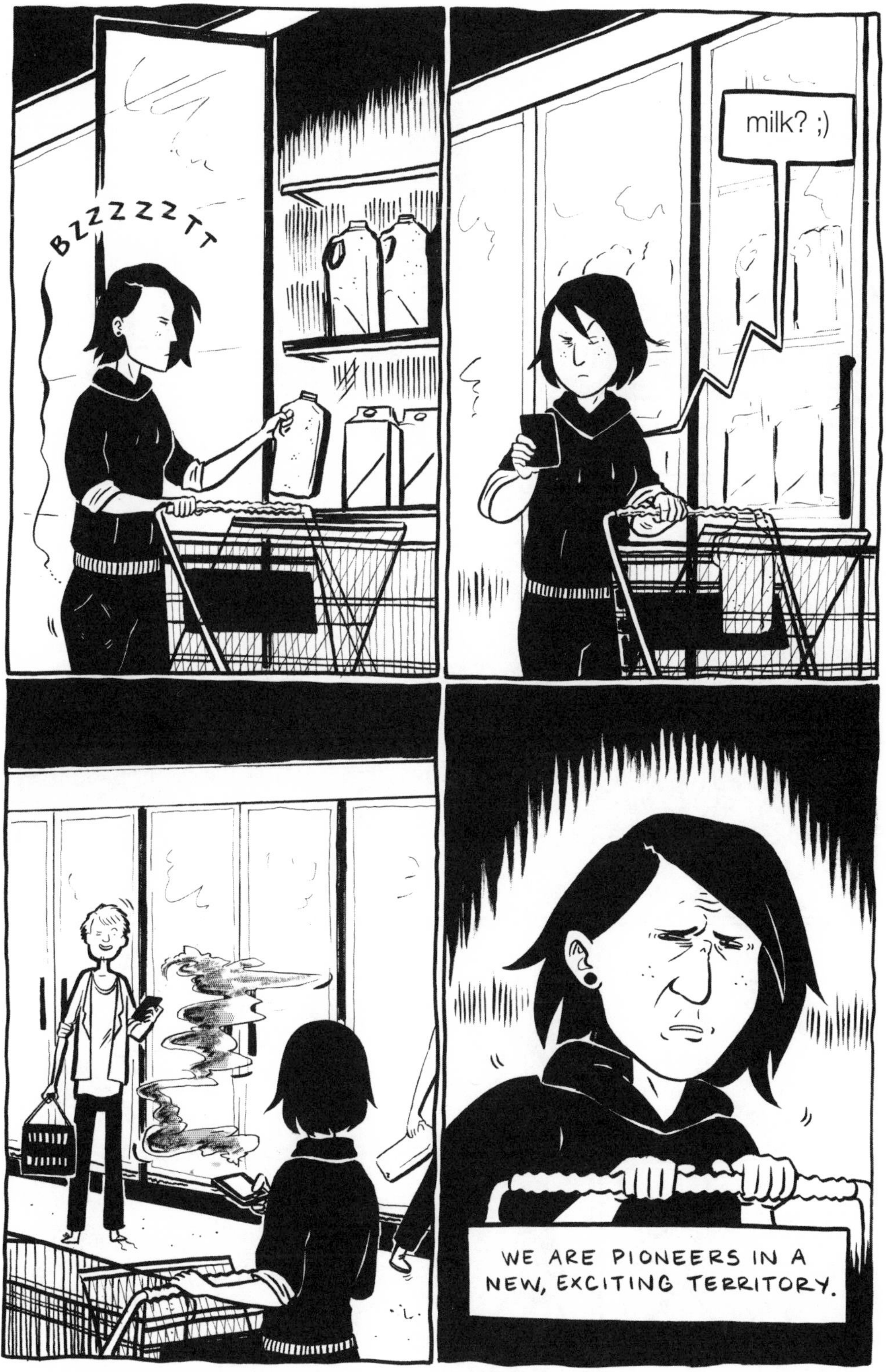
BZZZZZZTT
milk? ;)
WE ARE PIONEERS IN A NEW, EXCITING TERRITORY.

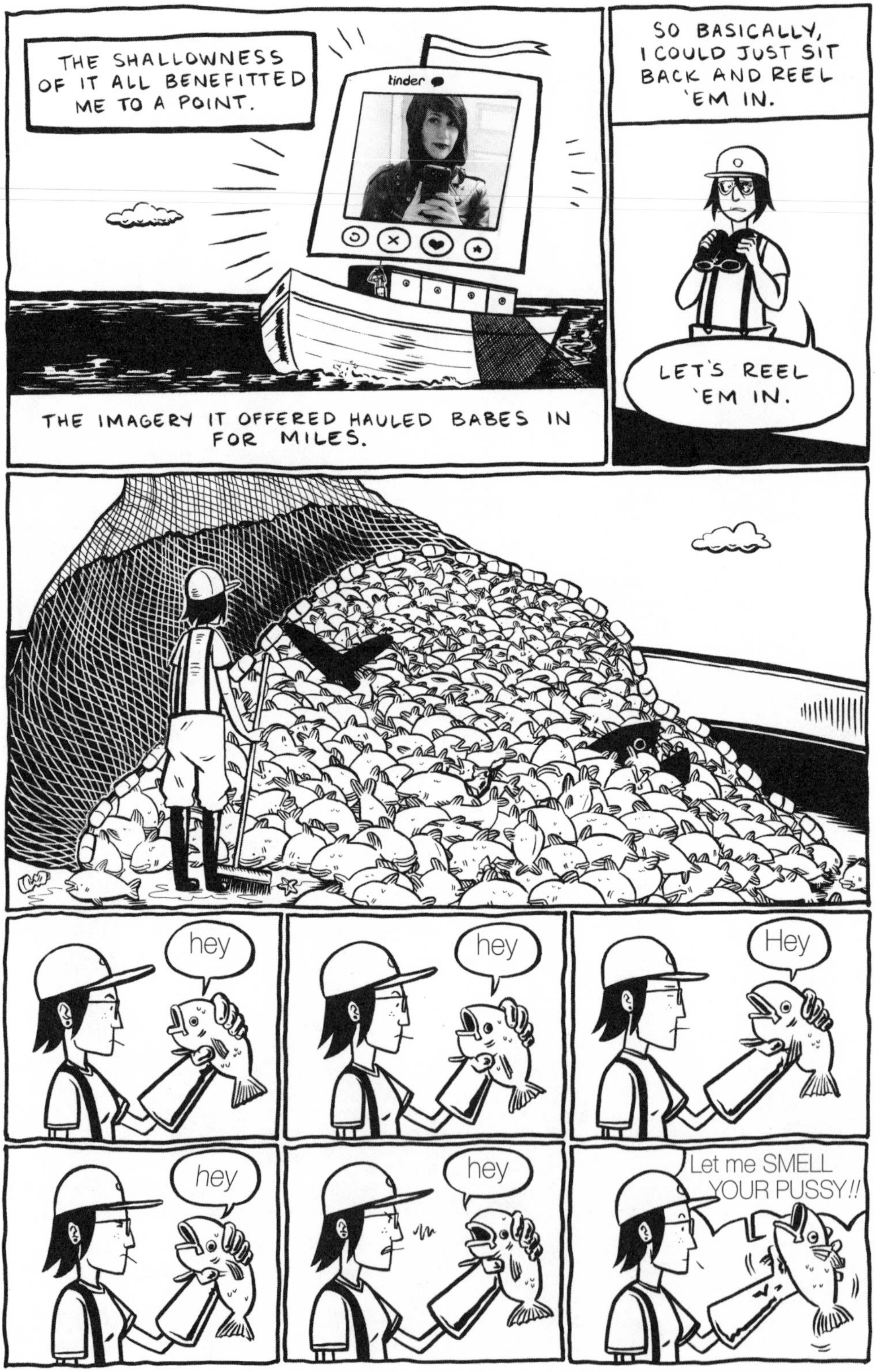

THE SHALLOWNESS OF IT ALL BENEFITTED ME TO A POINT.
tinder
THE IMAGERY IT OFFERED HAULED BABES IN FOR MILES.
SO BASICALLY, I COULD JUST SIT BACK AND REEL 'EM IN.
LET'S REEL 'EM IN.
hey
hey
Hey
hey
hey
Let me SMELL YOUR PUSSY!!

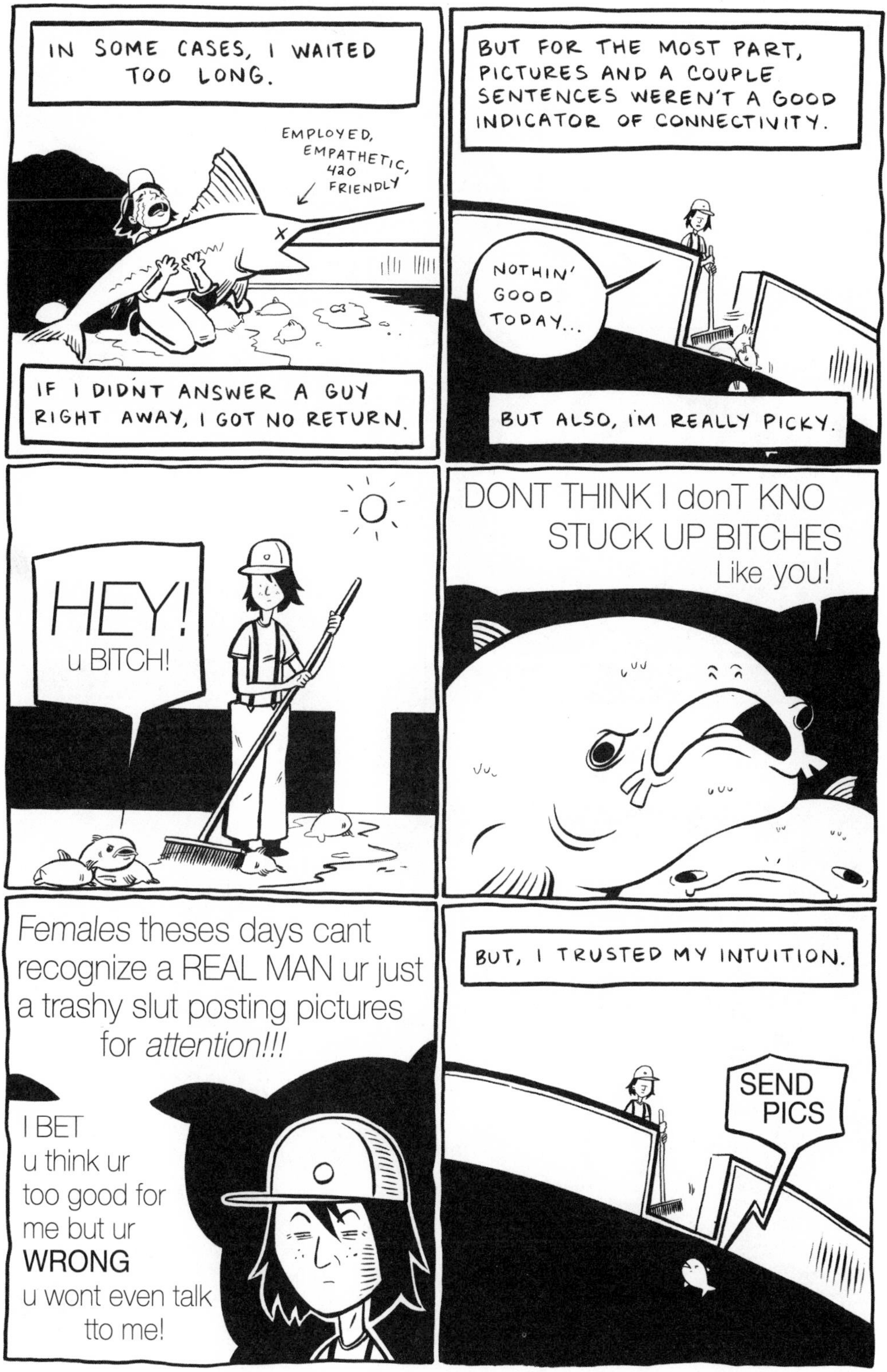
IN SOME CASES, I WAITED TOO LONG.
EMPLOYED, EMPATHETIC, 420 FRIENDLY
IF I DIDN'T ANSWER A GUY RIGHT AWAY, I GOT NO RETURN.
BUT FOR THE MOST PART, PICTURES AND A COUPLE SENTENCES WEREN'T A GOOD INDICATOR OF CONNECTIVITY.
NOTHIN' GOOD TODAY...
BUT ALSO, I'M REALLY PICKY.
HEY! u BITCH!
DONT THINK I donT KNO STUCK UP BITCHES Like you!
Females theses days cant recognize a REAL MAN ur just a trashy slut posting pictures for attention!!!
I BET u think ur too good for me but ur WRONG u wont even talk tto me!
BUT, I TRUSTED MY INTUITION.
SEND PICS

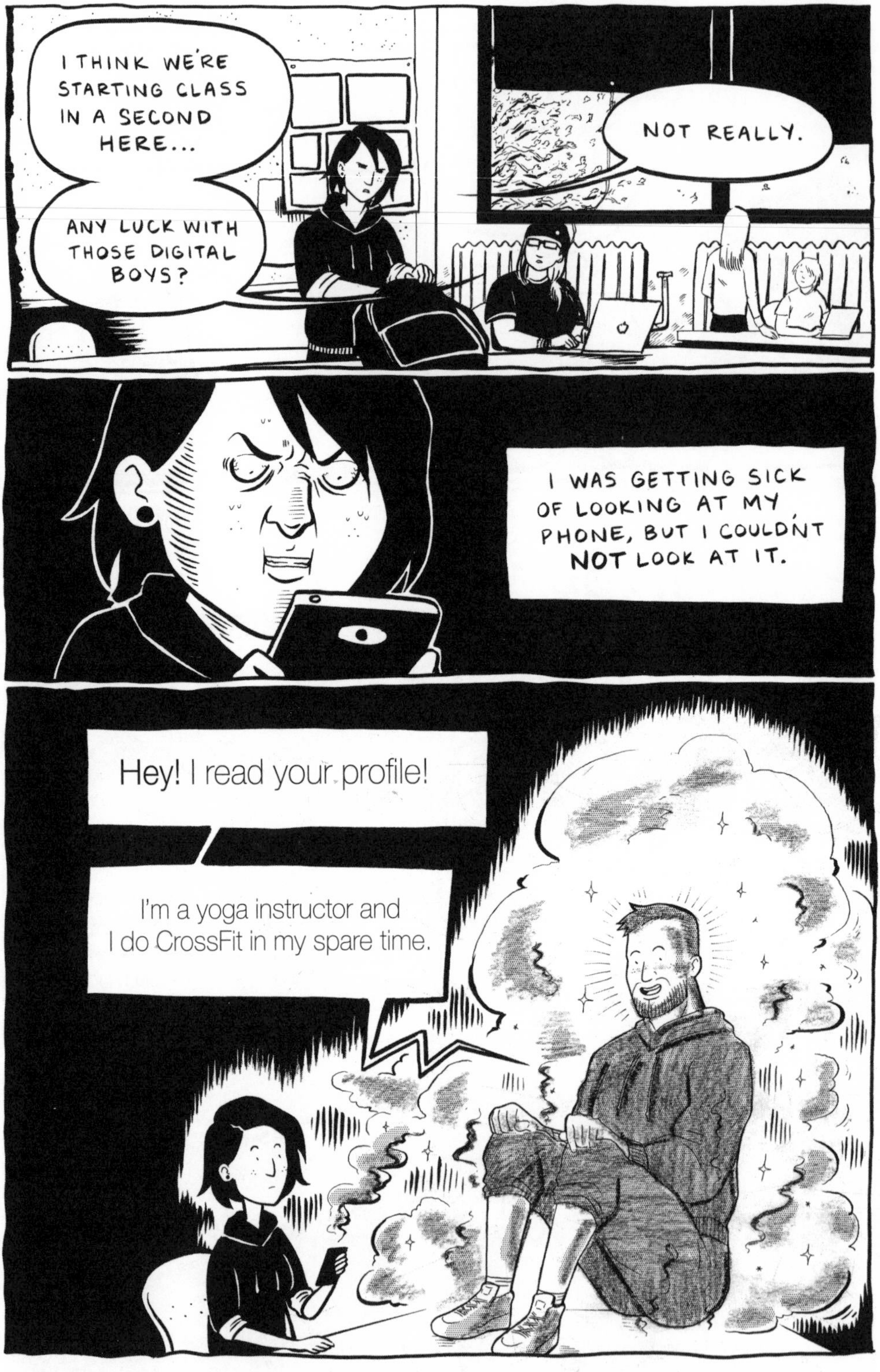
I THINK WE'RE STARTING CLASS IN A SECOND HERE...
ANY LUCK WITH THOSE DIGITAL BOYS?
NOT REALLY.
I WAS GETTING SICK OF LOOKING AT MY PHONE, BUT I COULDN'T NOT LOOK AT IT.
Hey! I read your profile!
I'm a yoga instructor and I do CrossFit in my spare time.

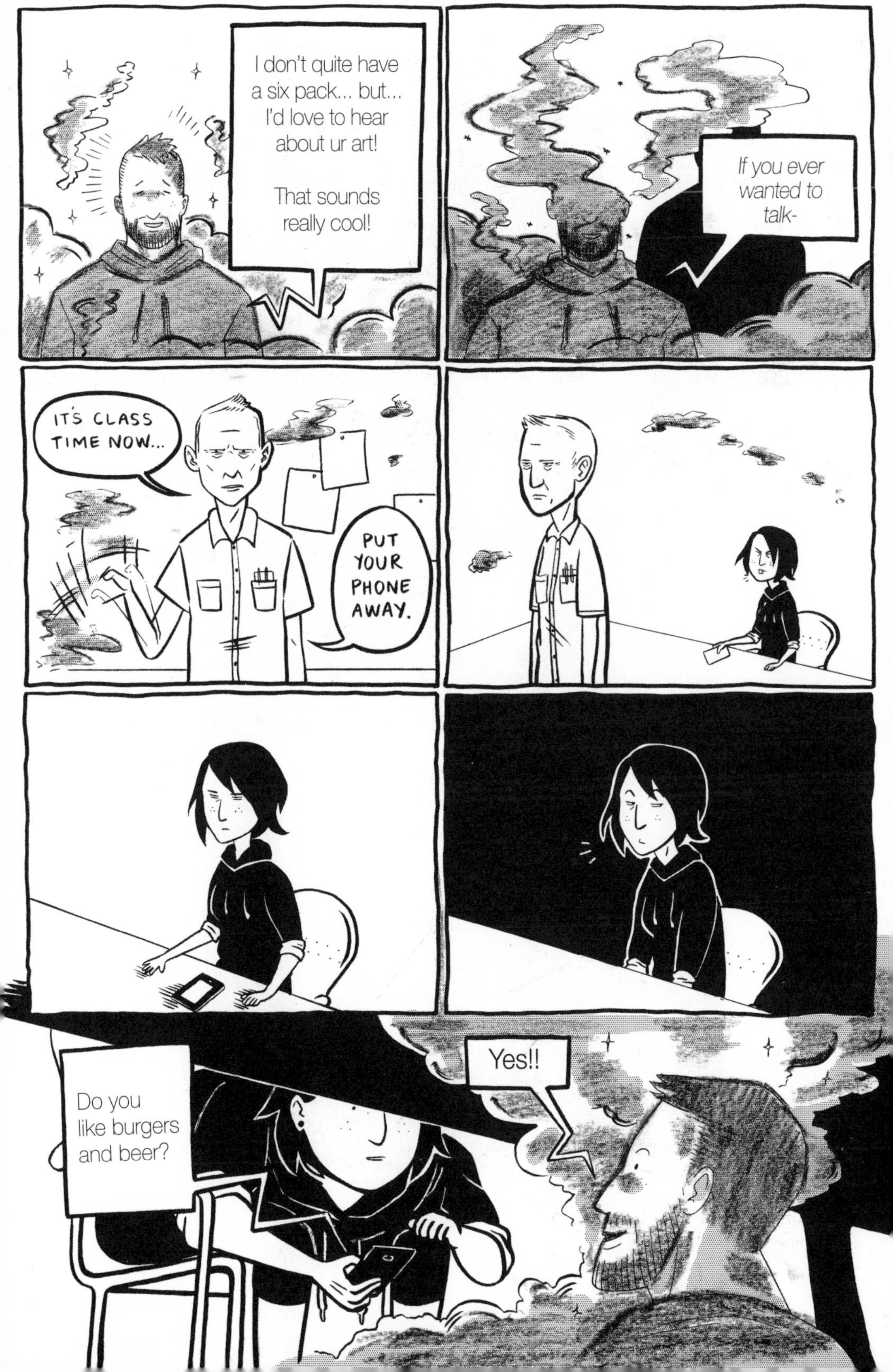
I don't quite have a six pack... but... I'd love to hear about ur art!

That sounds really cool!
If you ever wanted to talk-
IT'S CLASS TIME NOW...
PUT YOUR PHONE AWAY.
Do you like burgers and beer?
Yes!!

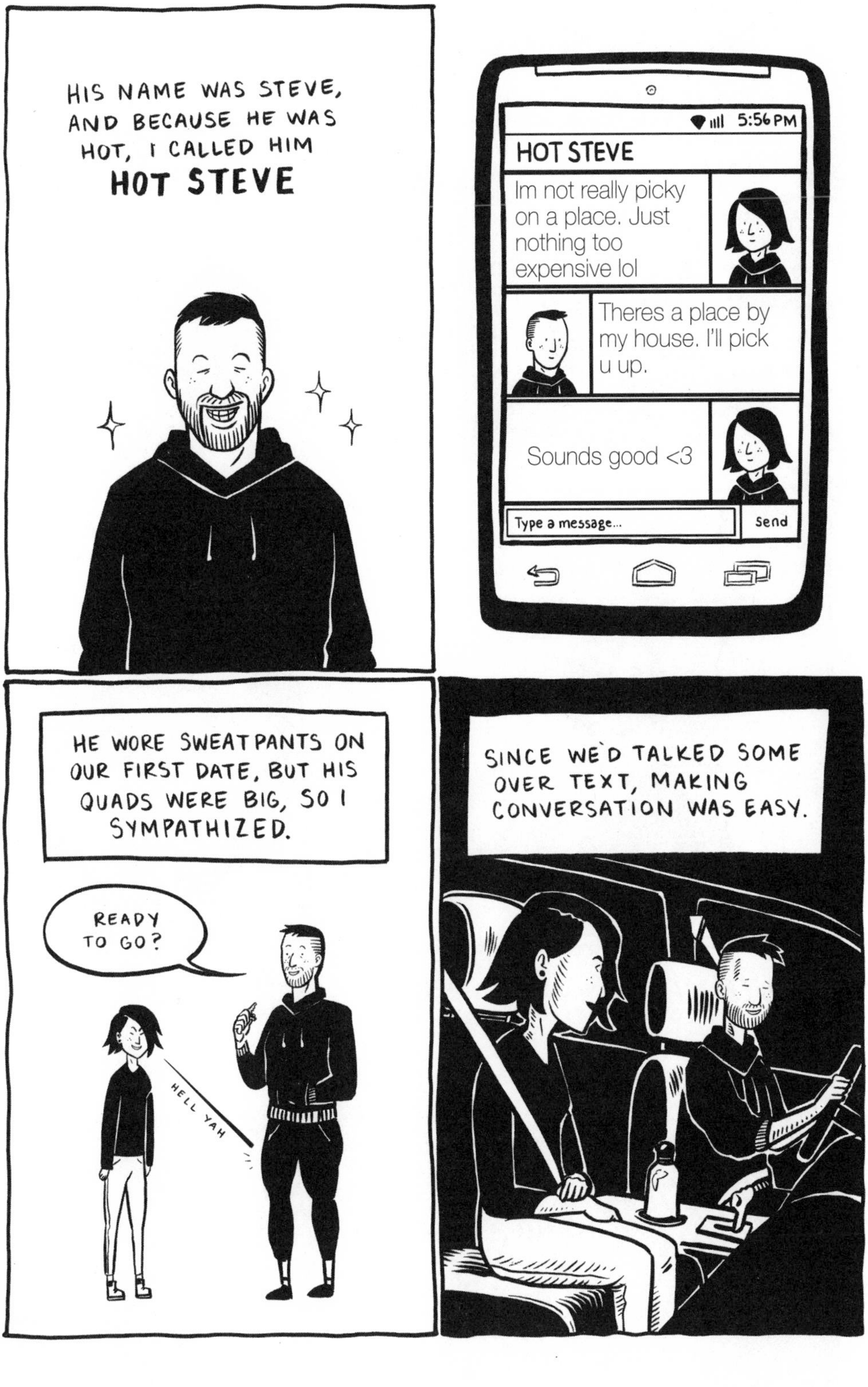
HIS NAME WAS STEVE, AND BECAUSE HE WAS HOT, I CALLED HIM
HOT STEVE
5:56 PM
HOT STEVE
Im not really picky on a place. Just nothing too expensive lol
Theres a place by my house. I'll pick u up.
Sounds good <3
Type a message...
Send
HE WORE SWEATPANTS ON OUR FIRST DATE, BUT HIS QUADS WERE BIG, SO I SYMPATHIZED.
READY TO GO?
HELL YAH
SINCE WE'D TALKED SOME OVER TEXT, MAKING CONVERSATION WAS EASY.

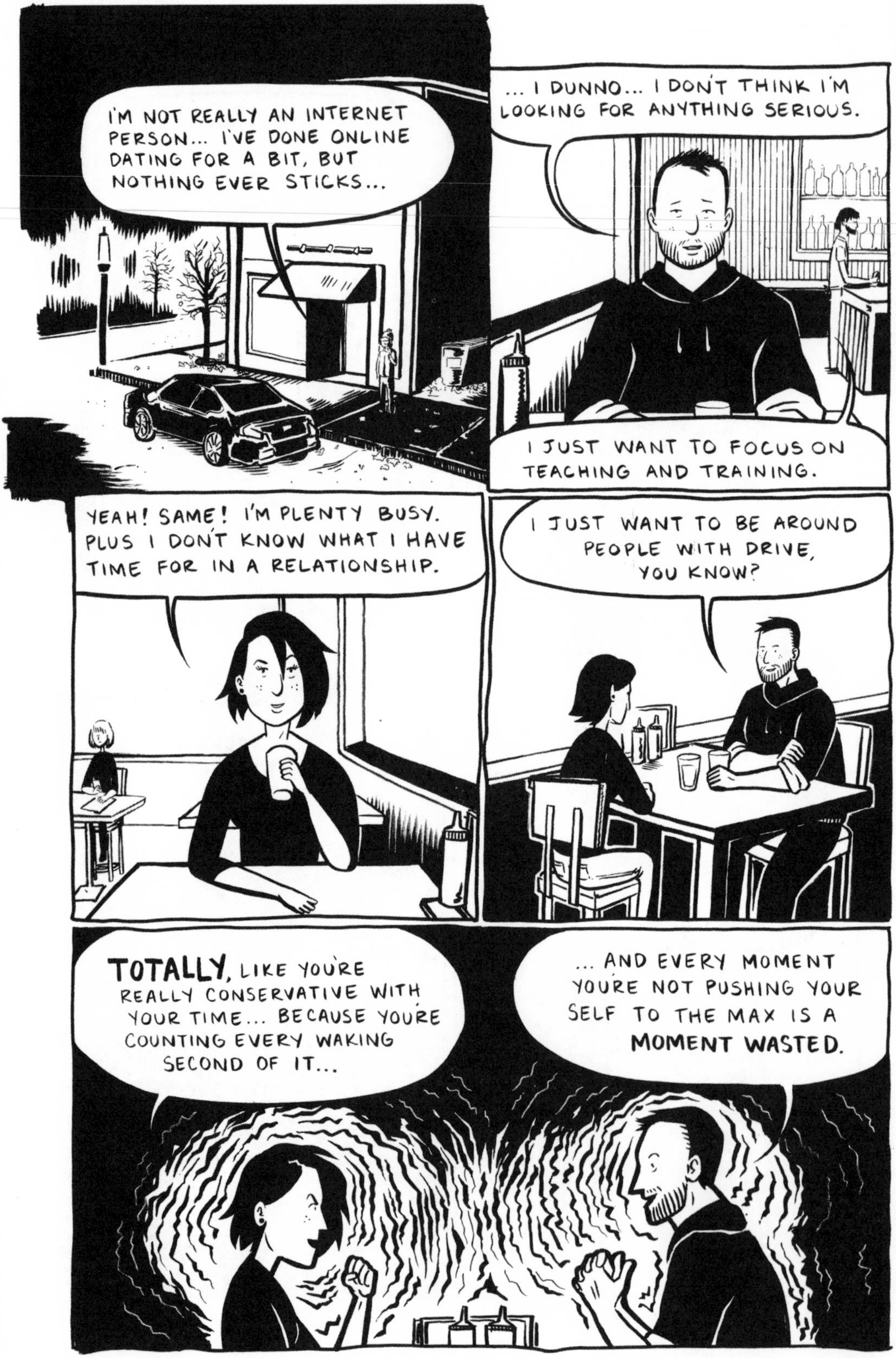
I'M NOT REALLY AN INTERNET PERSON... I'VE DONE ONLINE DATING FOR A BIT, BUT NOTHING EVER STICKS...
... I DUNNO... I DON'T THINK I'M LOOKING FOR ANYTHING SERIOUS.
I JUST WANT TO FOCUS ON TEACHING AND TRAINING.
YEAH! SAME! I'M PLENTY BUSY. PLUS I DON'T KNOW WHAT I HAVE TIME FOR IN A RELATIONSHIP.
I JUST WANT TO BE AROUND PEOPLE WITH DRIVE, YOU KNOW?
TOTALLY, LIKE YOU'RE REALLY CONSERVATIVE WITH YOUR TIME... BECAUSE YOU'RE COUNTING EVERY WAKING SECOND OF IT...
... AND EVERY MOMENT YOU'RE NOT PUSHING YOUR SELF TO THE MAX IS A MOMENT WASTED.

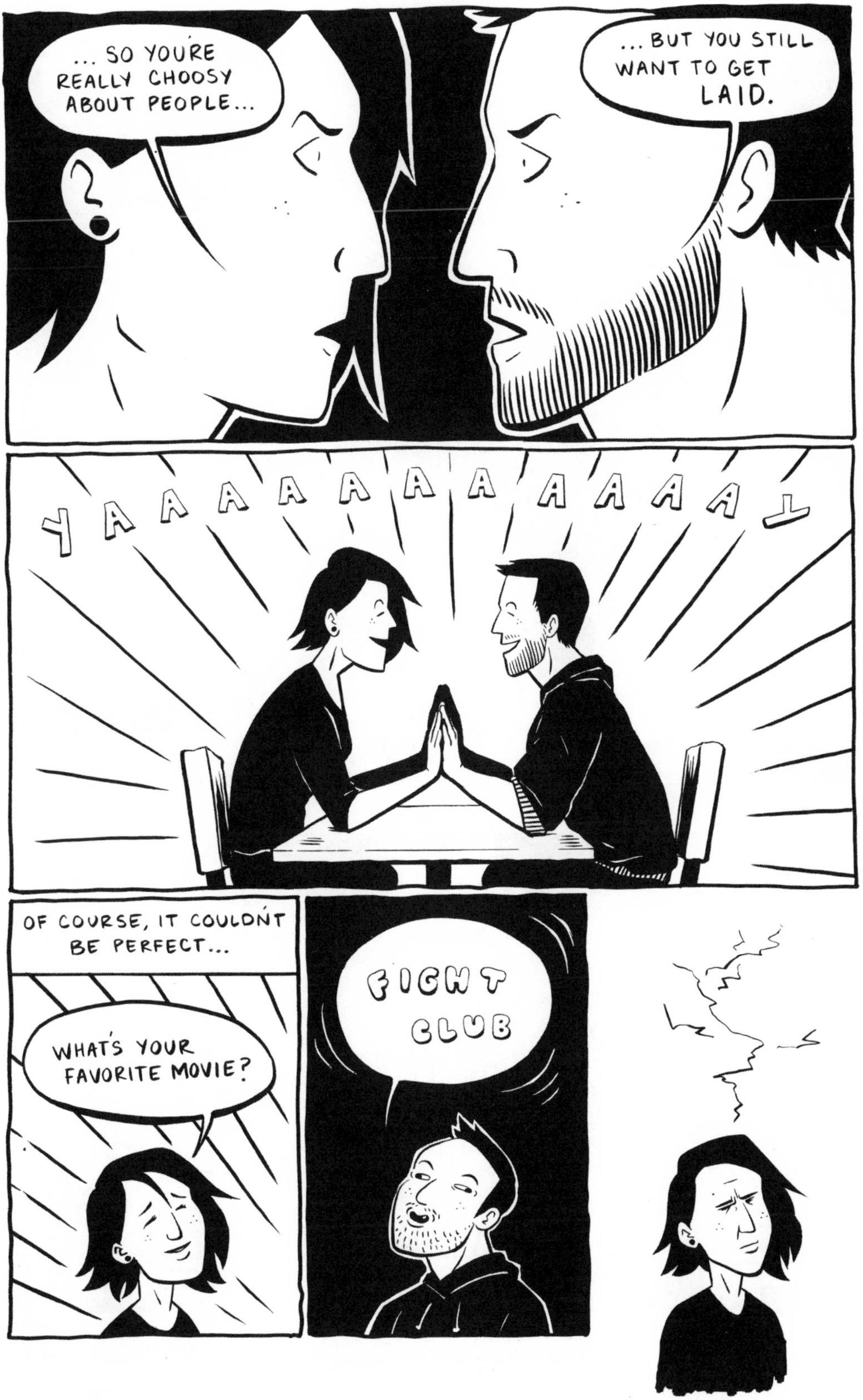
... SO YOU'RE REALLY CHOOSY ABOUT PEOPLE...
... BUT YOU STILL WANT TO GET LAID.
YAAAAAAAAAAAL
OF COURSE, IT COULDN'T BE PERFECT...
WHAT'S YOUR FAVORITE MOVIE?
FIGHT CLUB

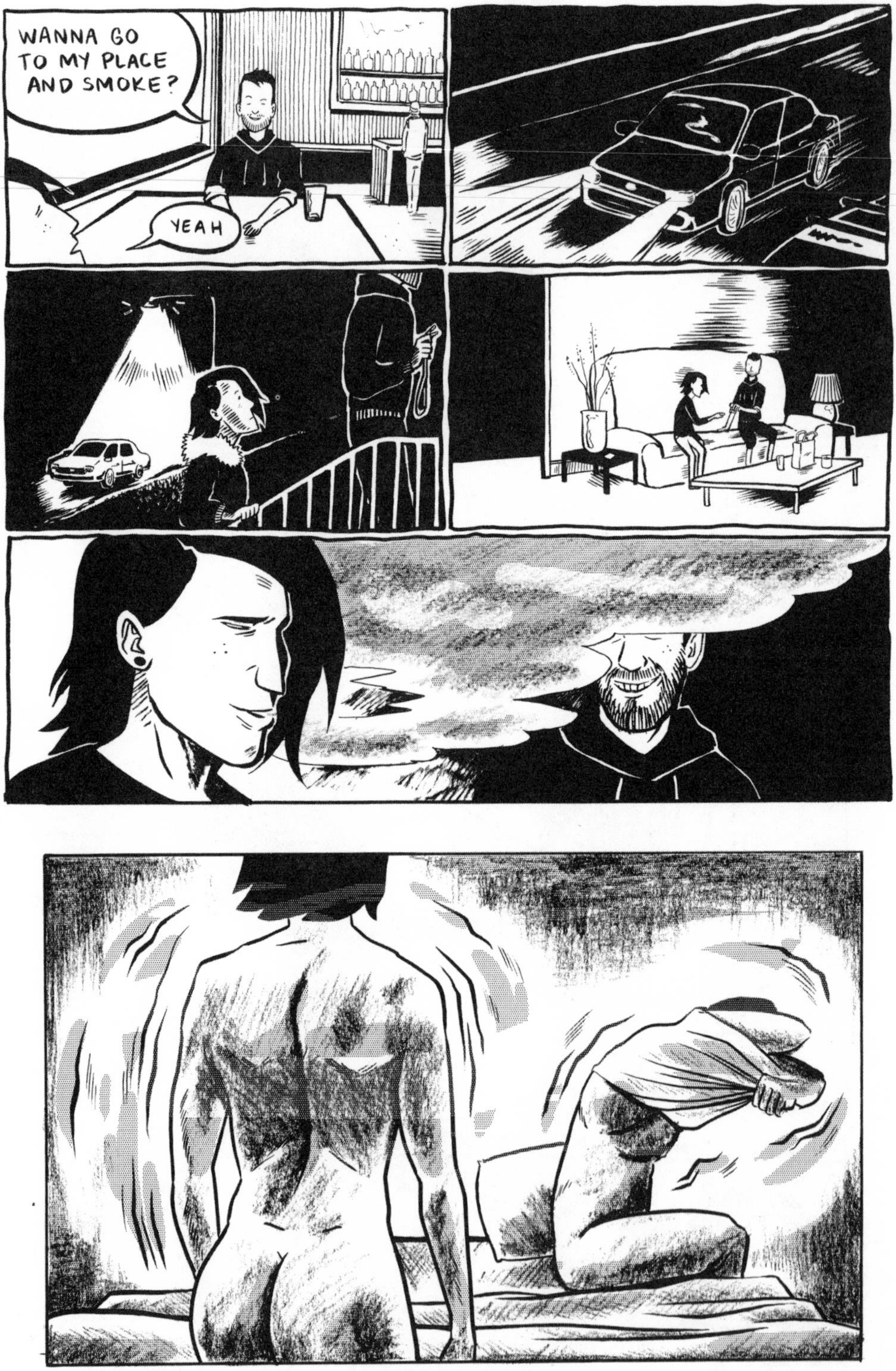
WANNA GO TO MY PLACE AND SMOKE?
YEAH

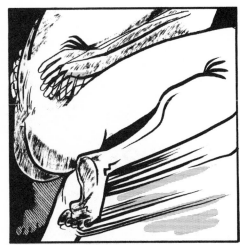

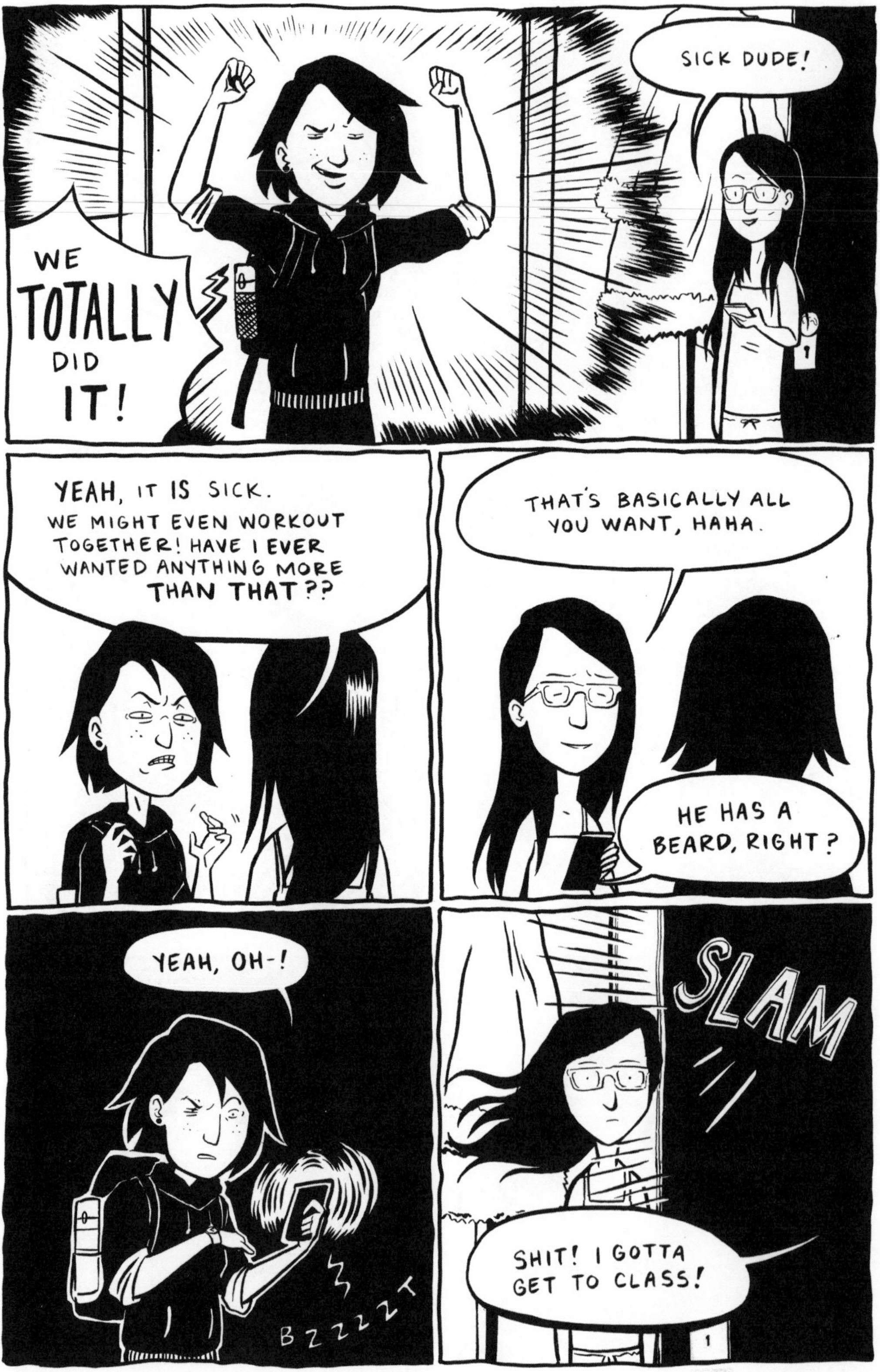
WE TOTALLY DID IT!
SICK DUDE!
YEAH, IT IS SICK. WE MIGHT EVEN WORKOUT TOGETHER! HAVE I EVER WANTED ANYTHING MORE THAN THAT??
THAT'S BASICALLY ALL YOU WANT, HAHA.
HE HAS A BEARD, RIGHT?
YEAH, OH-!
BZZZZT
SLAM
SHIT! I GOTTA GET TO CLASS!

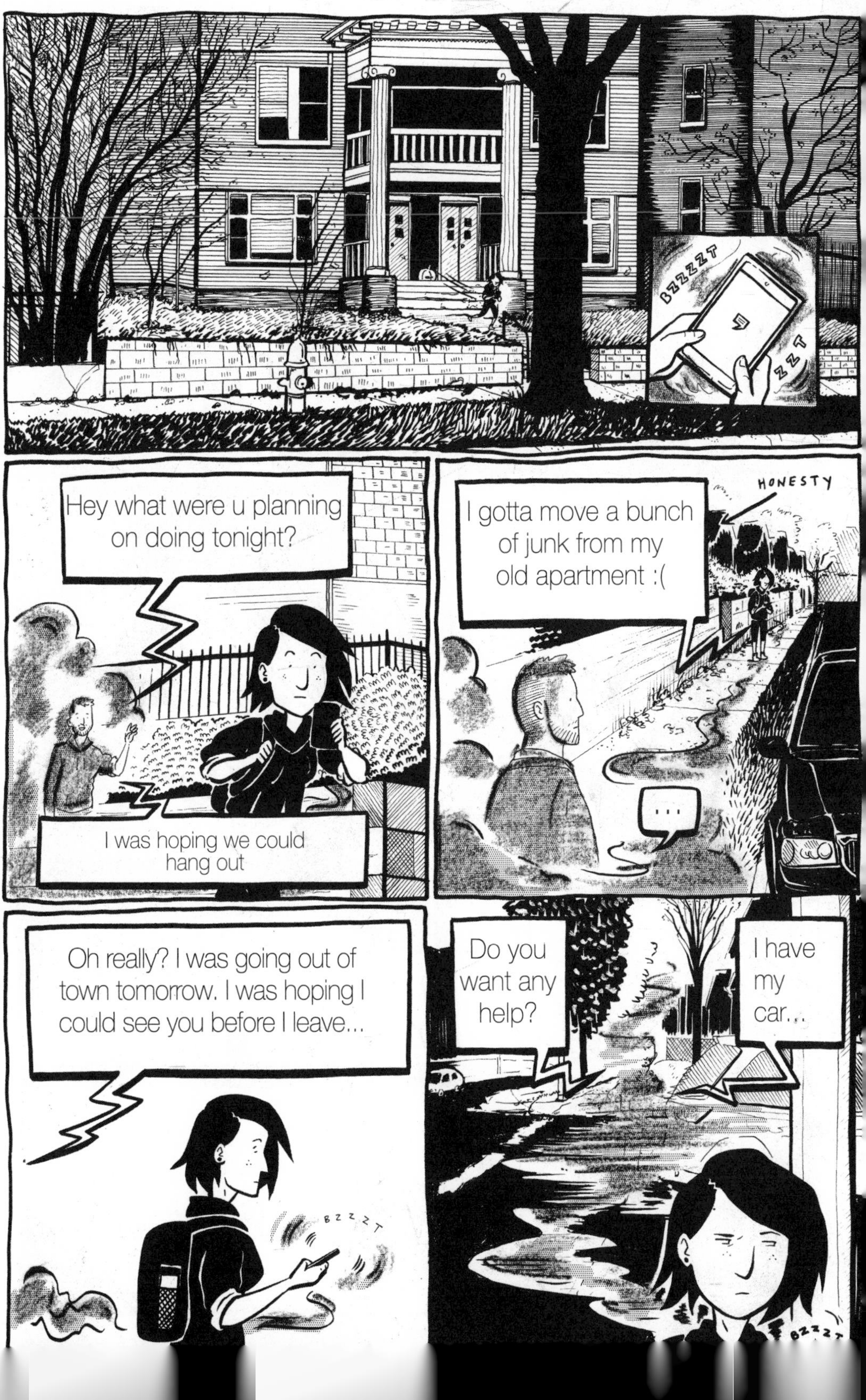
BZZZZT
ZZT
Hey what were u planning on doing tonight?
I was hoping we could hang out
HONESTY
I gotta move a bunch of junk from my old apartment :(
....
Oh really? I was going out of town tomorrow. I was hoping I could see you before I leave...
BZZZT
Do you want any help?
I have my car...
BZZZT

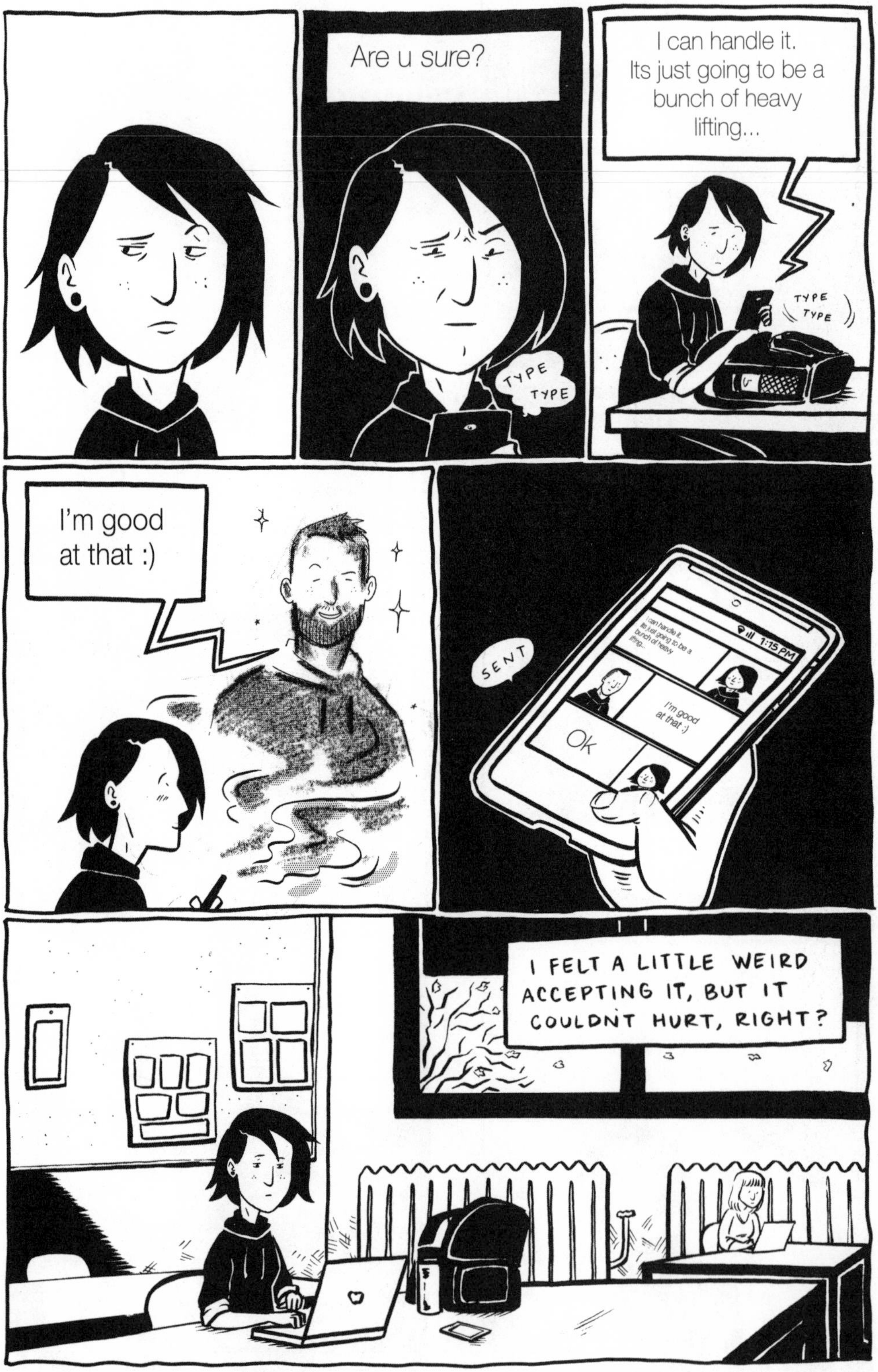
Are u sure?
TYPE TYPE
I can handle it. Its just going to be a bunch of heavy lifting...
TYPE TYPE
I'm good at that :)
SENT
Ok
I FELT A LITTLE WEIRD ACCEPTING IT, BUT IT COULDN'T HURT, RIGHT?

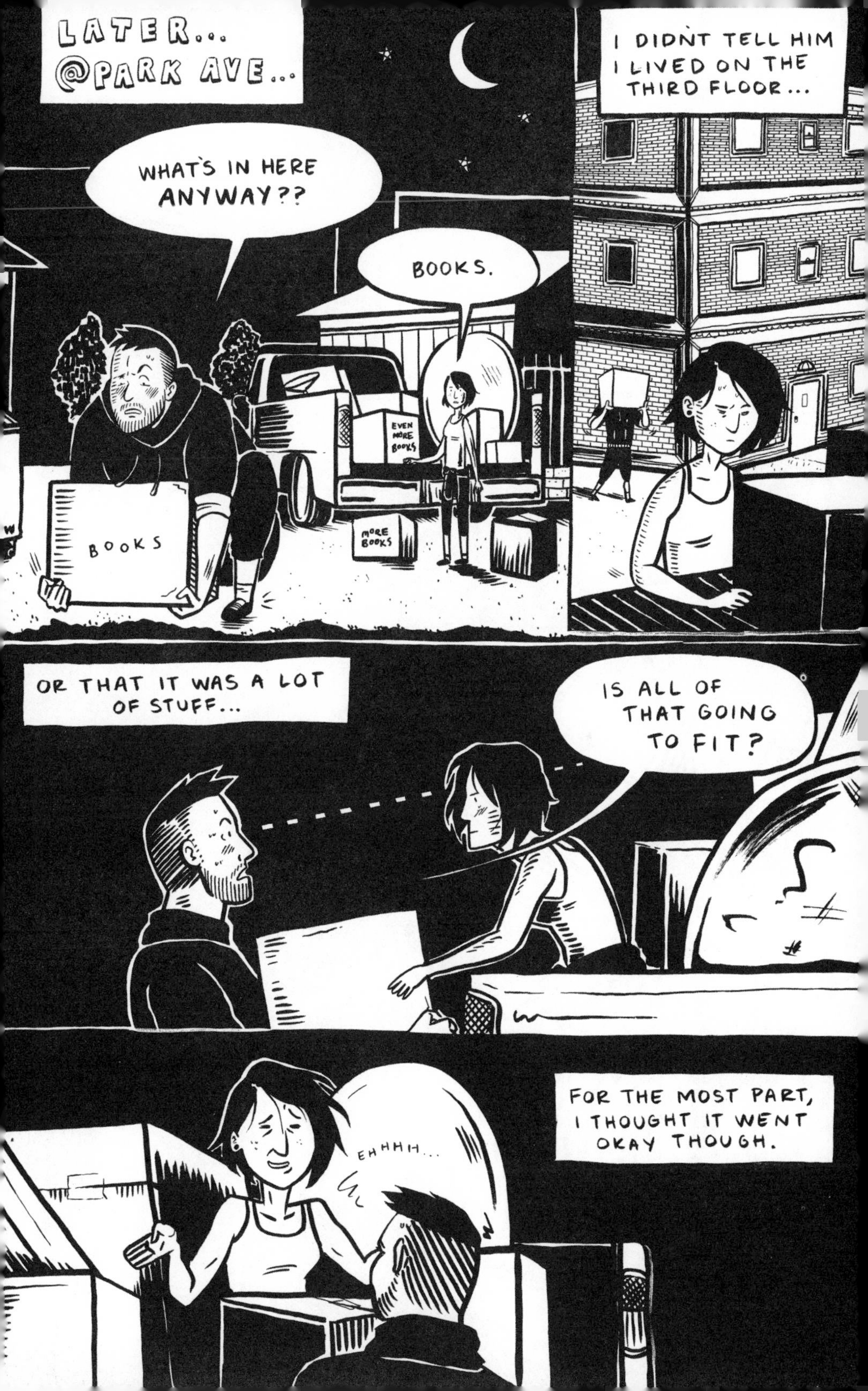
LATER...
@PARK AVE...
WHAT'S IN HERE ANYWAY??
BOOKS.
EVEN MORE BOOKS
MORE BOOKS
BOOKS
I DIDN'T TELL HIM I LIVED ON THE THIRD FLOOR...
OR THAT IT WAS A LOT OF STUFF...
IS ALL OF THAT GOING TO FIT?
EHHHH...
FOR THE MOST PART, I THOUGHT IT WENT OKAY THOUGH.

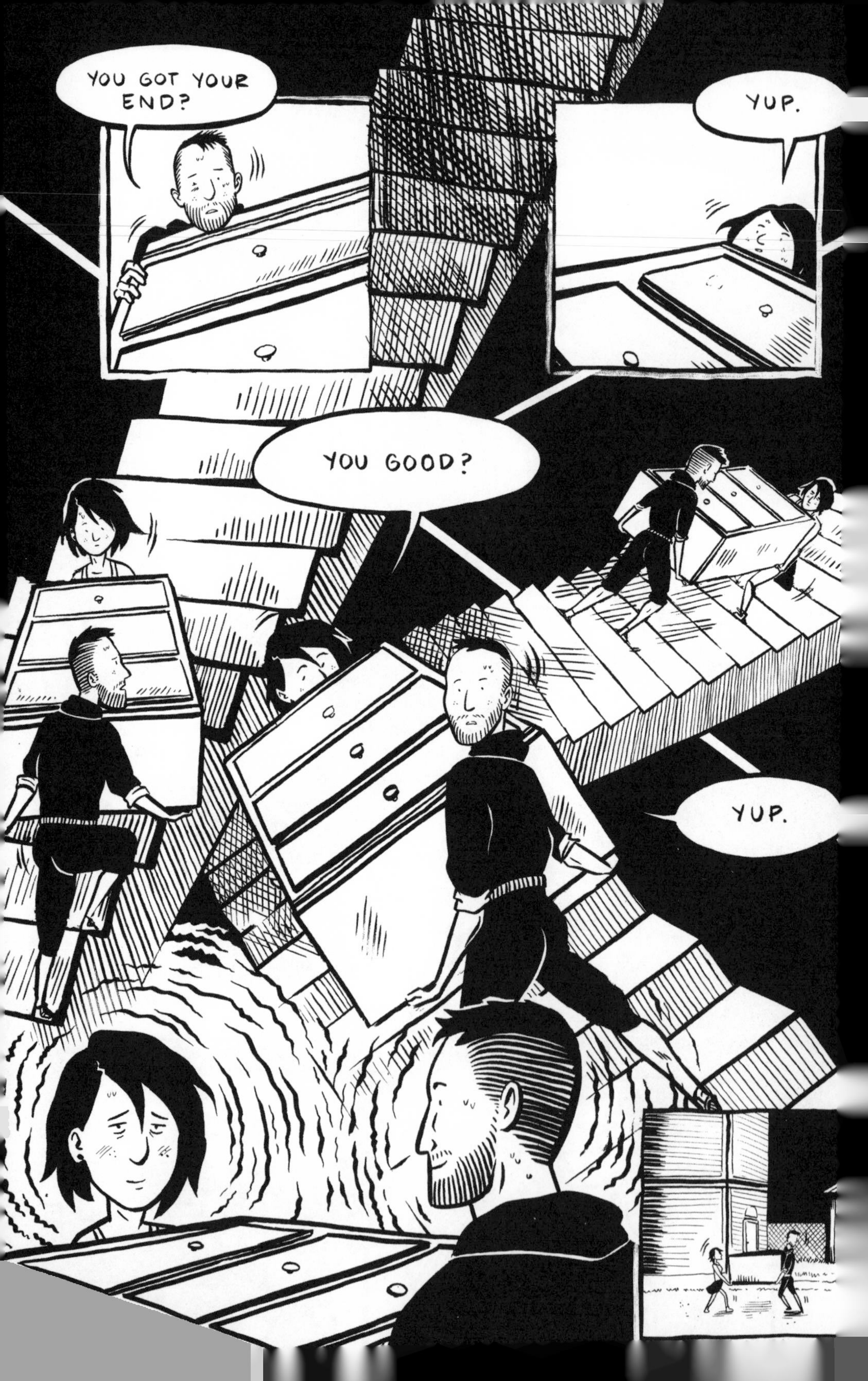
YOU GOT YOUR END?
YUP.
YOU GOOD?
YUP.

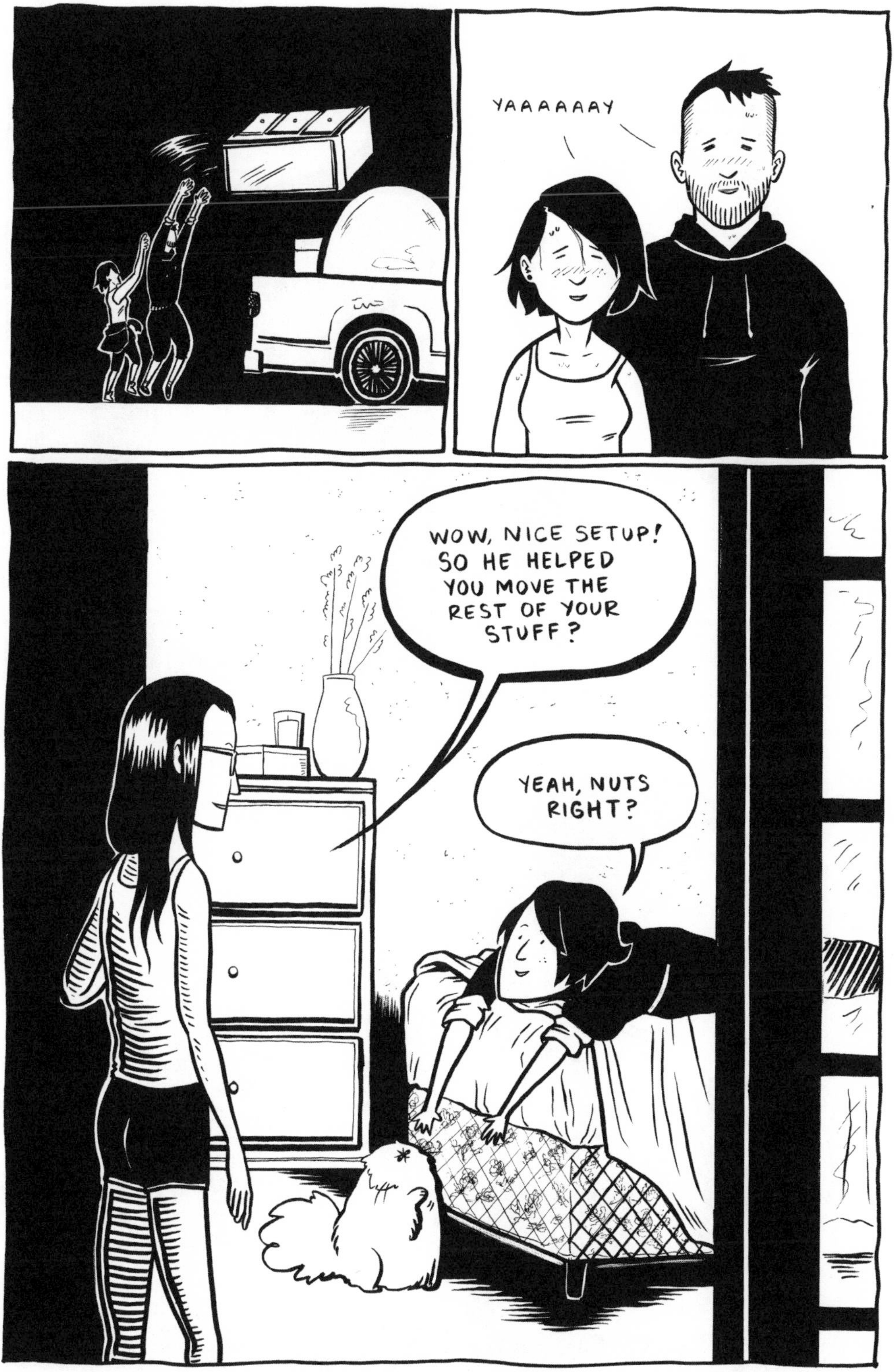
YAAAAAAY
WOW, NICE SETUP! SO HE HELPED YOU MOVE THE REST OF YOUR STUFF?
YEAH, NUTS RIGHT?

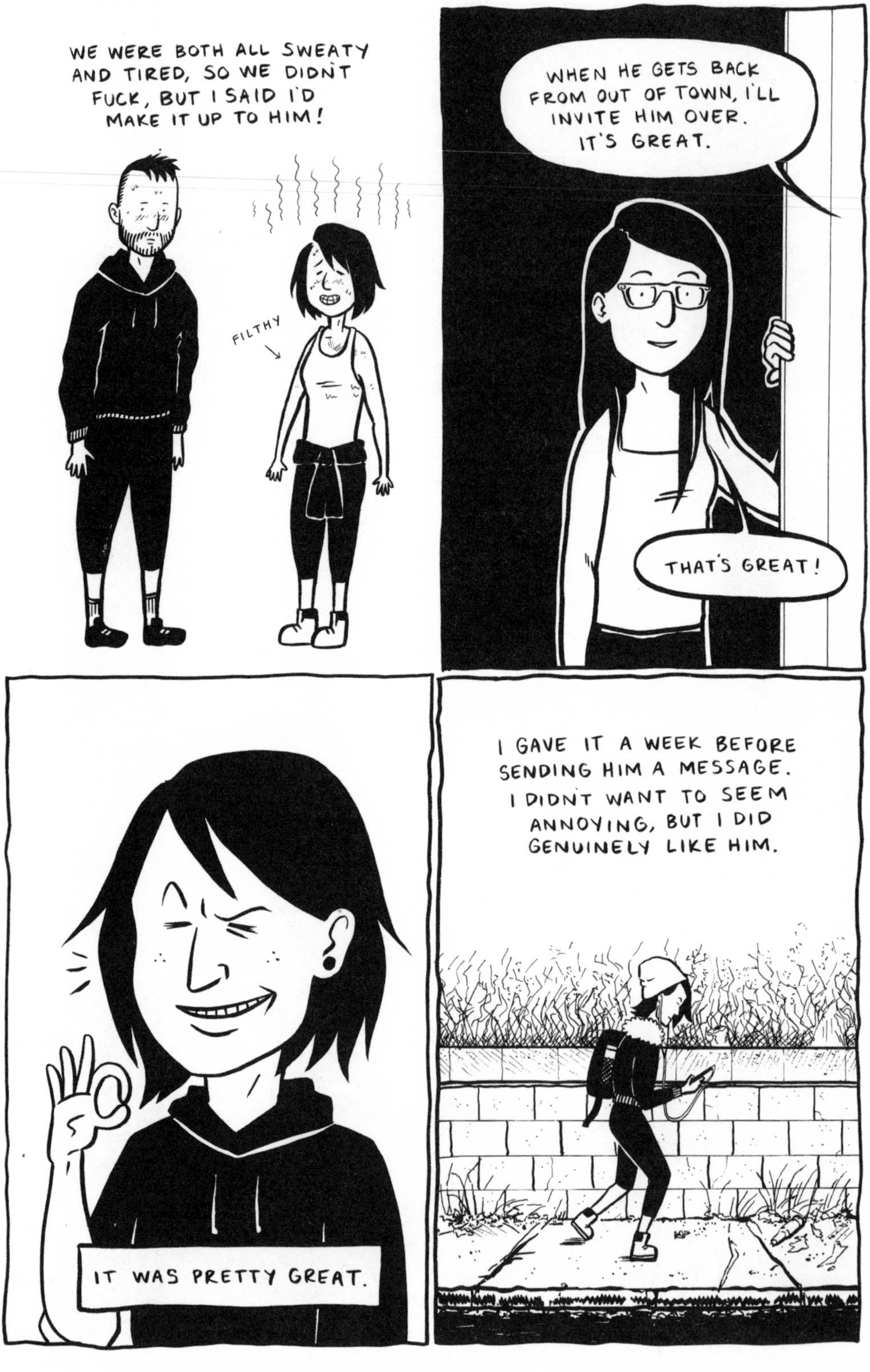
WE WERE BOTH ALL SWEATY AND TIRED, SO WE DIDN'T FUCK, BUT I SAID I'D MAKE IT UP TO HIM!
FILTHY
WHEN HE GETS BACK FROM OUT OF TOWN, I'LL INVITE HIM OVER. IT'S GREAT.
THAT'S GREAT!
IT WAS PRETTY GREAT.
I GAVE IT A WEEK BEFORE SENDING HIM A MESSAGE. I DIDN'T WANT TO SEEM ANNOYING, BUT I DID GENUINELY LIKE HIM.

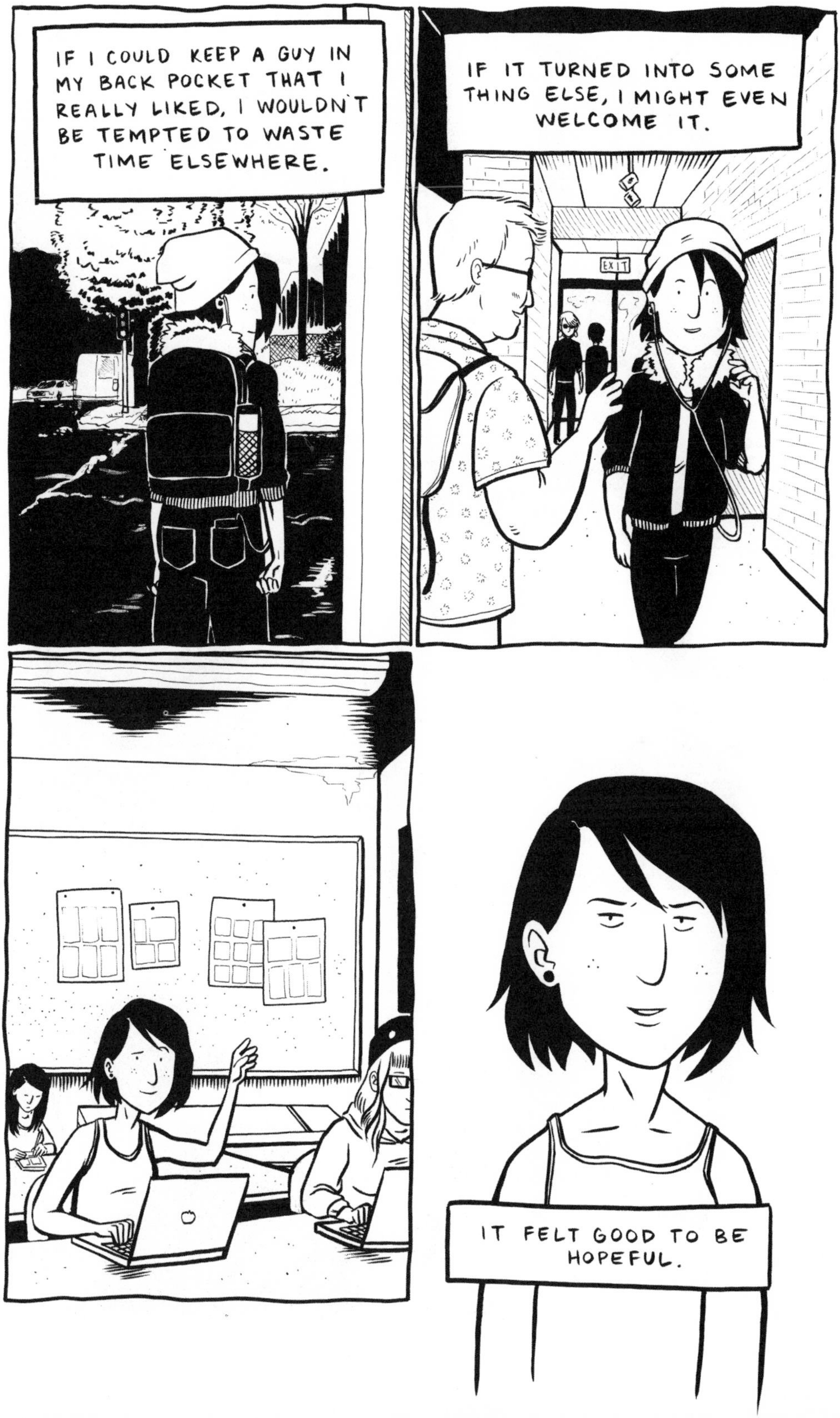
IF I COULD KEEP A GUY IN MY BACK POCKET THAT I REALLY LIKED, I WOULDN'T BE TEMPTED TO WASTE TIME ELSEWHERE.
IF IT TURNED INTO SOME THING ELSE, I MIGHT EVEN WELCOME IT.
EXIT
IT FELT GOOD TO BE HOPEFUL.

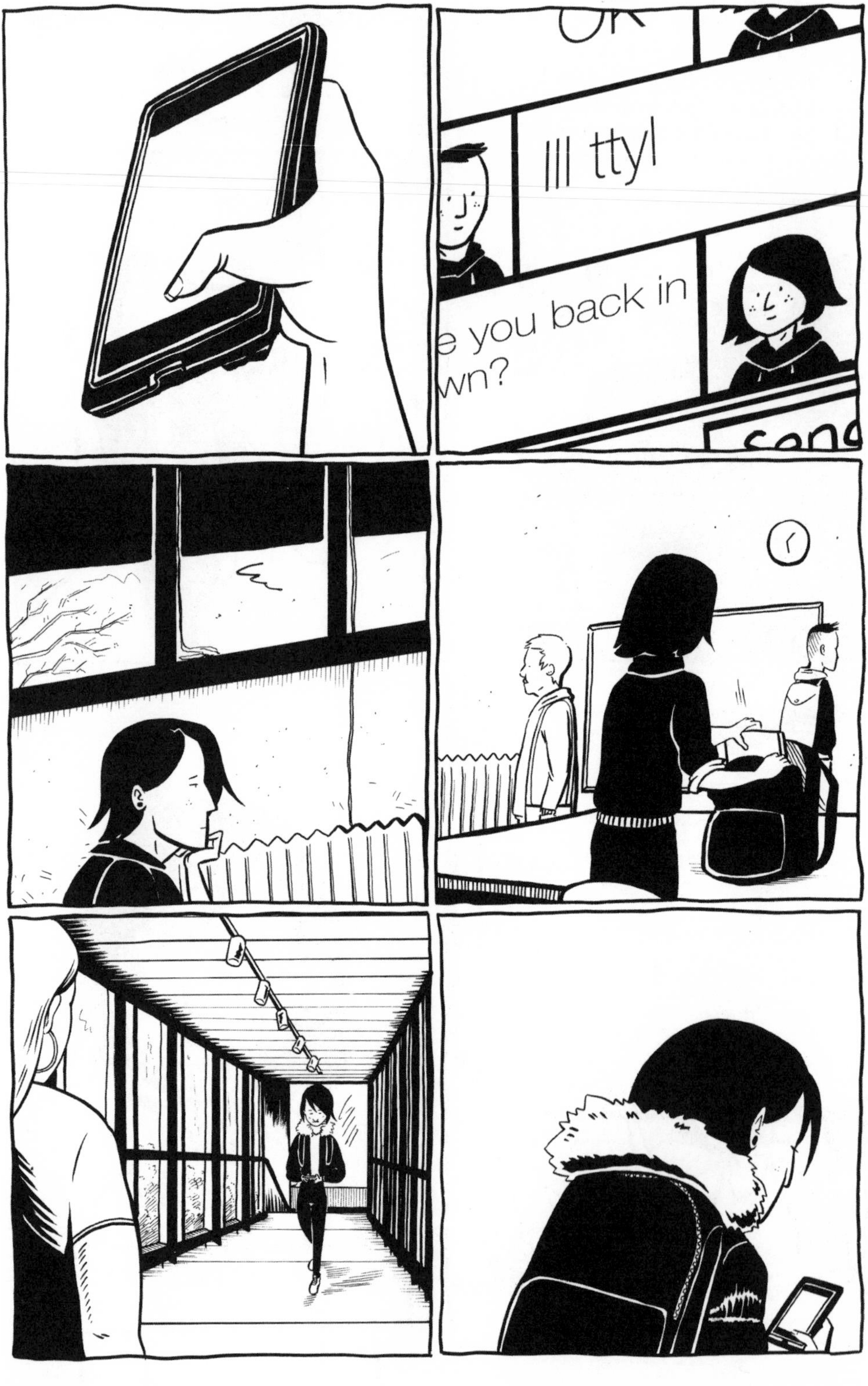
OK
Ill ttyl
e you back in
wn?

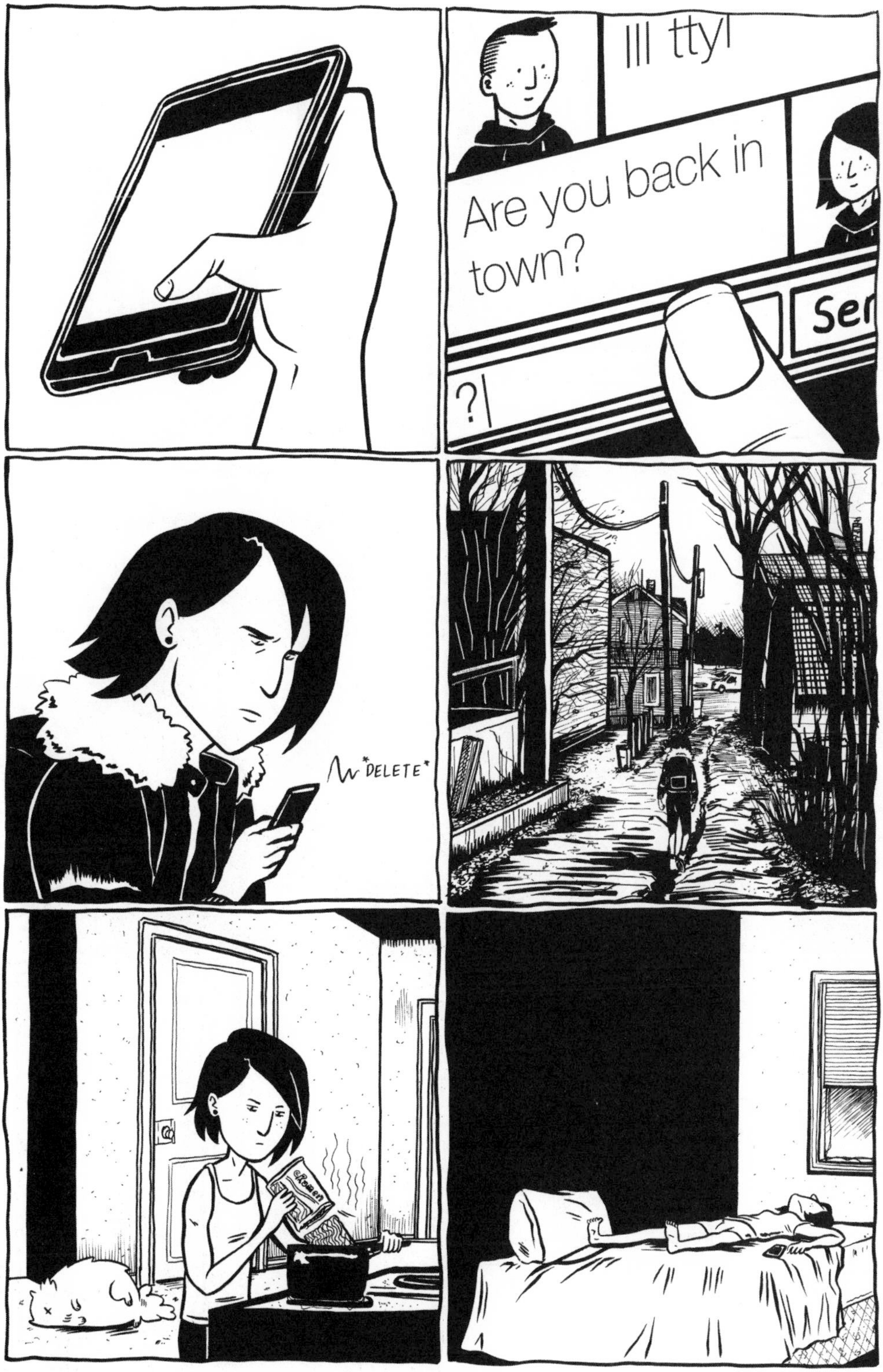
lll ttyl
Are you back in town?
?
Ser
DELETE
Ramen

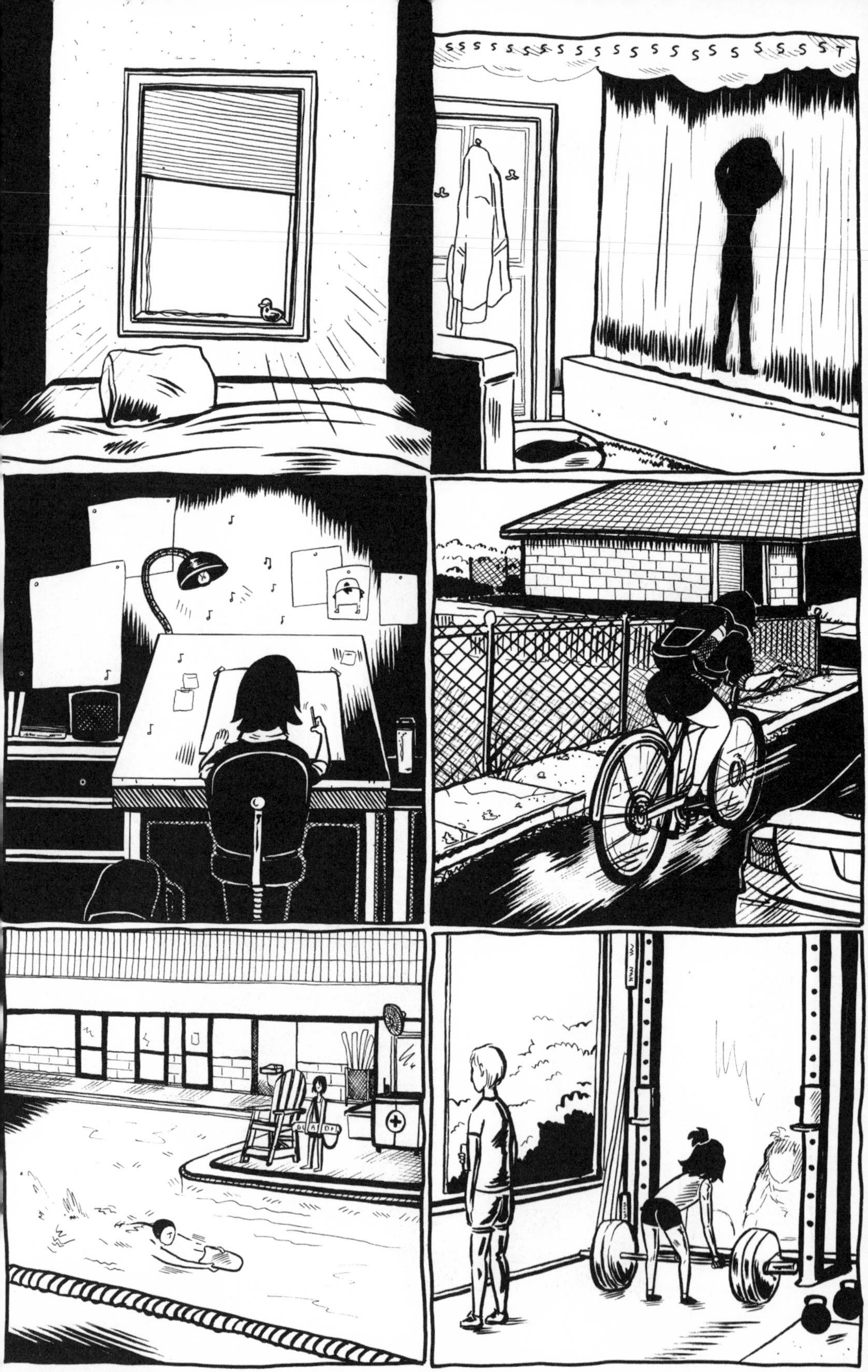
SSSSSSSSSSSSSSSSSSSSST

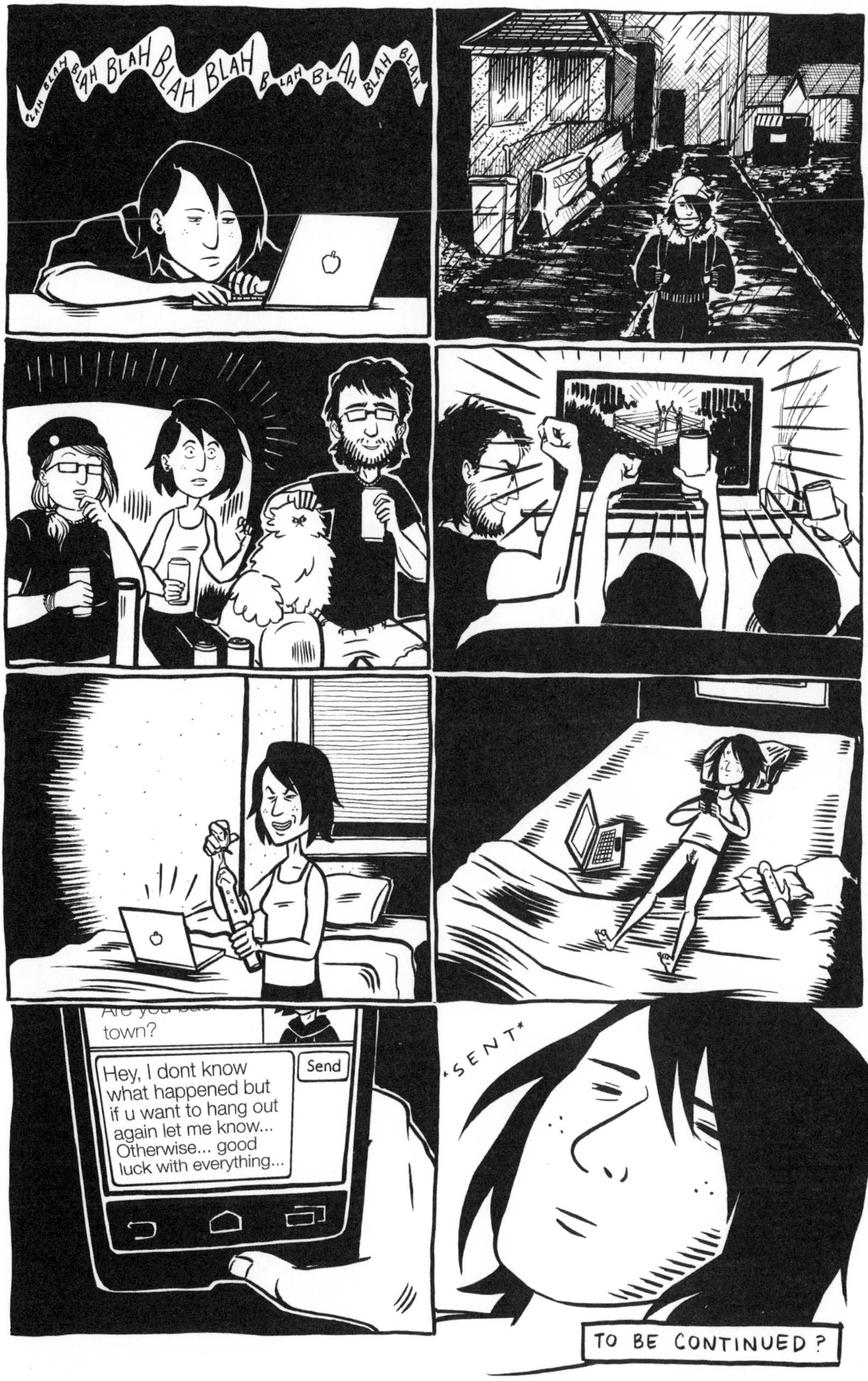
BLAH BLAH BLAH BLAH BLAH BLAH BLAH BLAH BLAH BLAH BLAH BLAH
town?
Hey, I dont know what happened but if u want to hang out again let me know... Otherwise... good luck with everything...
Send
SENT
TO BE CONTINUED?

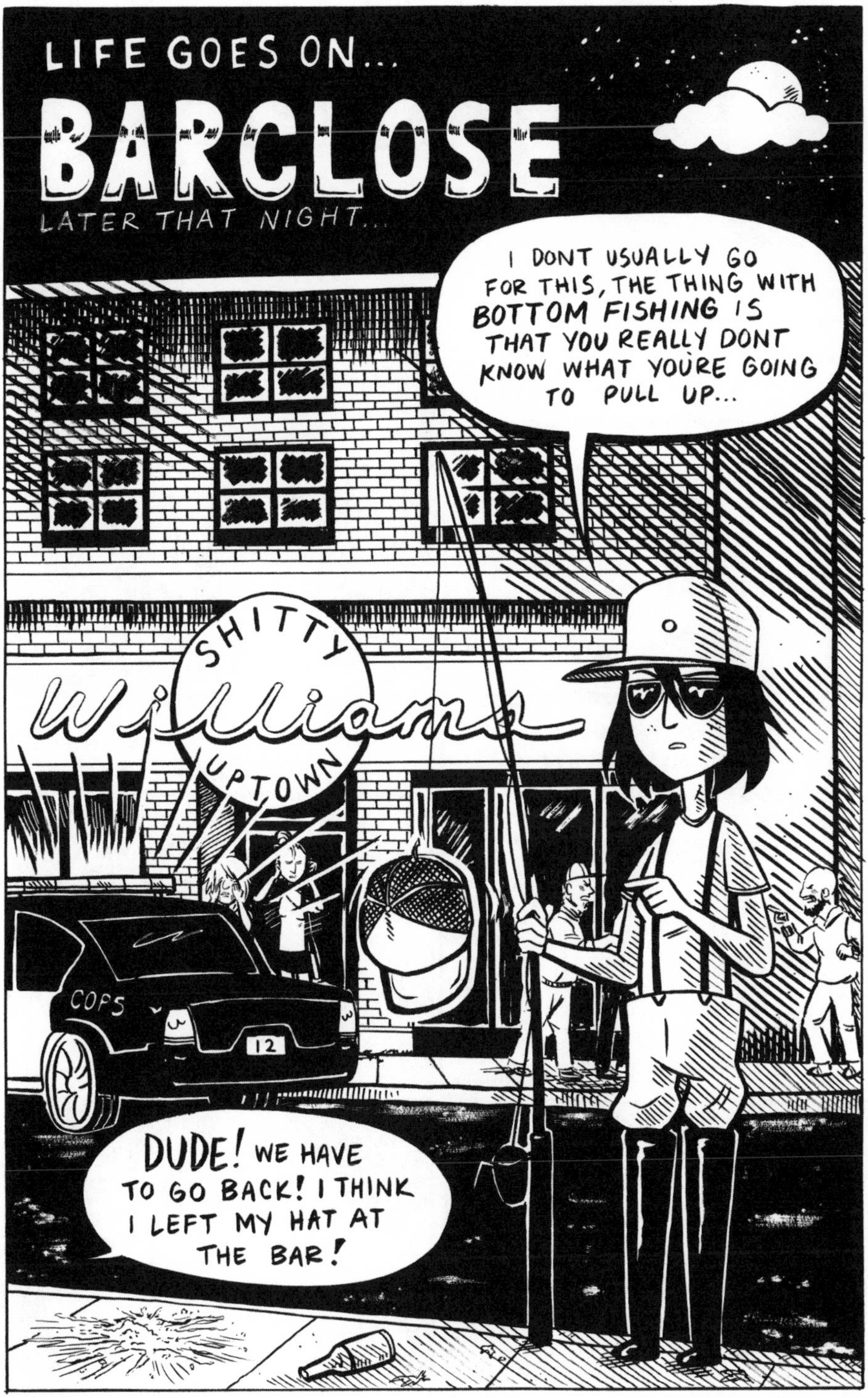
LIFE GOES ON...
BARCLOSE
LATER THAT NIGHT...
I DONT USUALLY GO FOR THIS, THE THING WITH BOTTOM FISHING IS THAT YOU REALLY DONT KNOW WHAT YOU'RE GOING TO PULL UP...
SHITTY
Williams
UPTOWN
COPS
12
DUDE! WE HAVE TO GO BACK! I THINK I LEFT MY HAT AT THE BAR!

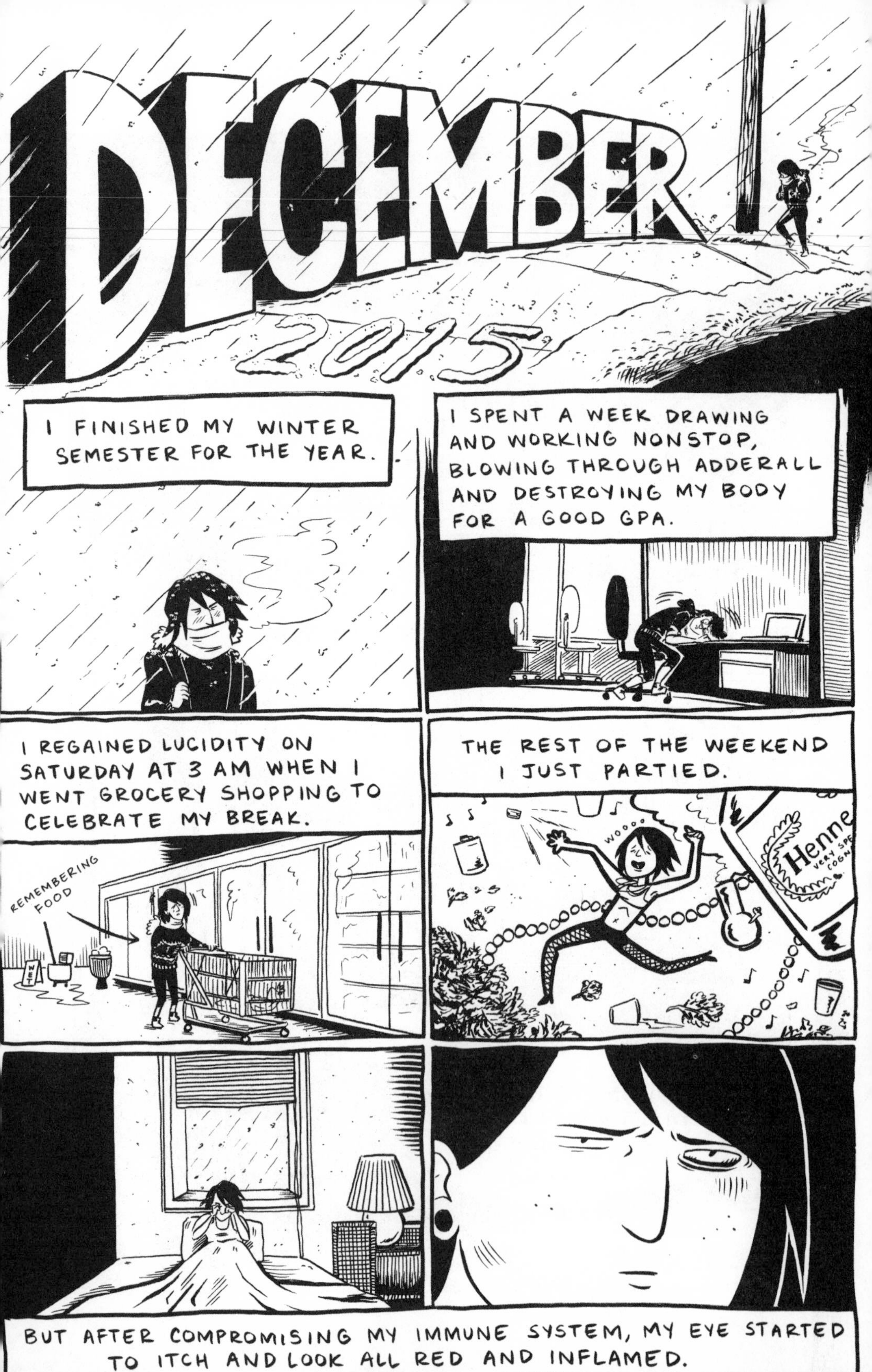
DECEMBER
2015
I FINISHED MY WINTER SEMESTER FOR THE YEAR.
I SPENT A WEEK DRAWING AND WORKING NONSTOP, BLOWING THROUGH ADDERALL AND DESTROYING MY BODY FOR A GOOD GPA.
I REGAINED LUCIDITY ON SATURDAY AT 3 AM WHEN I WENT GROCERY SHOPPING TO CELEBRATE MY BREAK.
REMEMBERING FOOD
THE REST OF THE WEEKEND I JUST PARTIED.
WOOOO
BUT AFTER COMPROMISING MY IMMUNE SYSTEM, MY EYE STARTED TO ITCH AND LOOK ALL RED AND INFLAMED.

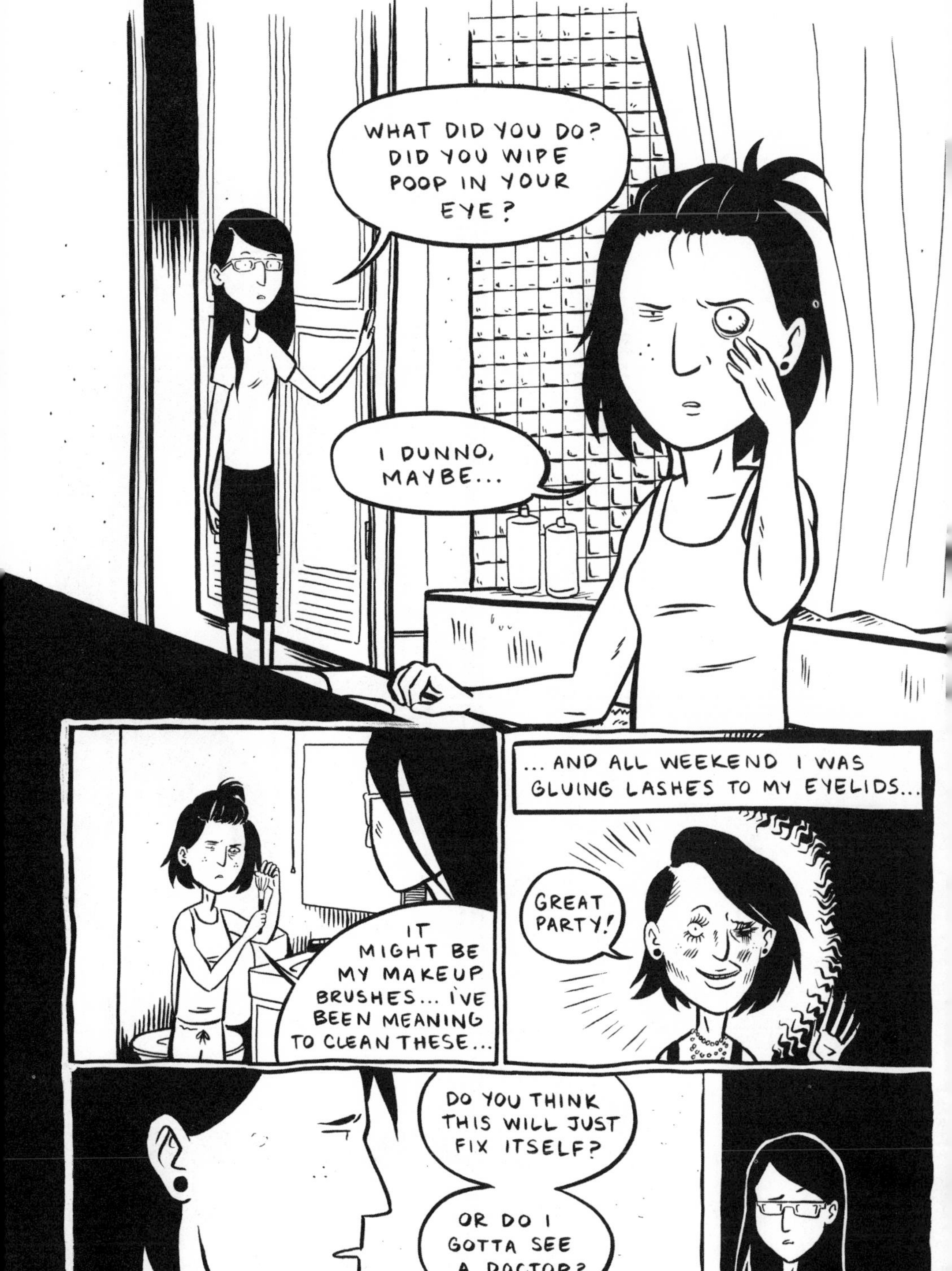
WHAT DID YOU DO? DID YOU WIPE POOP IN YOUR EYE?
I DUNNO, MAYBE...
IT MIGHT BE MY MAKEUP BRUSHES... I'VE BEEN MEANING TO CLEAN THESE...
... AND ALL WEEKEND I WAS GLUING LASHES TO MY EYELIDS...
GREAT PARTY!
DO YOU THINK THIS WILL JUST FIX ITSELF?
OR DO I GOTTA SEE A DOCTOR?
UHHHH...

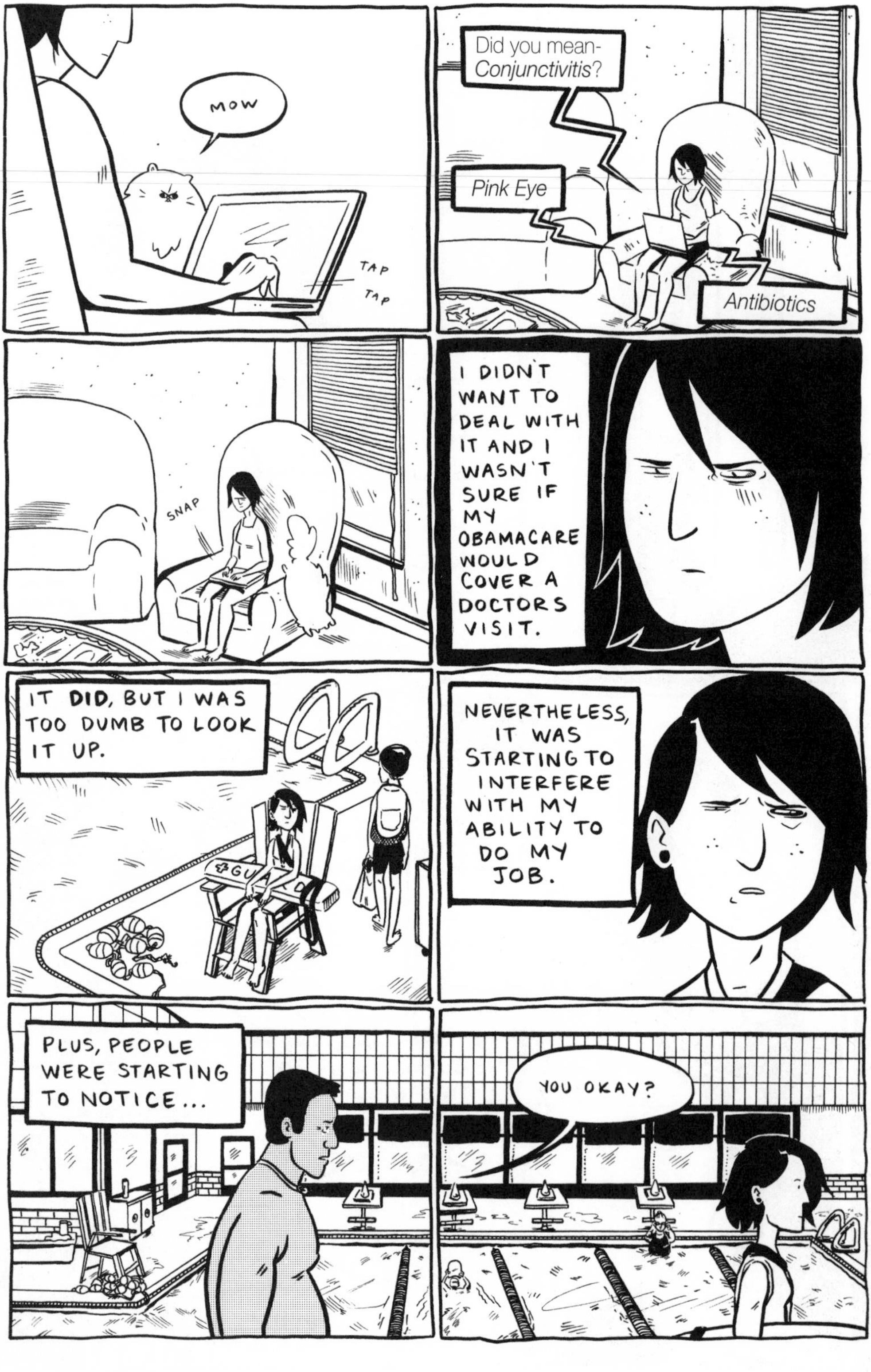
MOW
TAP
TAP
Did you mean-
Conjunctivitis?
Pink Eye
Antibiotics
SNAP
I DIDN'T WANT TO DEAL WITH IT AND I WASN'T SURE IF MY OBAMACARE WOULD COVER A DOCTORS VISIT.
IT DID, BUT I WAS TOO DUMB TO LOOK IT UP.
NEVERTHELESS, IT WAS STARTING TO INTERFERE WITH MY ABILITY TO DO MY JOB.
PLUS, PEOPLE WERE STARTING TO NOTICE...
YOU OKAY?

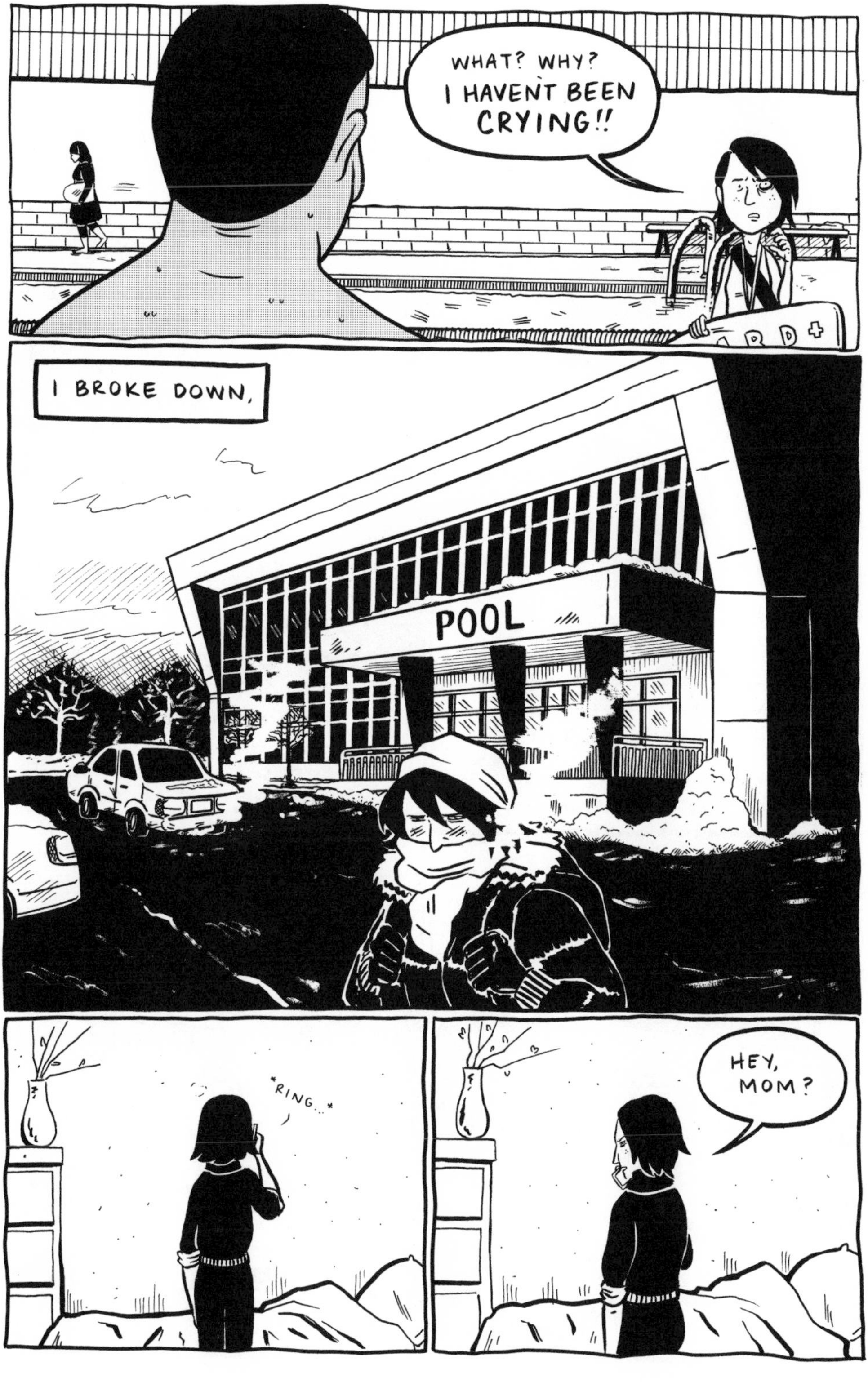
WHAT? WHY? I HAVEN'T BEEN CRYING!!
I BROKE DOWN,
POOL
RING...
HEY, MOM?

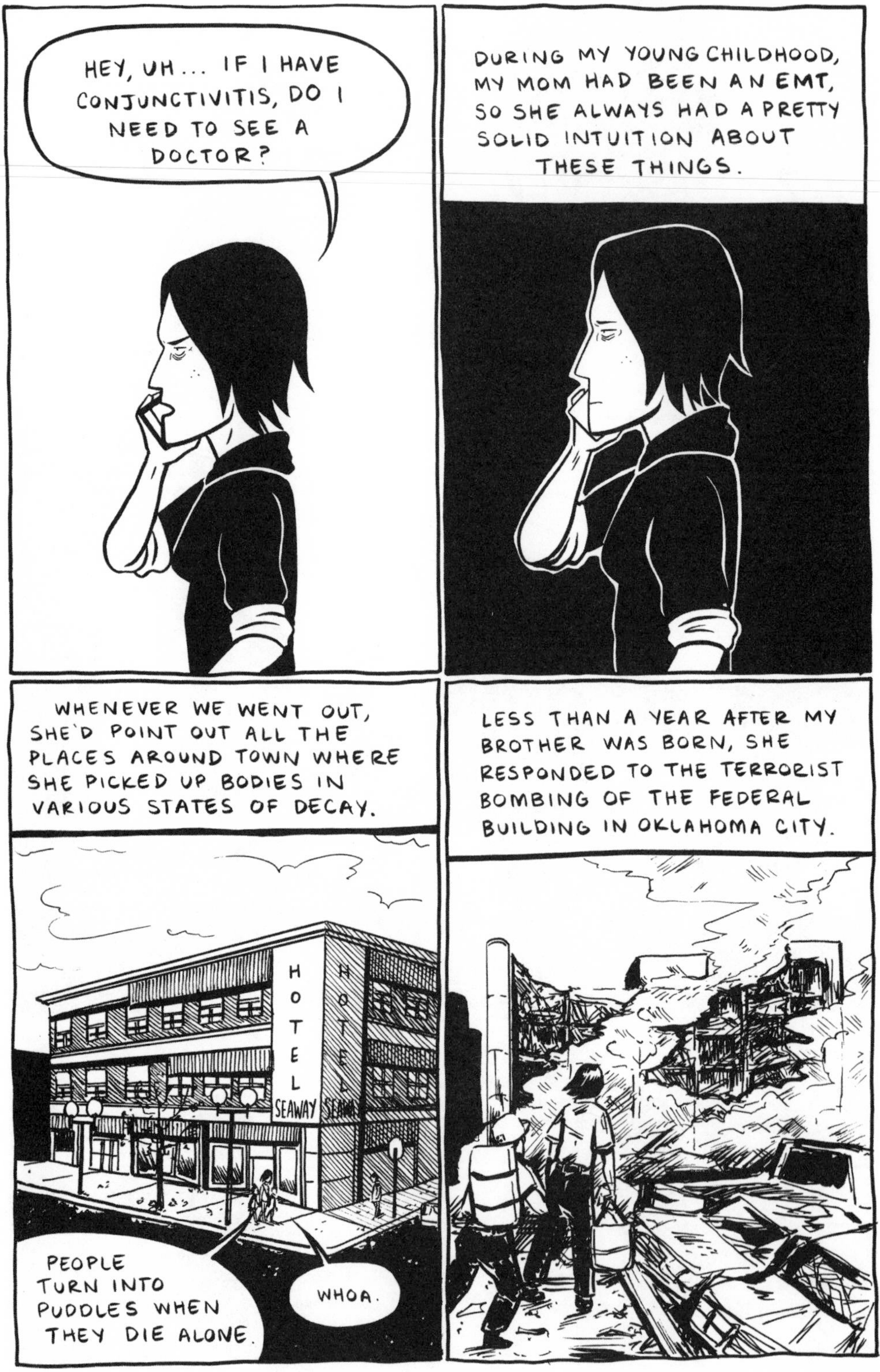
HEY, UH... IF I HAVE CONJUNCTIVITIS, DO I NEED TO SEE A DOCTOR?
DURING MY YOUNG CHILDHOOD, MY MOM HAD BEEN AN EMT, SO SHE ALWAYS HAD A PRETTY SOLID INTUITION ABOUT THESE THINGS.
WHENEVER WE WENT OUT, SHE'D POINT OUT ALL THE PLACES AROUND TOWN WHERE SHE PICKED UP BODIES IN VARIOUS STATES OF DECAY.
HOTEL
SEAWAY
PEOPLE TURN INTO PUDDLES WHEN THEY DIE ALONE.
WHOA.
LESS THAN A YEAR AFTER MY BROTHER WAS BORN, SHE RESPONDED TO THE TERRORIST BOMBING OF THE FEDERAL BUILDING IN OKLAHOMA CITY.

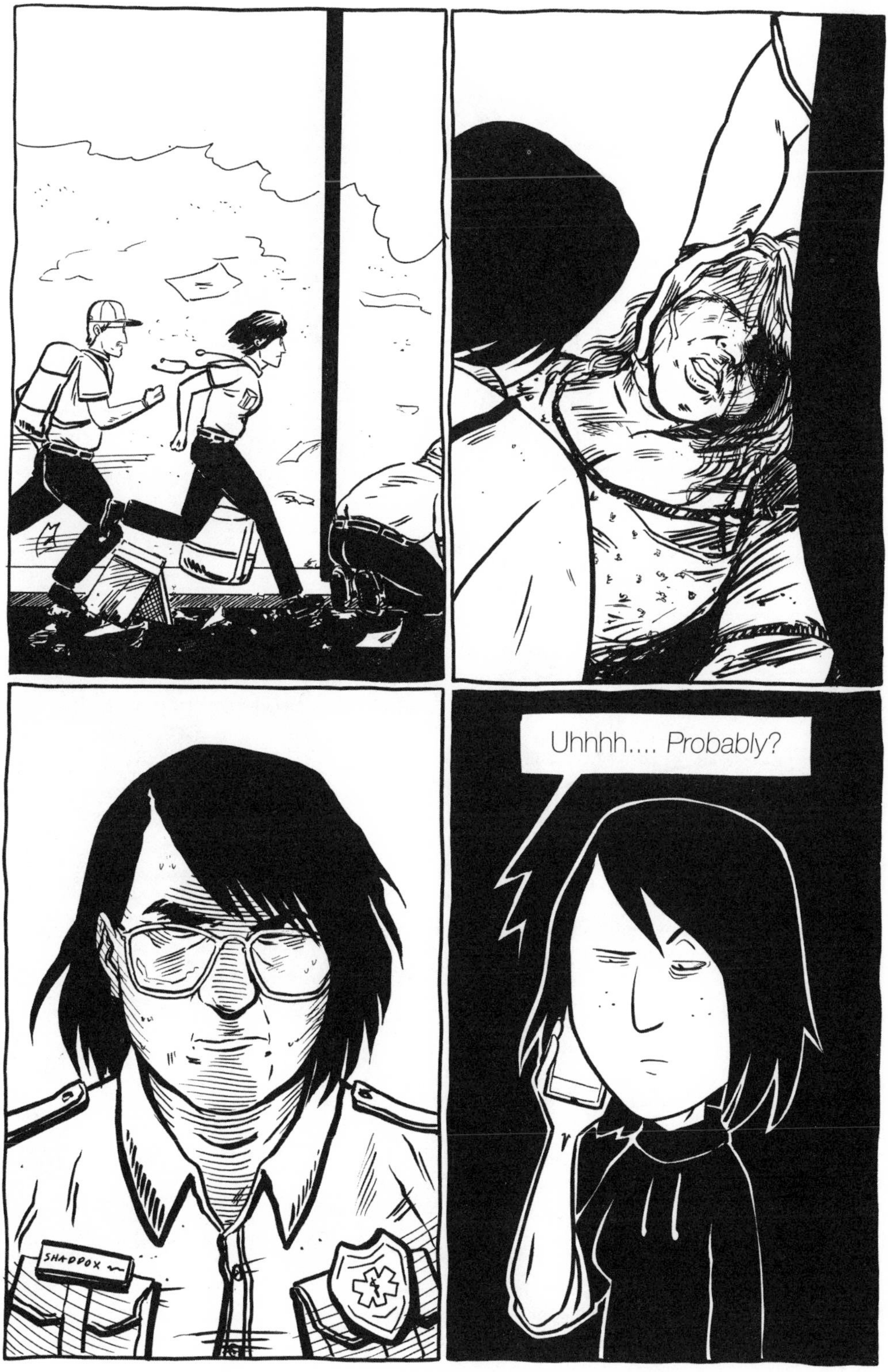
SHADDOX
Uhhhh.... *Probably?*

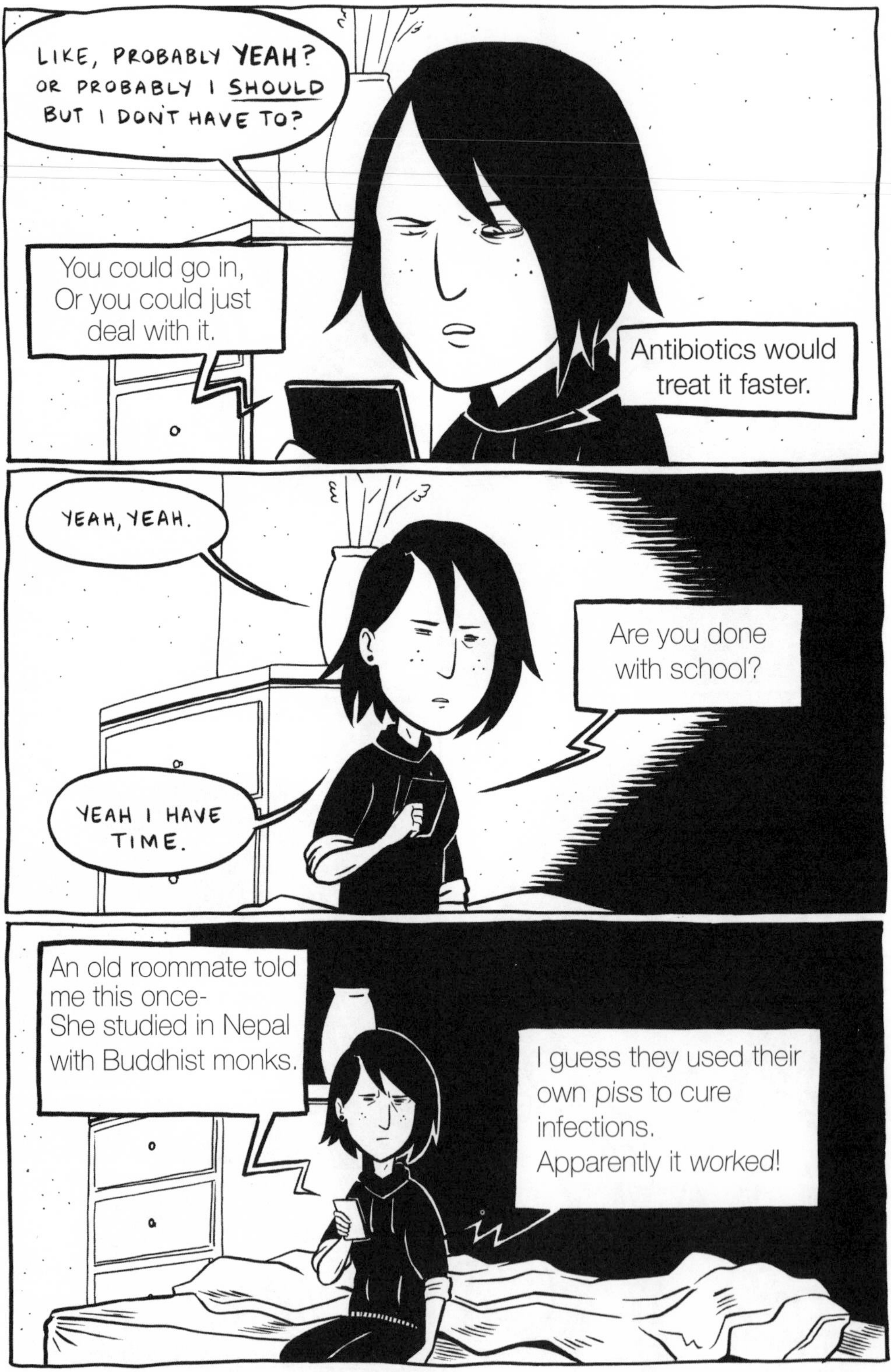
LIKE, PROBABLY YEAH? OR PROBABLY I SHOULD BUT I DON'T HAVE TO?
You could go in, Or you could just deal with it.
Antibiotics would treat it faster.
YEAH, YEAH.
Are you done with school?
YEAH I HAVE TIME.
An old roommate told me this once- She studied in Nepal with Buddhist monks.
I guess they used their own *piss* to cure infections. Apparently it *worked*!

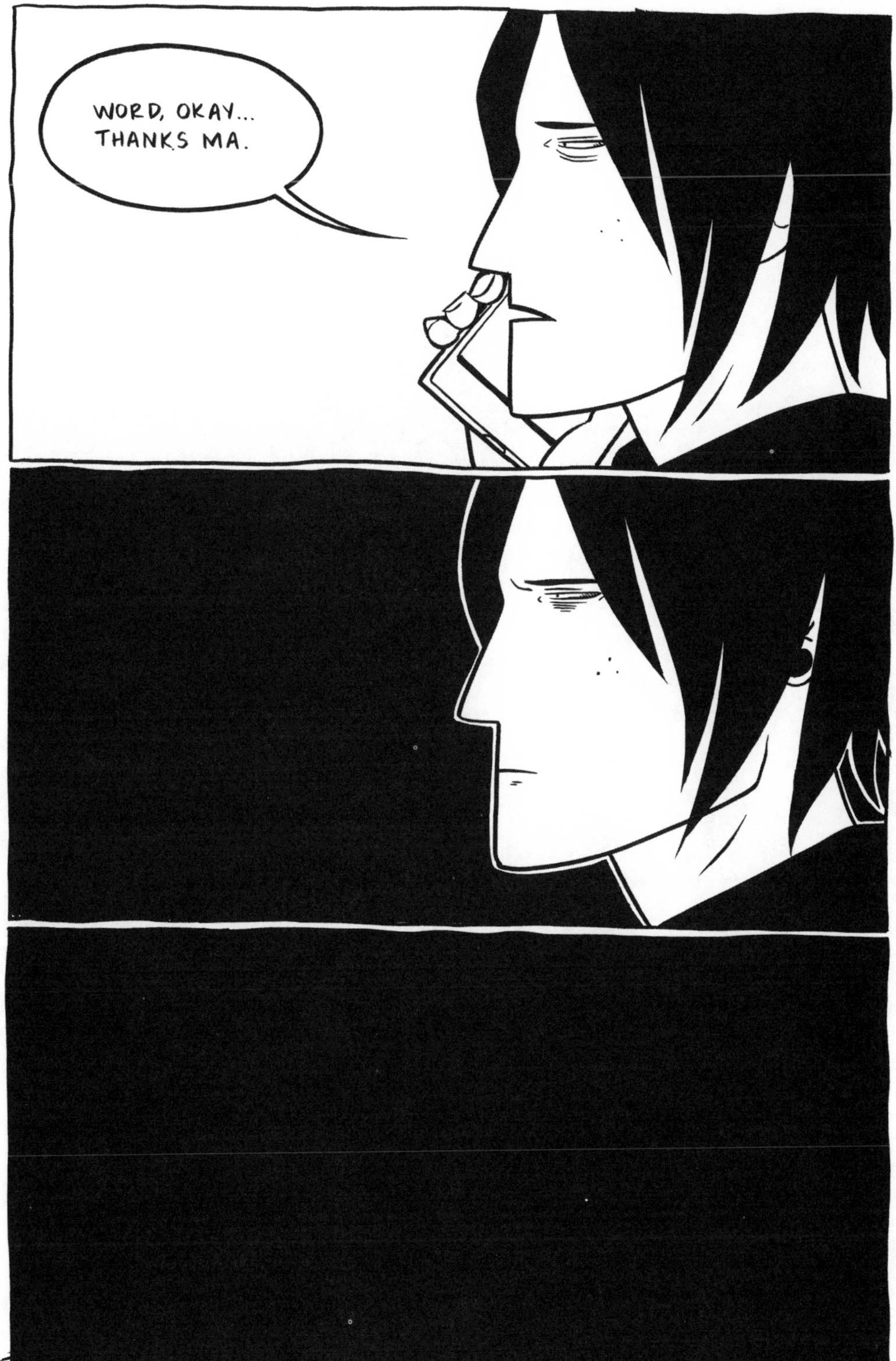
WORD, OKAY... THANKS MA.

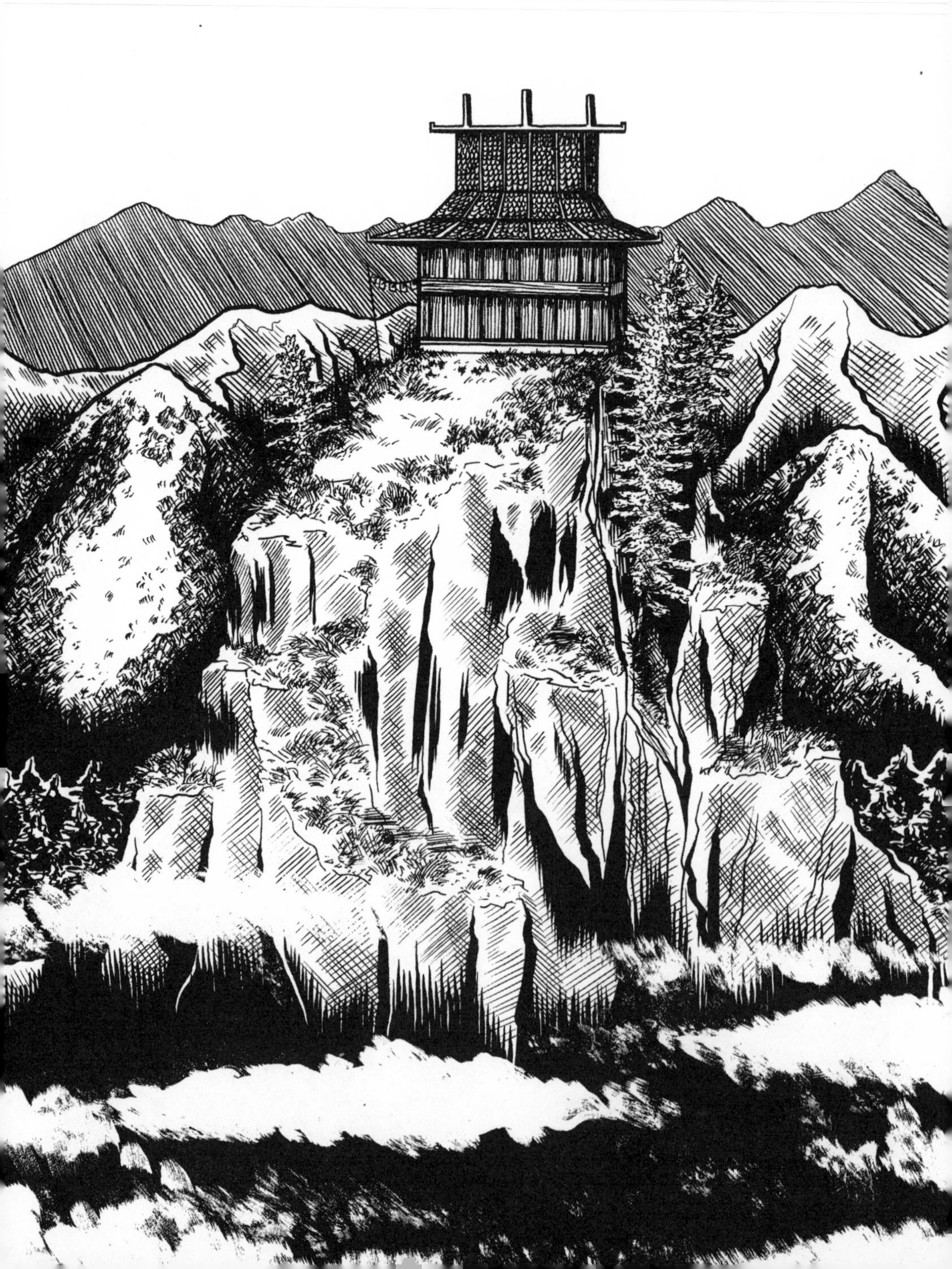

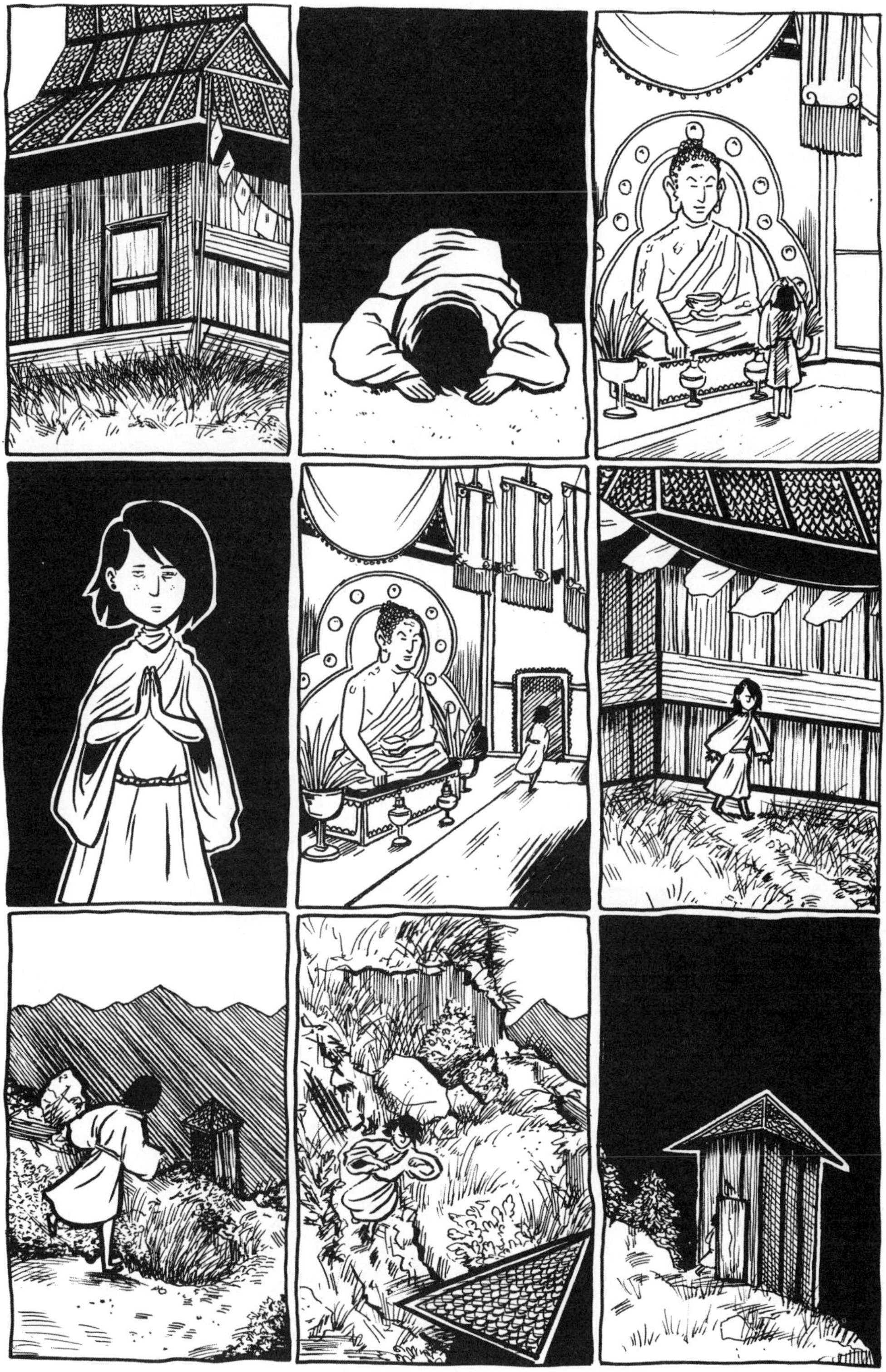

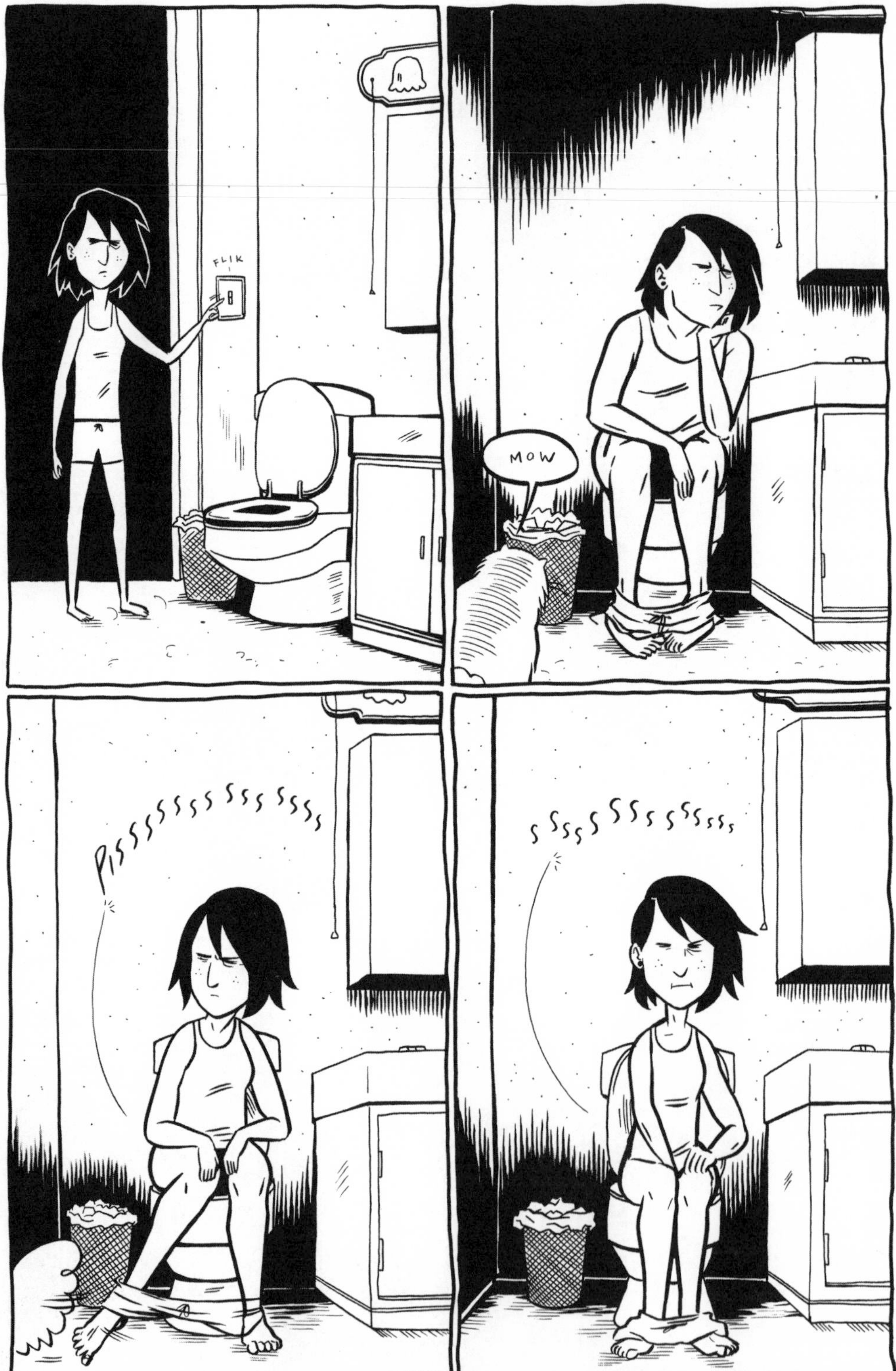
FLIK
MOW
PISSSSSSSSSSSSSSS
SSSSSSSSSSSSSSSS

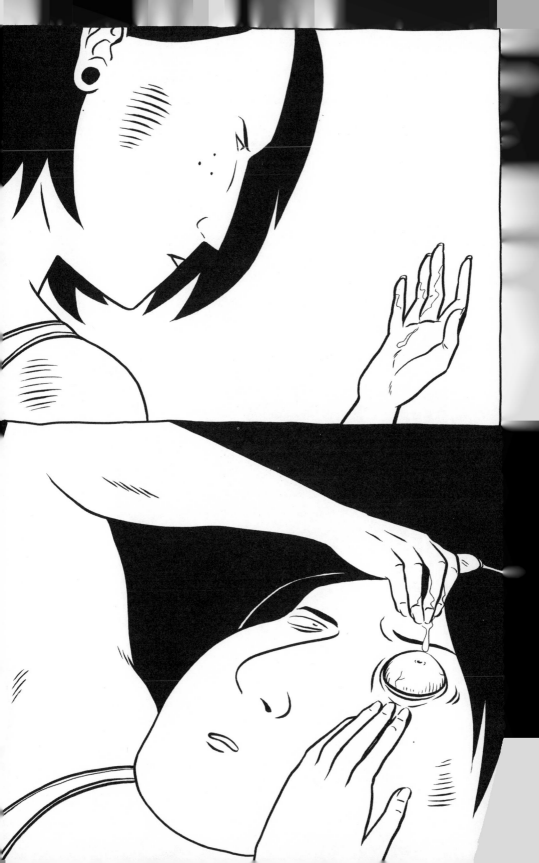

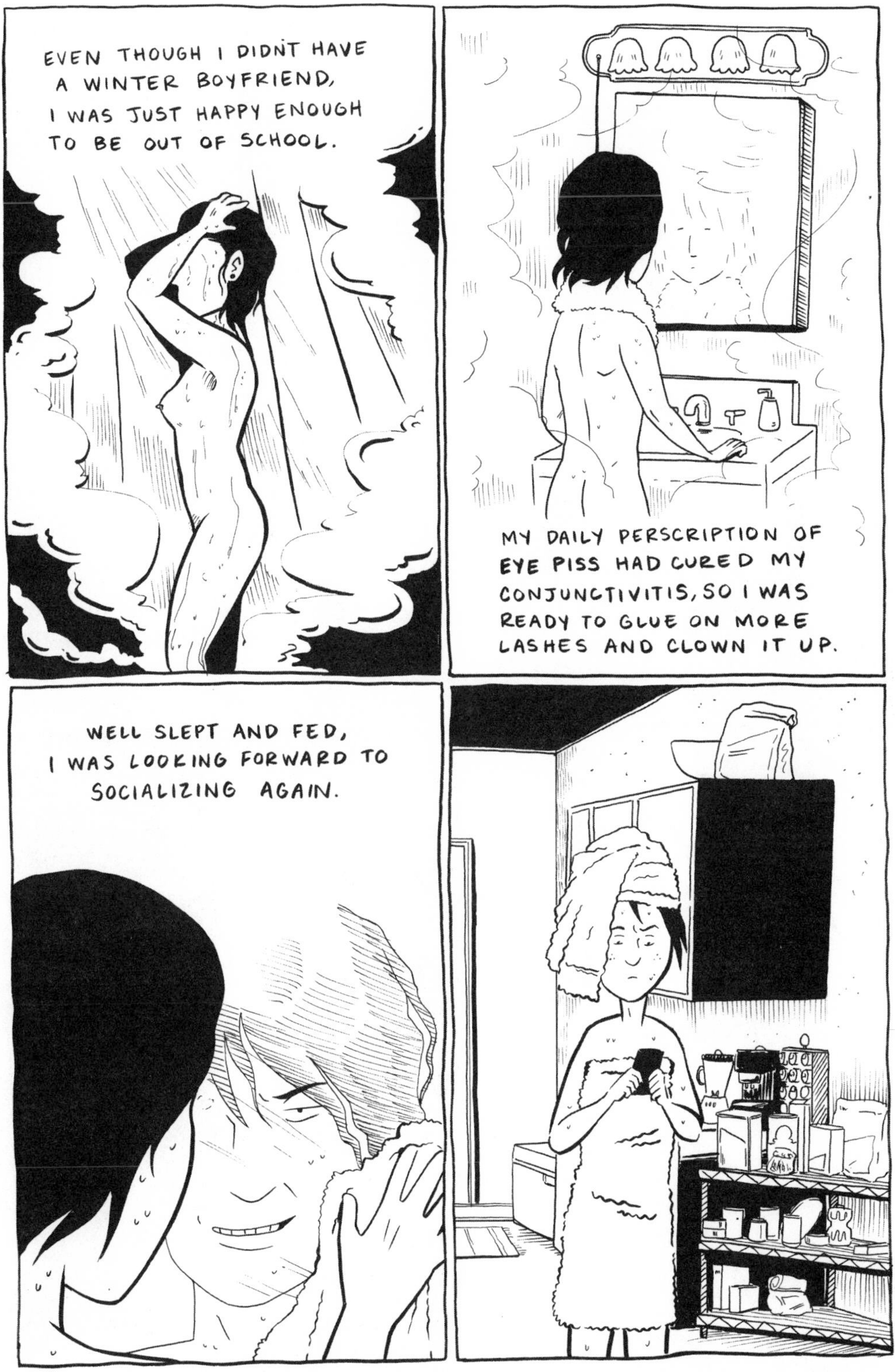
EVEN THOUGH I DIDN'T HAVE A WINTER BOYFRIEND, I WAS JUST HAPPY ENOUGH TO BE OUT OF SCHOOL.
MY DAILY PERSCRIPTION OF EYE PISS HAD CURED MY CONJUNCTIVITIS, SO I WAS READY TO GLUE ON MORE LASHES AND CLOWN IT UP.
WELL SLEPT AND FED, I WAS LOOKING FORWARD TO SOCIALIZING AGAIN.

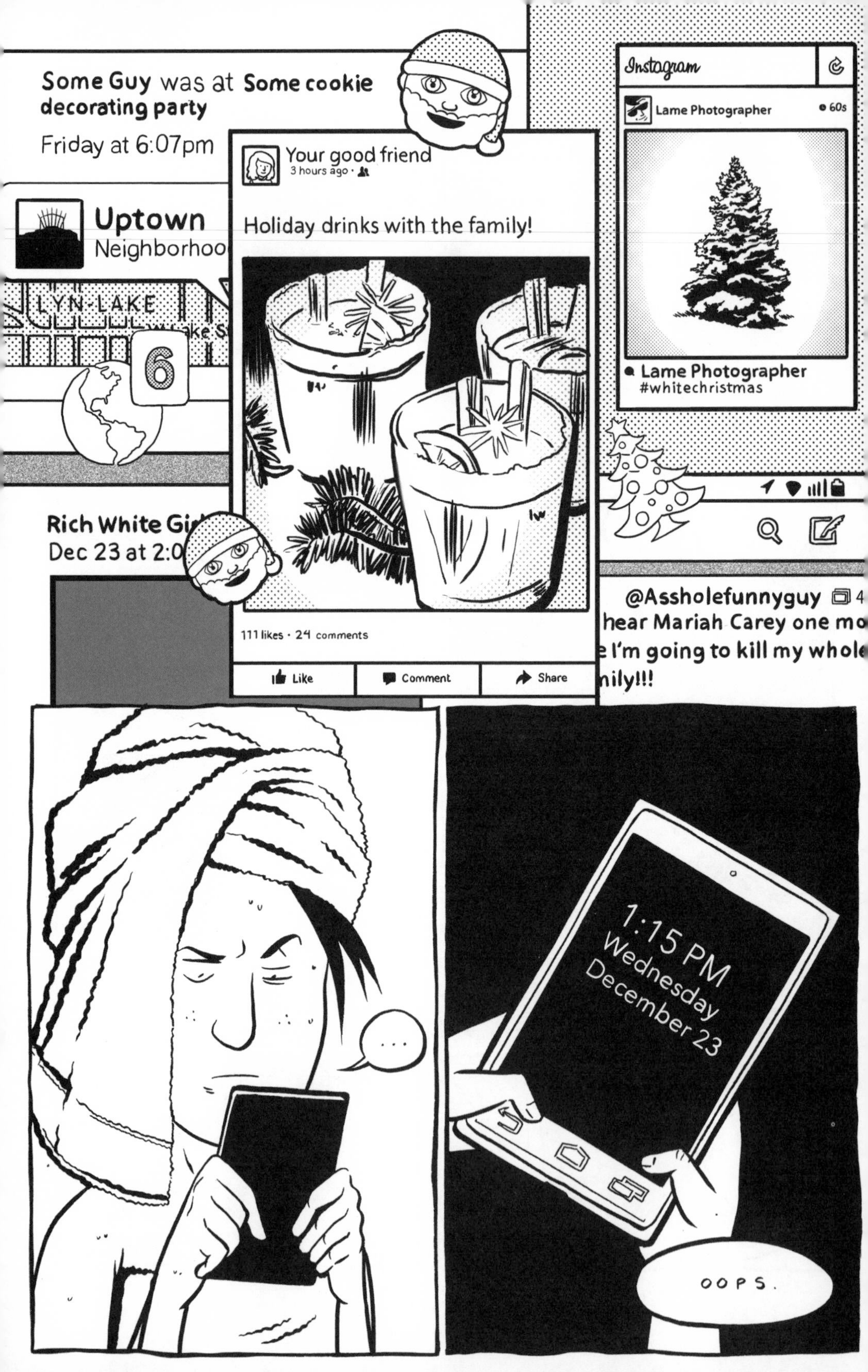

Some Guy was at Some cookie decorating party
Friday at 6:07pm
Uptown
Neighborhoo
LYN-LAKE
6
Your good friend
3 hours ago ·
Holiday drinks with the family!
111 likes · 24 comments
Like
Comment
Share
Instagram
Lame Photographer
60s
Lame Photographer
#whitechristmas
Rich White Gi
Dec 23 at 2:0
@Assholefunnyguy
hear Mariah Carey one mo
I'm going to kill my whol
nily!!!
...
1:15 PM
Wednesday
December 23
OOPS.

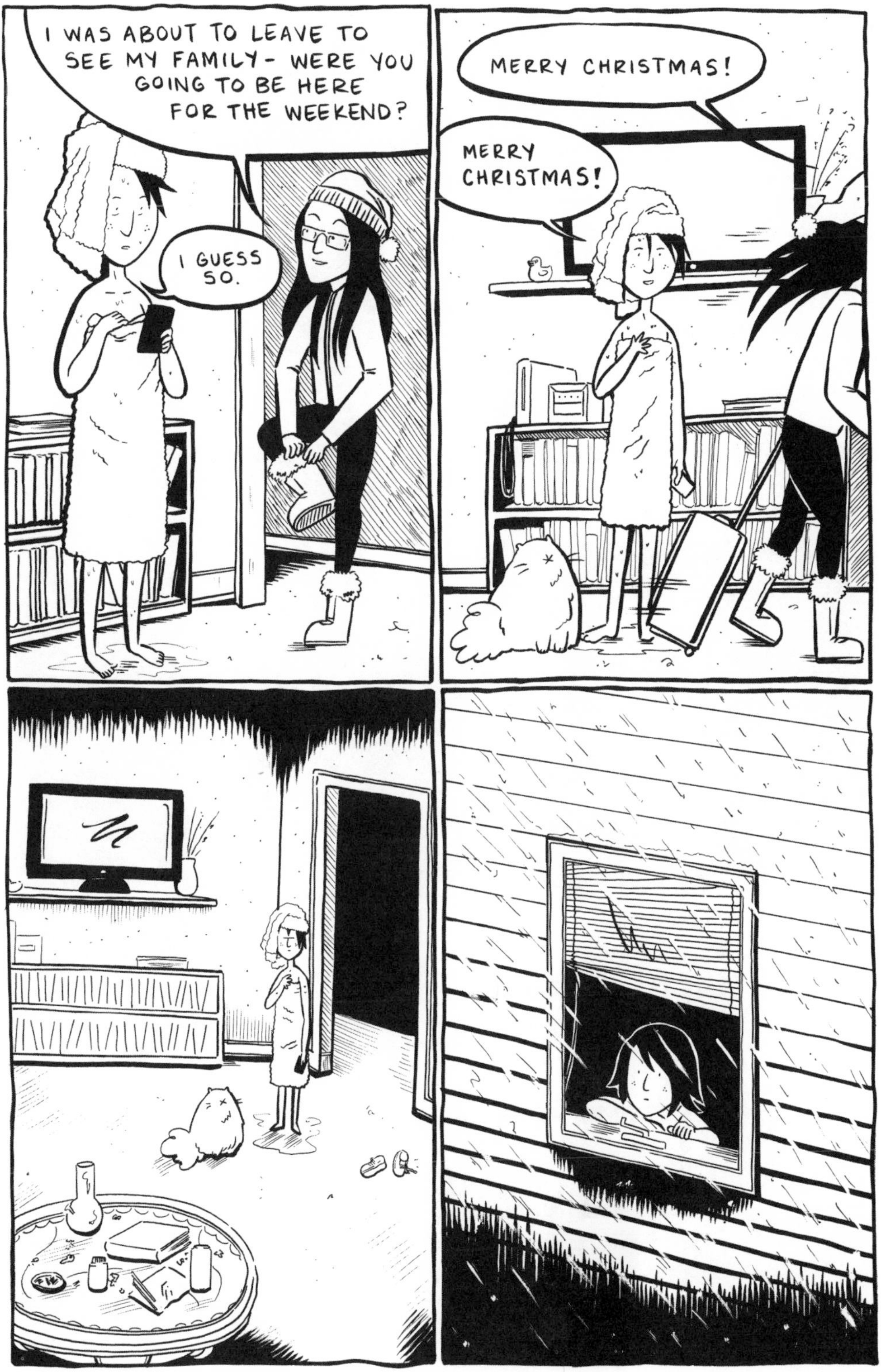
I WAS ABOUT TO LEAVE TO SEE MY FAMILY- WERE YOU GOING TO BE HERE FOR THE WEEKEND?
I GUESS SO.
MERRY CHRISTMAS!
MERRY CHRISTMAS!

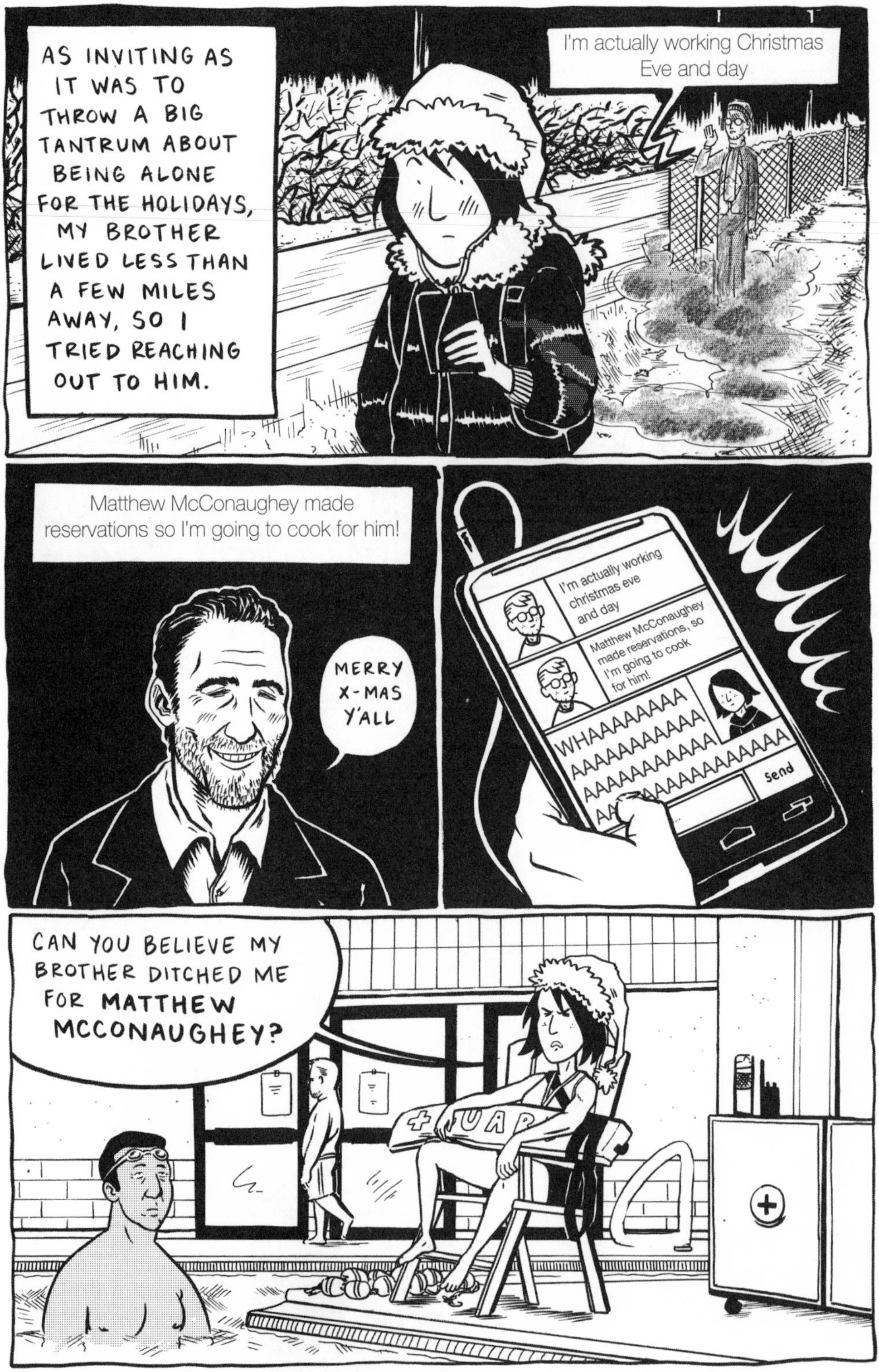
AS INVITING AS IT WAS TO THROW A BIG TANTRUM ABOUT BEING ALONE FOR THE HOLIDAYS, MY BROTHER LIVED LESS THAN A FEW MILES AWAY, SO I TRIED REACHING OUT TO HIM.
I'm actually working Christmas Eve and day
Matthew McConaughey made reservations so I'm going to cook for him!
MERRY X-MAS Y'ALL
I'm actually working christmas eve and day
Matthew McConaughey made reservations, so I'm going to cook for him!
WHAAAAAAAAAAAAAAAAAAAAAAAAAAAAAAAAAAAAAAAAAAAAAA
Send
CAN YOU BELIEVE MY BROTHER DITCHED ME FOR MATTHEW MCCONAUGHEY?

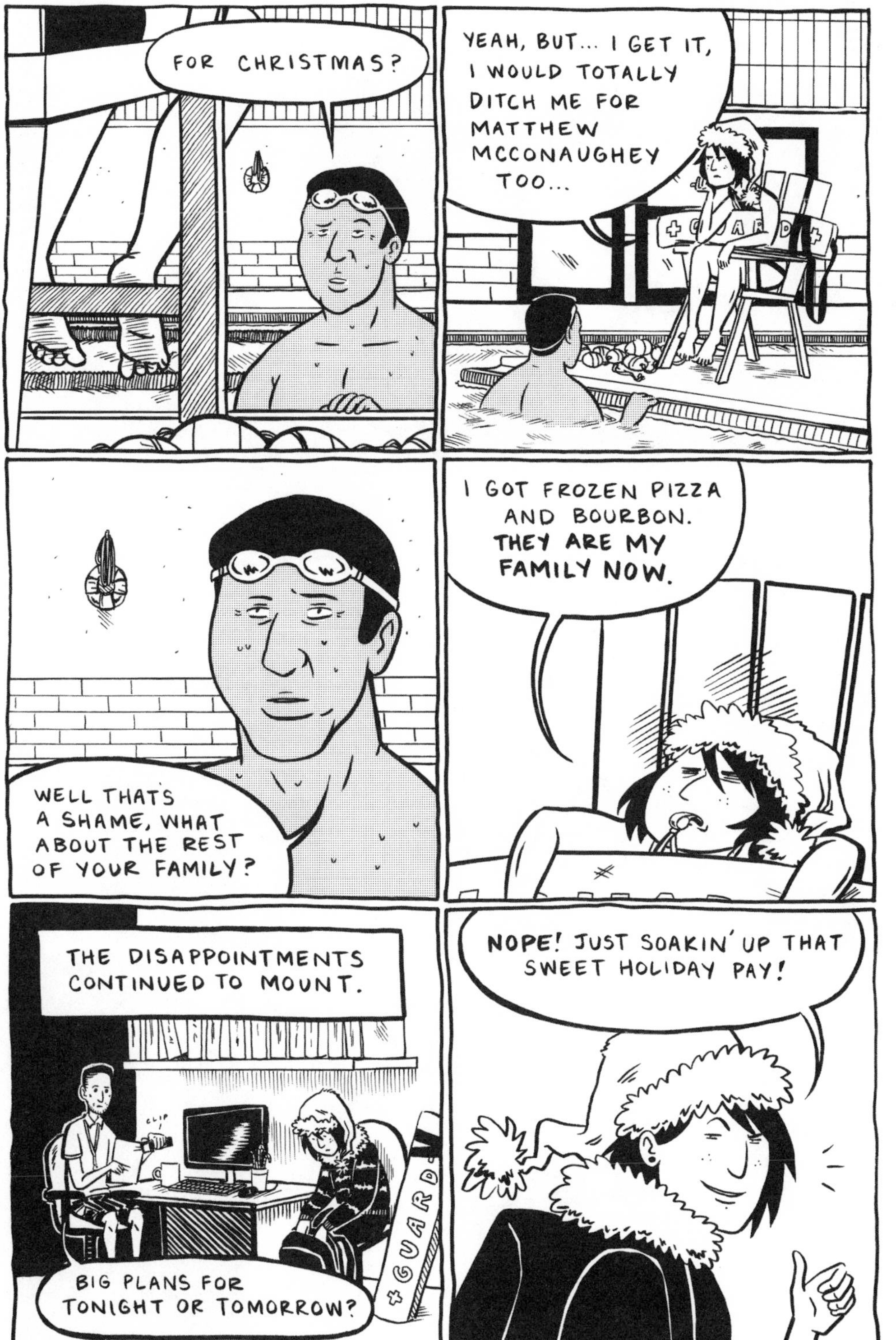
FOR CHRISTMAS?
YEAH, BUT... I GET IT, I WOULD TOTALLY DITCH ME FOR MATTHEW MCCONAUGHEY TOO...
+GUARD
WELL THATS A SHAME, WHAT ABOUT THE REST OF YOUR FAMILY?
I GOT FROZEN PIZZA AND BOURBON. THEY ARE MY FAMILY NOW.
THE DISAPPOINTMENTS CONTINUED TO MOUNT.
CLIP
BIG PLANS FOR TONIGHT OR TOMORROW?
+GUARD
NOPE! JUST SOAKIN' UP THAT SWEET HOLIDAY PAY!

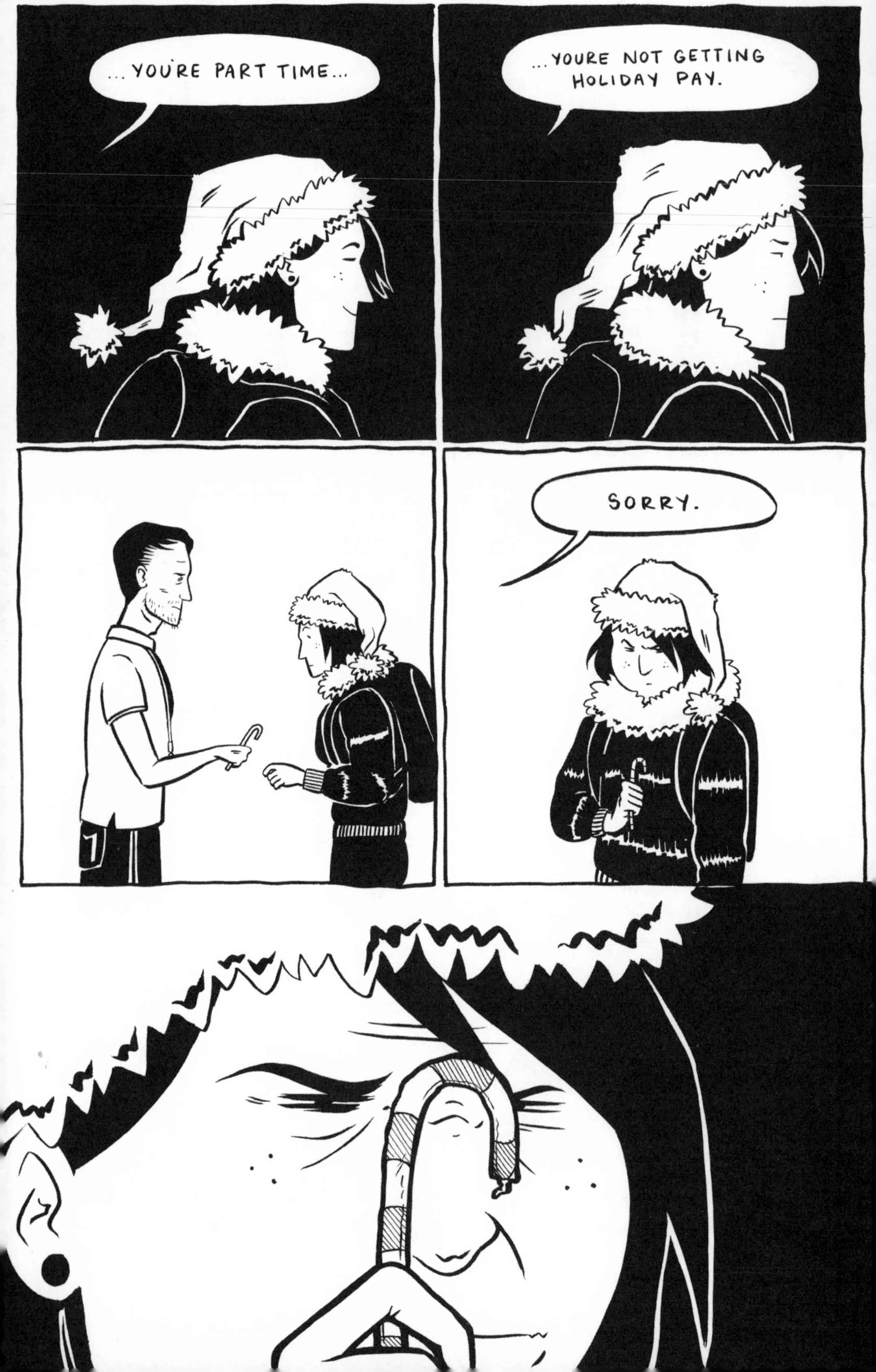
...YOU'RE PART TIME...
...YOURE NOT GETTING HOLIDAY PAY.
SORRY.

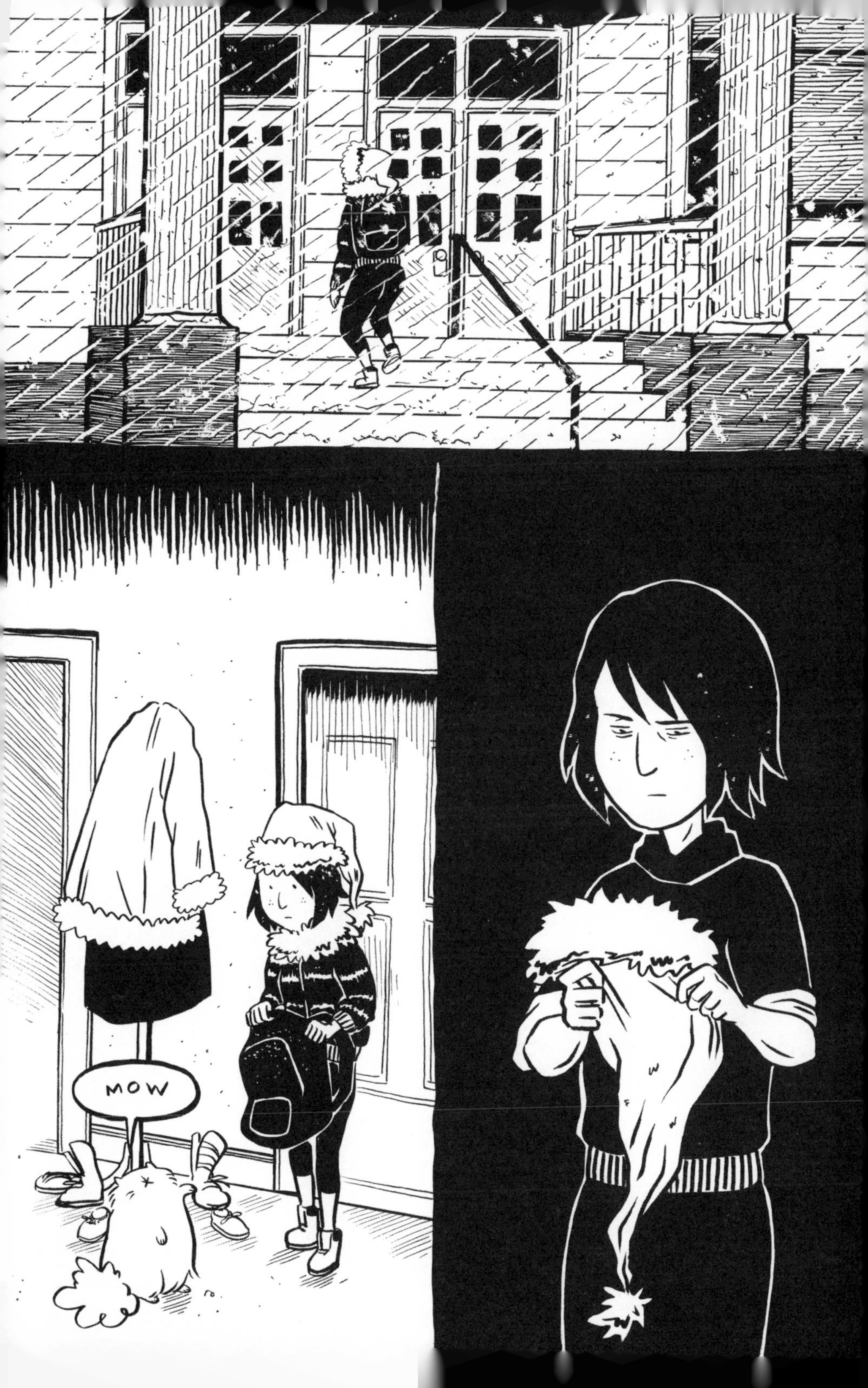
MOW

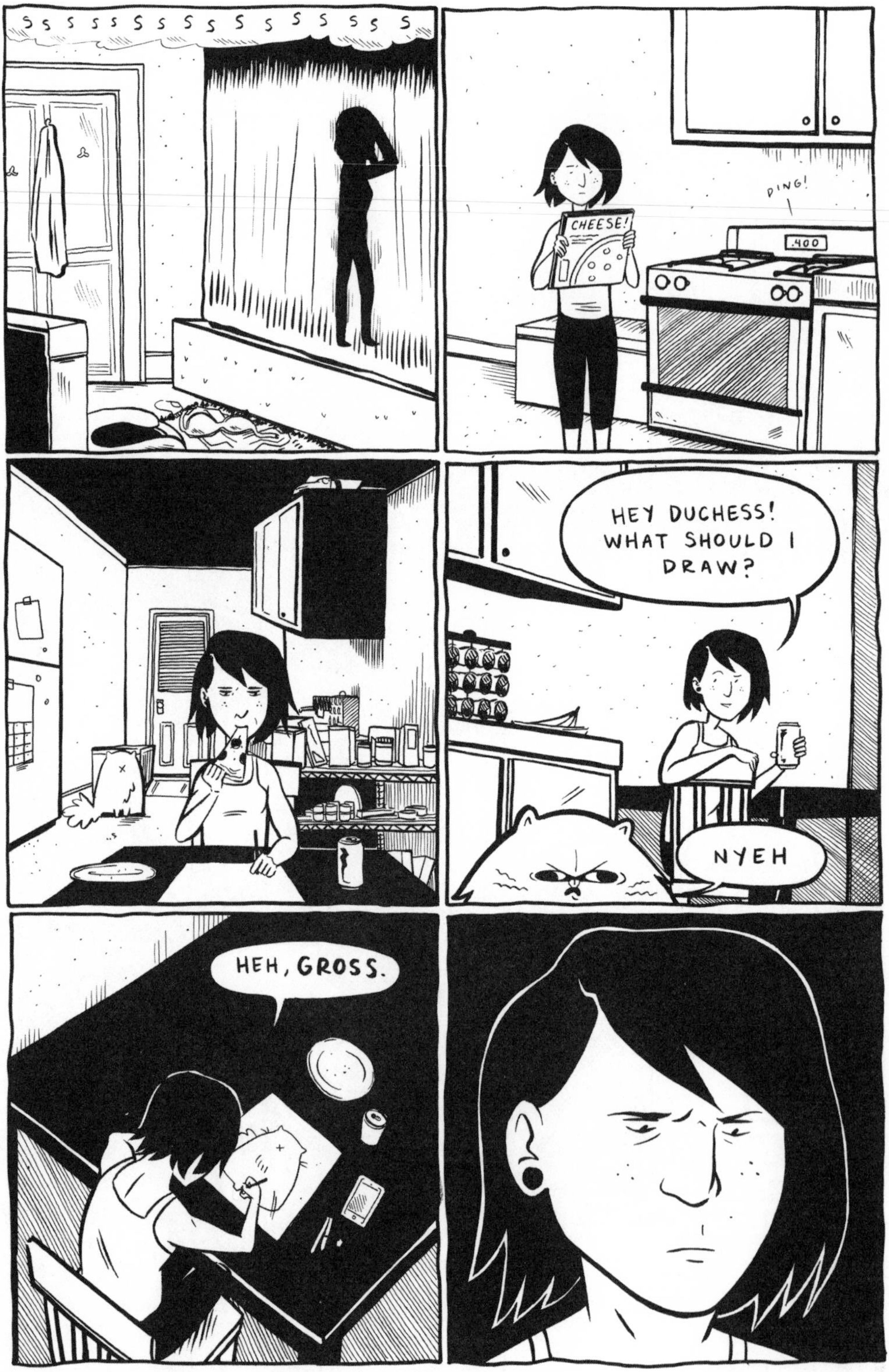
S S S S S S S S S S S S S S S S S
CHEESE!
DING!
.400
HEY DUCHESS! WHAT SHOULD I DRAW?
NYEH
HEH, GROSS.

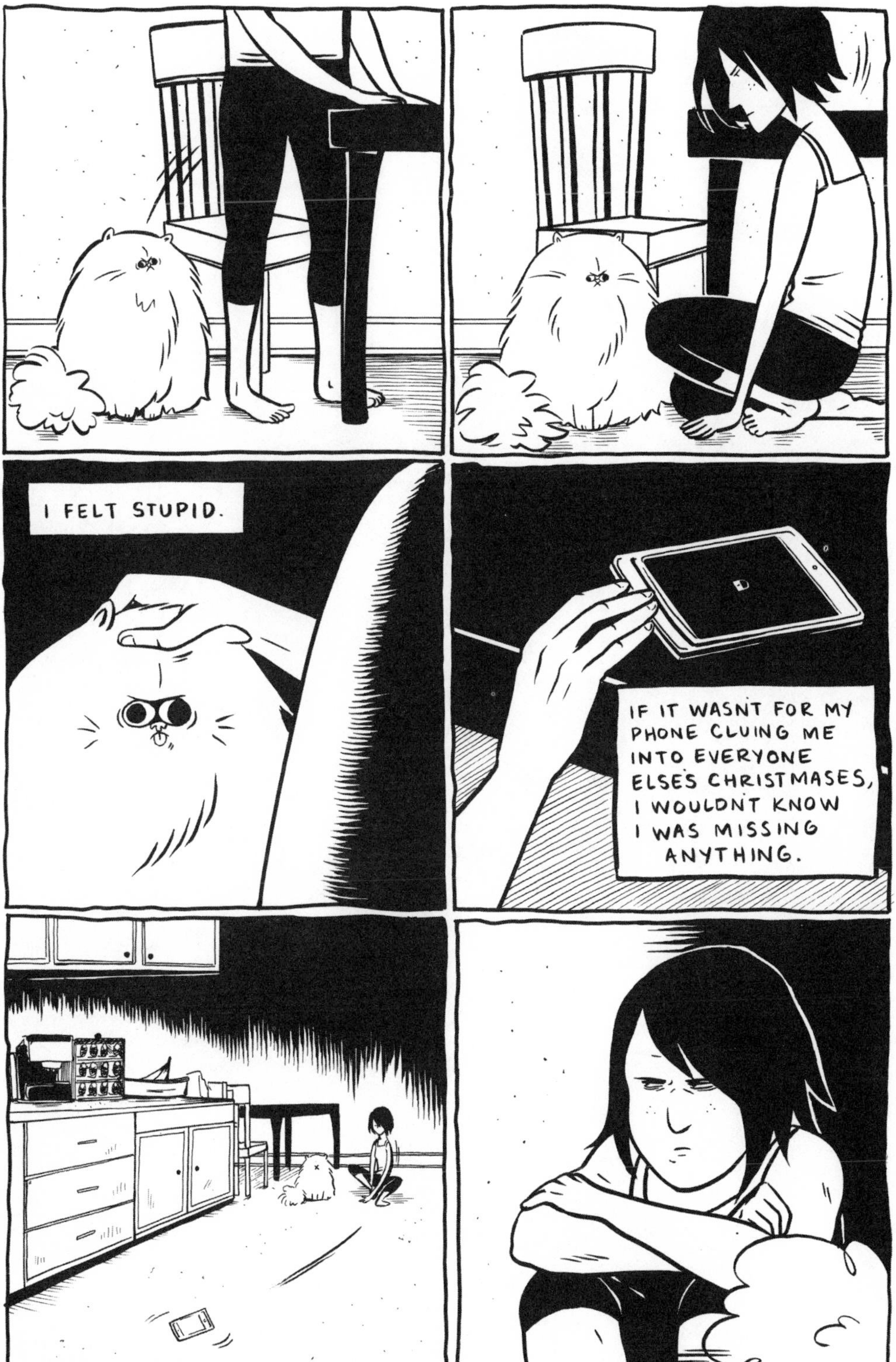
I FELT STUPID.
IF IT WASN'T FOR MY PHONE CLUING ME INTO EVERYONE ELSE'S CHRISTMASES, I WOULDN'T KNOW I WAS MISSING ANYTHING.

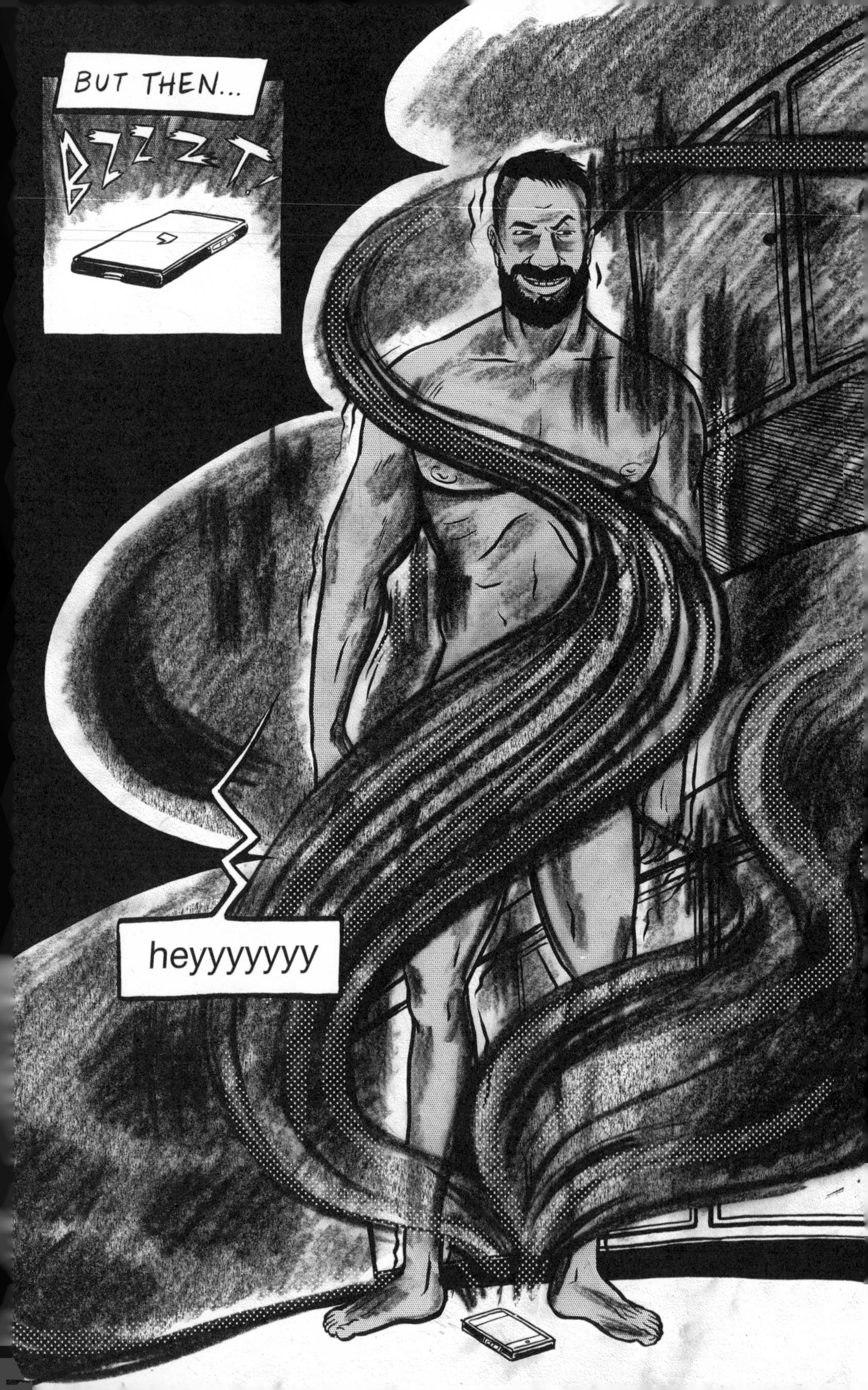
BUT THEN...
BZZZT!
heyyyyyyy

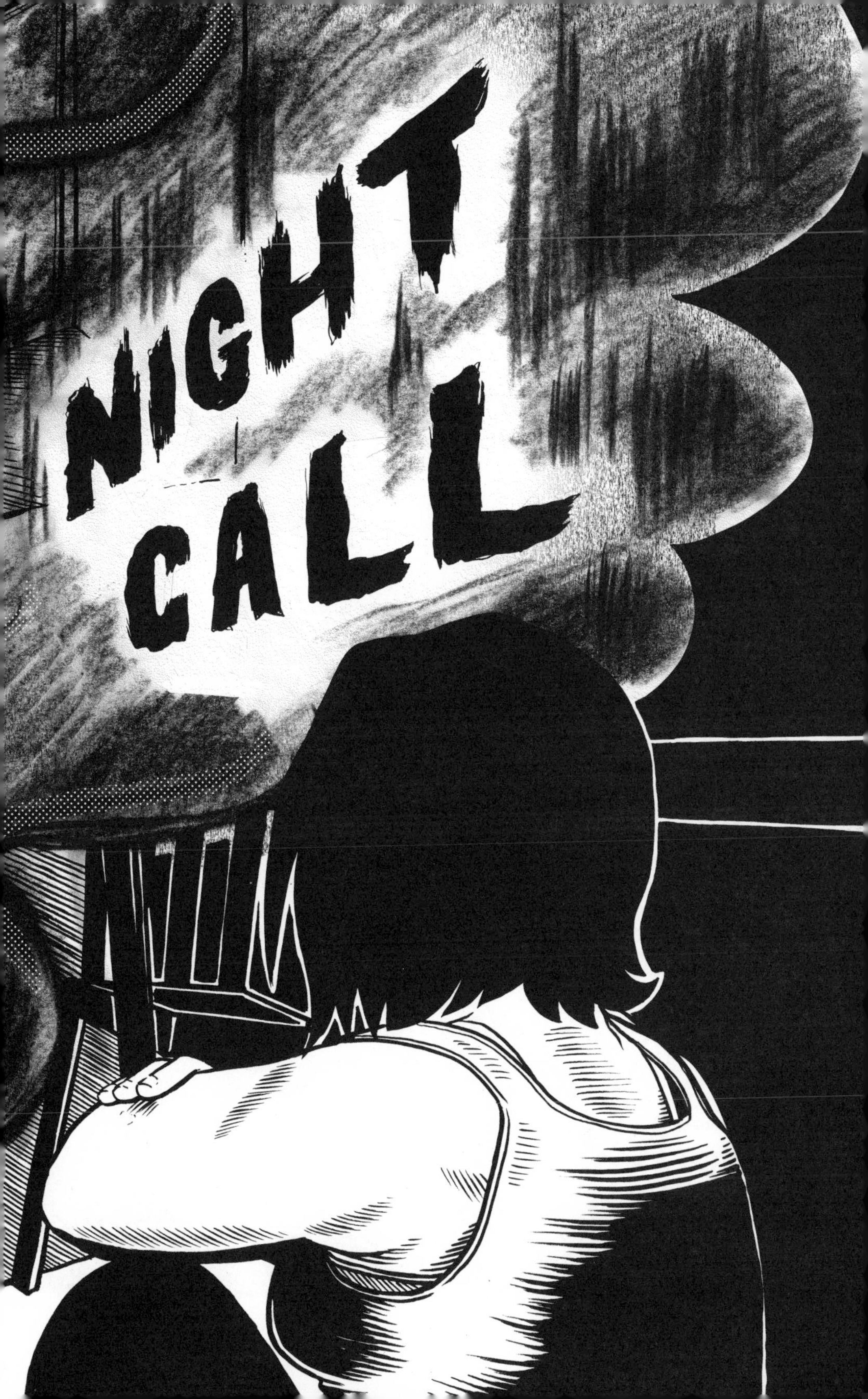
NIGHT CALL

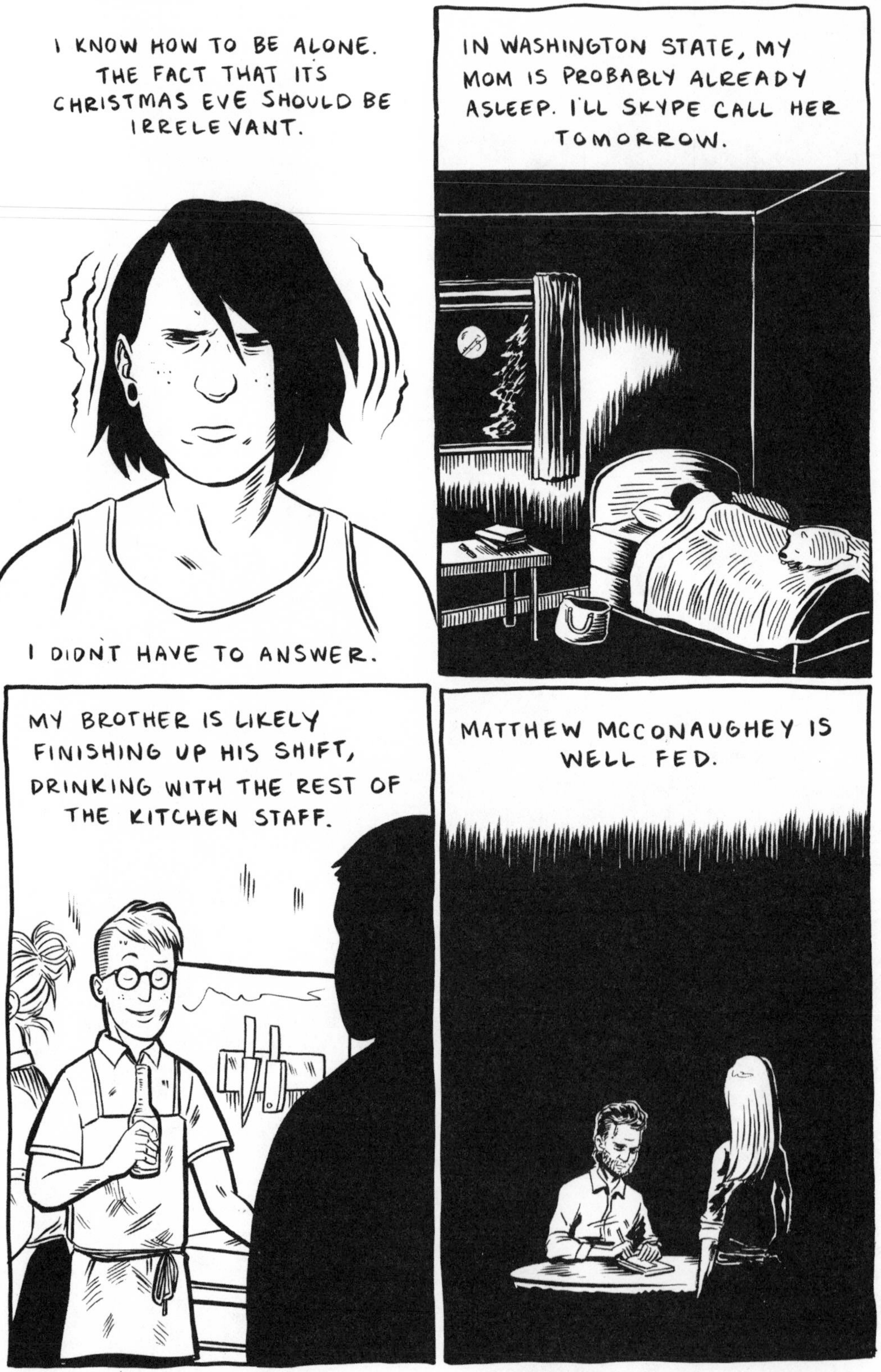
I KNOW HOW TO BE ALONE. THE FACT THAT ITS CHRISTMAS EVE SHOULD BE IRRELEVANT.
I DIDN'T HAVE TO ANSWER.
IN WASHINGTON STATE, MY MOM IS PROBABLY ALREADY ASLEEP. I'LL SKYPE CALL HER TOMORROW.
MY BROTHER IS LIKELY FINISHING UP HIS SHIFT, DRINKING WITH THE REST OF THE KITCHEN STAFF.
MATTHEW MCCONAUGHEY IS WELL FED.

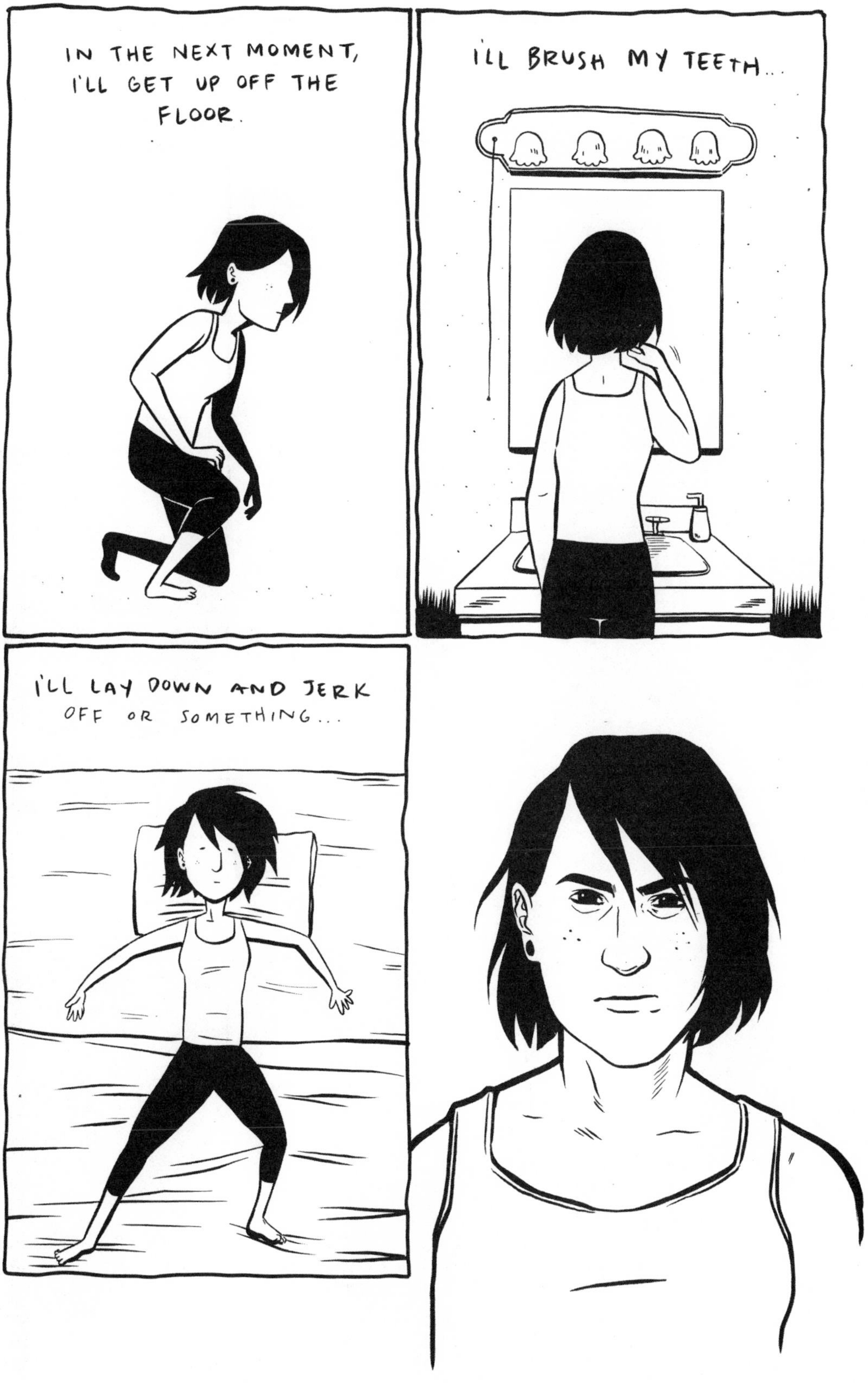
IN THE NEXT MOMENT, I'LL GET UP OFF THE FLOOR.
I'LL BRUSH MY TEETH...
I'LL LAY DOWN AND JERK OFF OR SOMETHING...

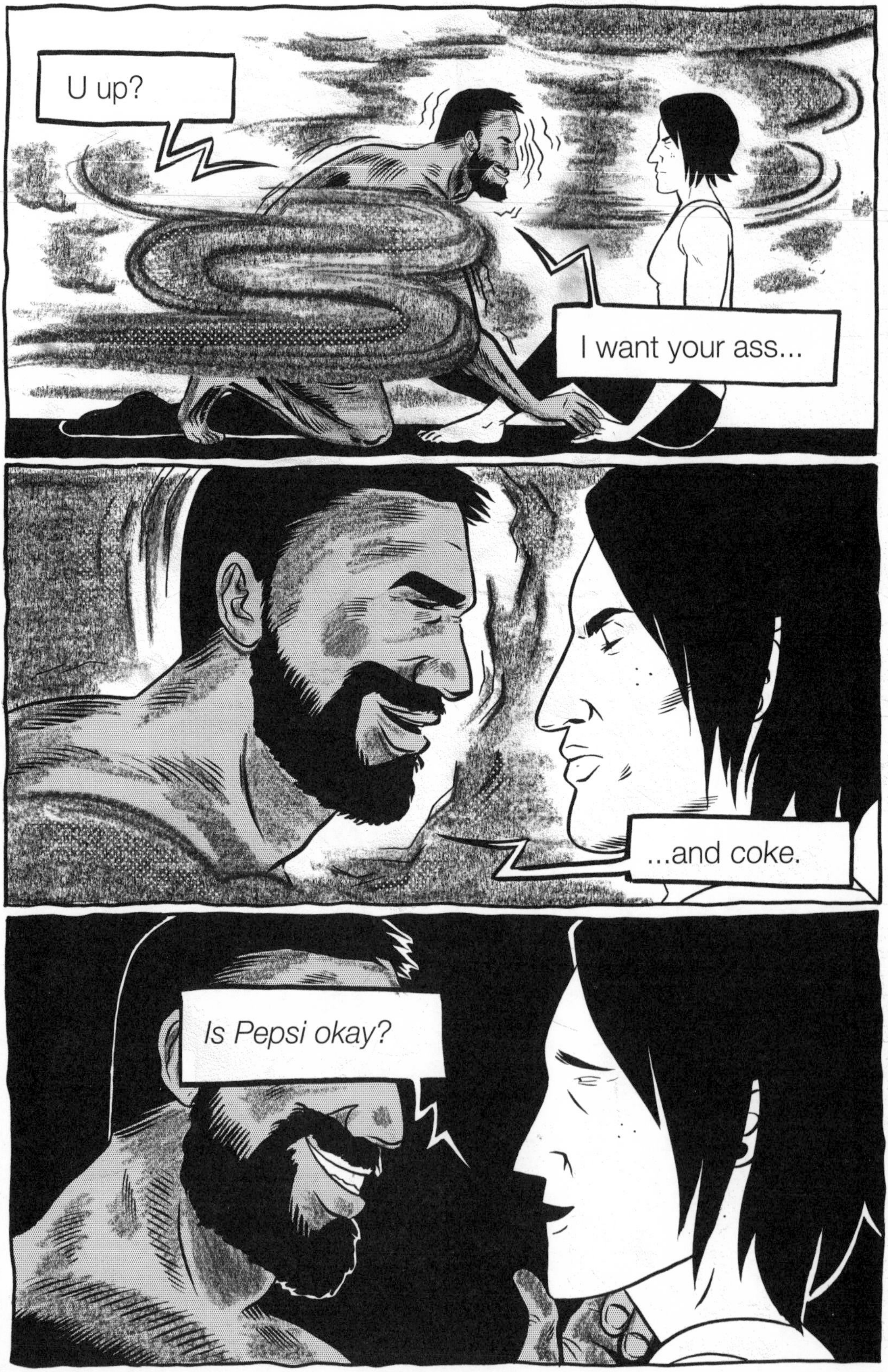
U up?
I want your ass...
...and coke.
Is Pepsi okay?

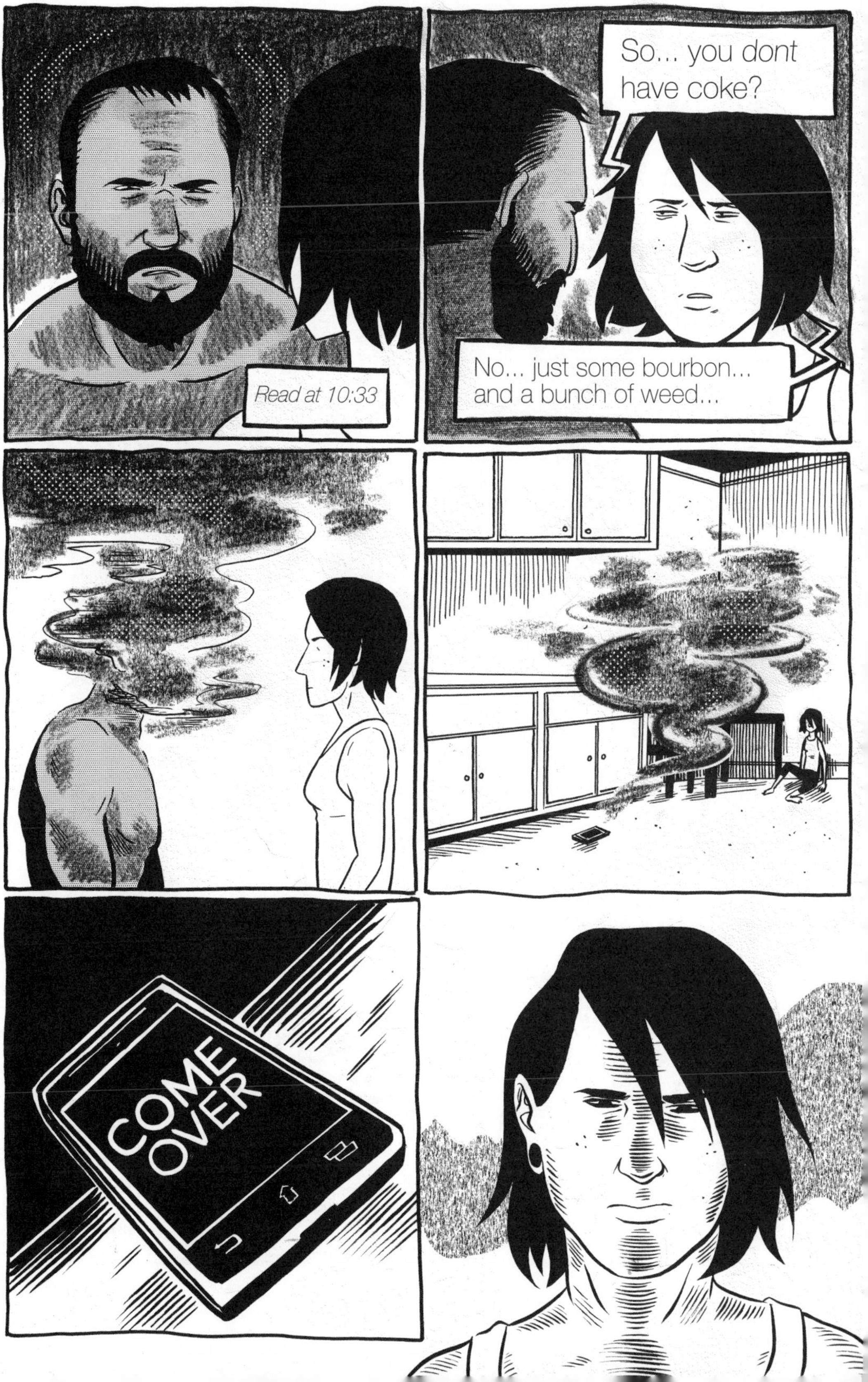
Read at 10:33
So... you dont have coke?
No... just some bourbon... and a bunch of weed...
COME OVER

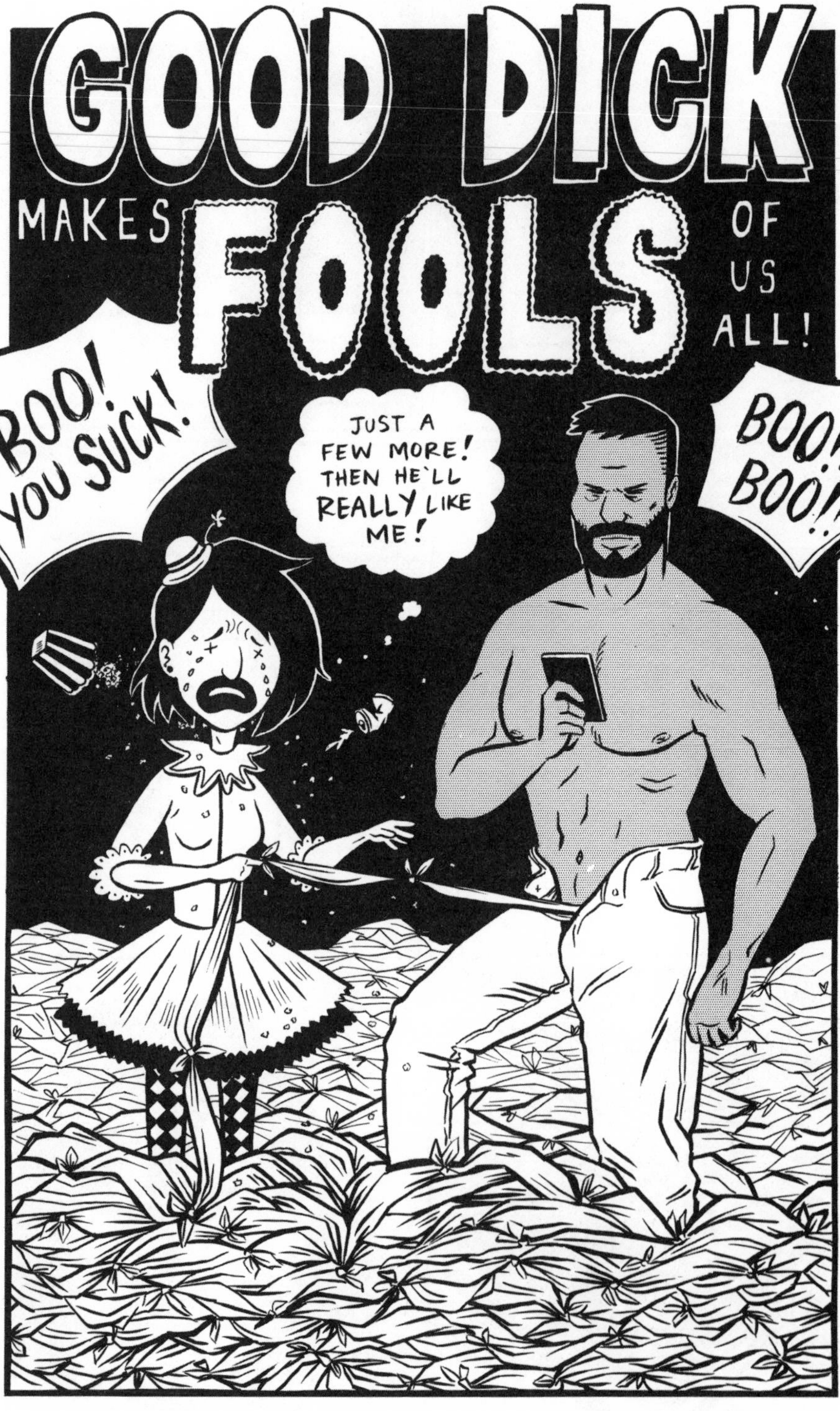
GOOD DICK
MAKES FOOLS OF US ALL!
BOO! YOU SUCK!
JUST A FEW MORE! THEN HE'LL REALLY LIKE ME!
BOO!! BOO!!

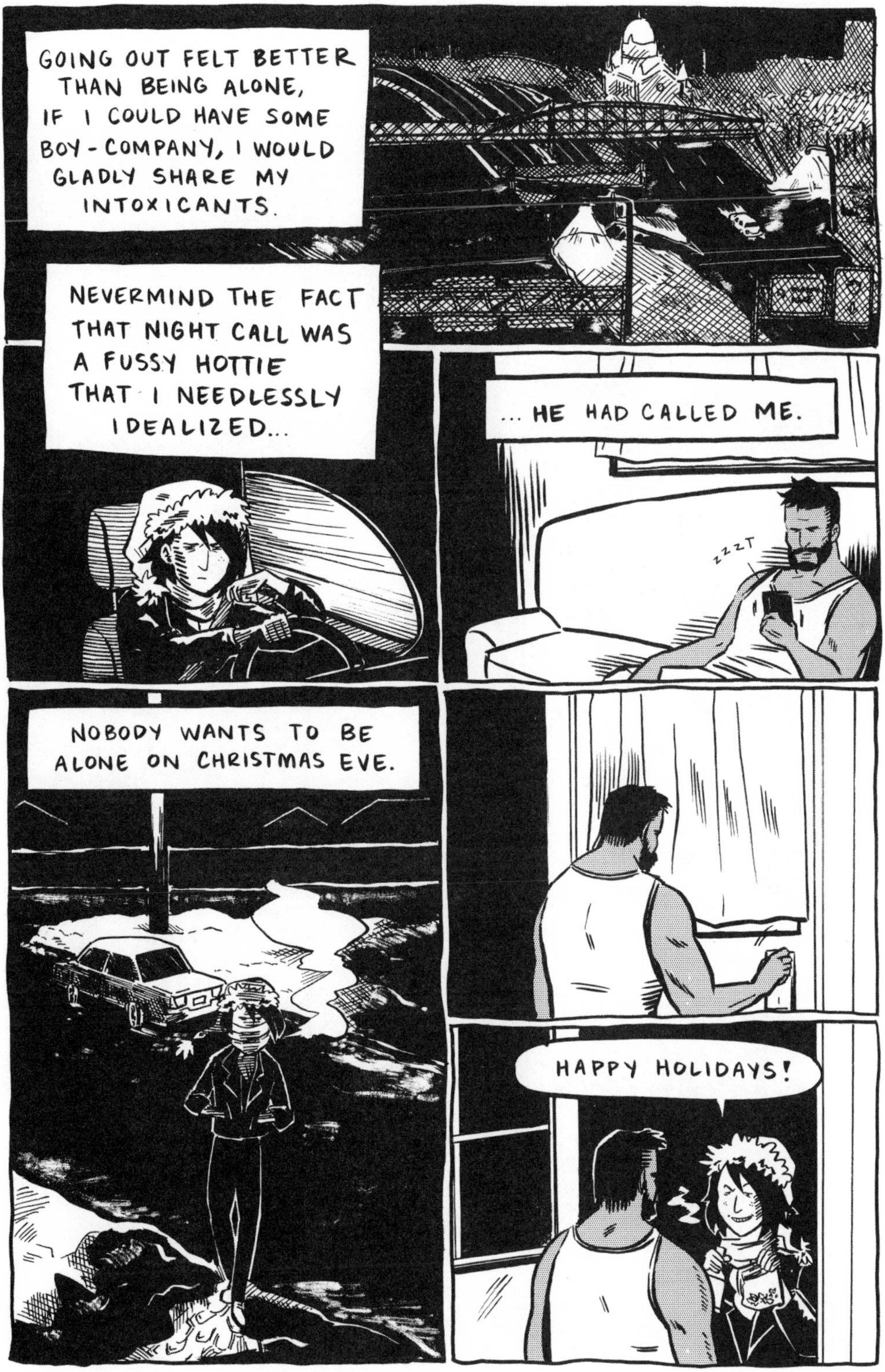
GOING OUT FELT BETTER THAN BEING ALONE, IF I COULD HAVE SOME BOY-COMPANY, I WOULD GLADLY SHARE MY INTOXICANTS.
NEVERMIND THE FACT THAT NIGHT CALL WAS A FUSSY HOTTIE THAT I NEEDLESSLY IDEALIZED...
... HE HAD CALLED ME.
ZZZT
NOBODY WANTS TO BE ALONE ON CHRISTMAS EVE.
HAPPY HOLIDAYS!

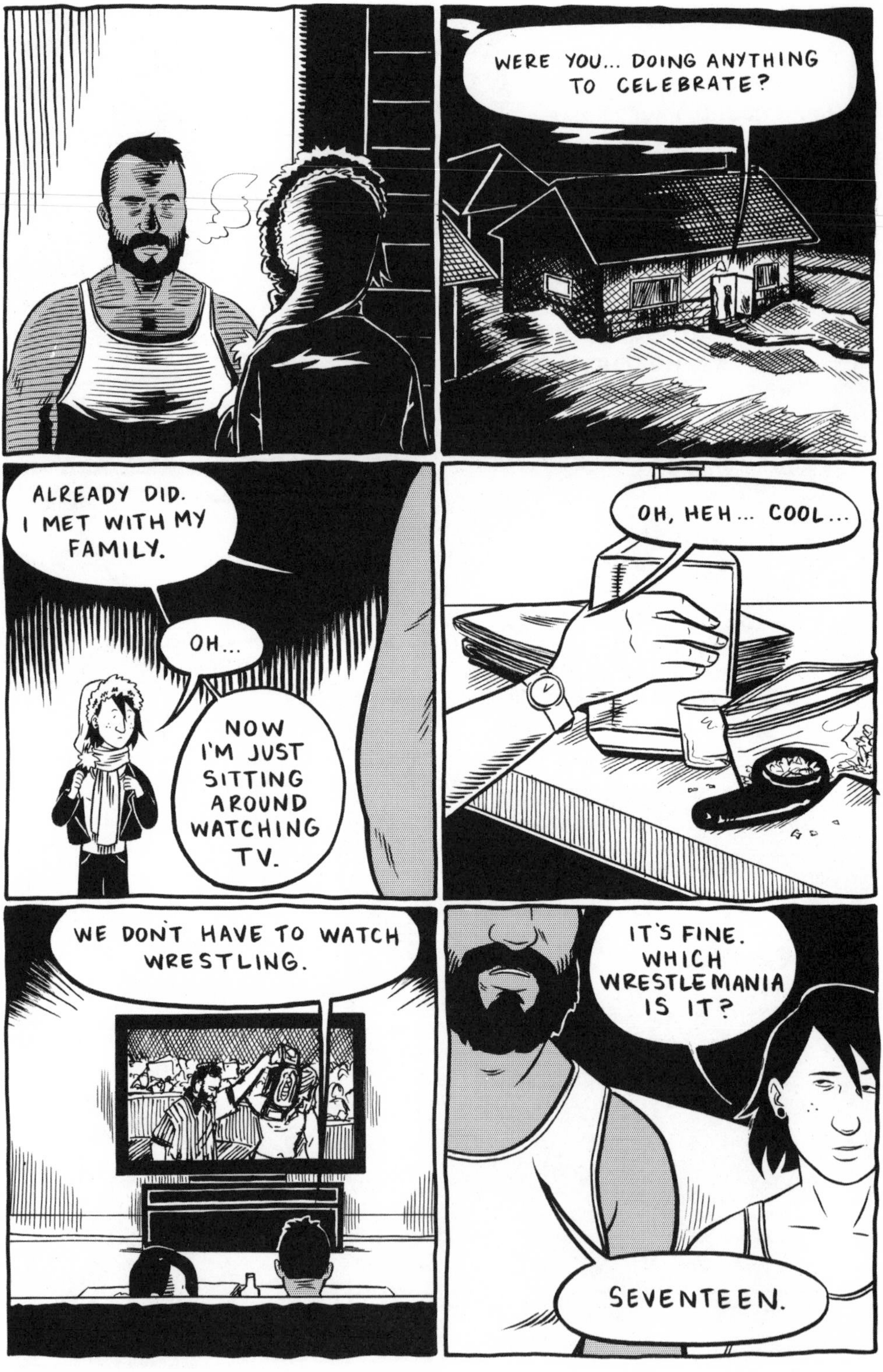
WERE YOU... DOING ANYTHING TO CELEBRATE?
ALREADY DID. I MET WITH MY FAMILY.
OH...
NOW I'M JUST SITTING AROUND WATCHING TV.
OH, HEH... COOL...
WE DON'T HAVE TO WATCH WRESTLING.
IT'S FINE. WHICH WRESTLEMANIA IS IT?
SEVENTEEN.

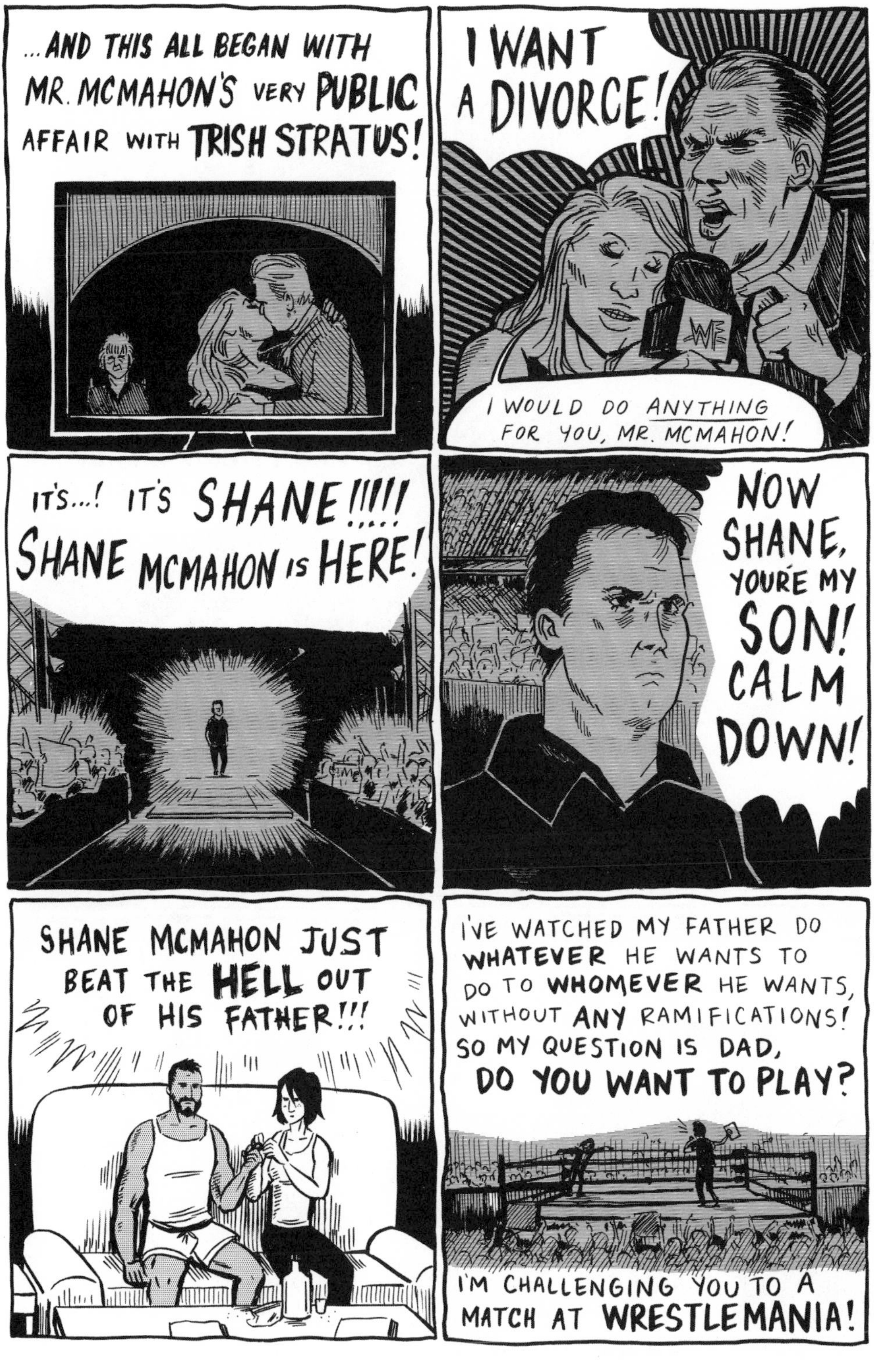

...AND THIS ALL BEGAN WITH MR. MCMAHON'S VERY PUBLIC AFFAIR WITH TRISH STRATUS!
I WANT A DIVORCE!
I WOULD DO ANYTHING FOR YOU, MR. MCMAHON!
WF
IT'S...! IT'S SHANE!!!!! SHANE MCMAHON IS HERE!
NOW SHANE, YOU'RE MY SON! CALM DOWN!
SHANE MCMAHON JUST BEAT THE HELL OUT OF HIS FATHER!!!
I'VE WATCHED MY FATHER DO WHATEVER HE WANTS TO DO TO WHOMEVER HE WANTS, WITHOUT ANY RAMIFICATIONS! SO MY QUESTION IS DAD, DO YOU WANT TO PLAY?
I'M CHALLENGING YOU TO A MATCH AT WRESTLEMANIA!

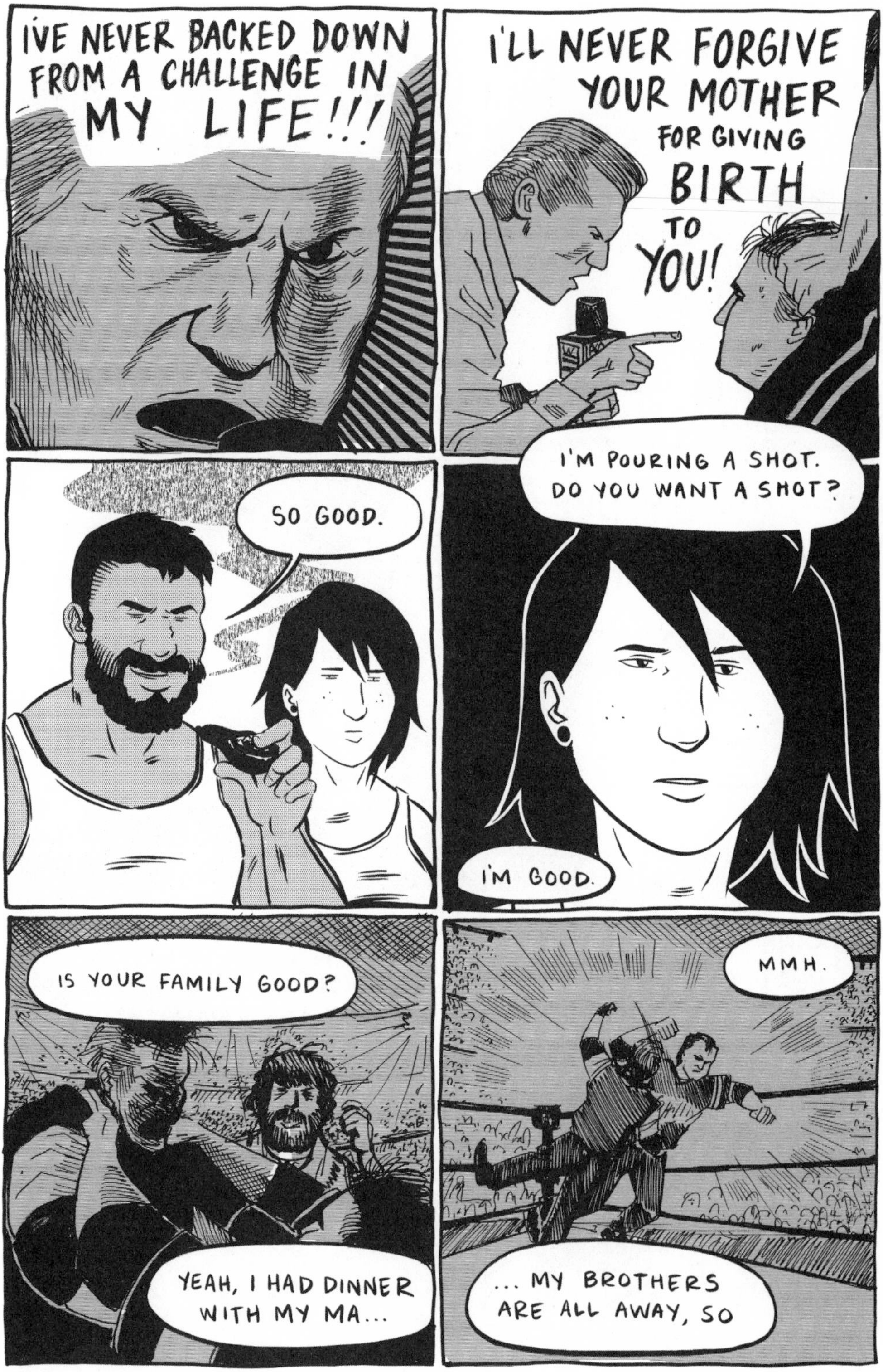
IVE NEVER BACKED DOWN FROM A CHALLENGE IN MY LIFE!!!
I'LL NEVER FORGIVE YOUR MOTHER FOR GIVING BIRTH TO YOU!
SO GOOD.
I'M POURING A SHOT. DO YOU WANT A SHOT?
I'M GOOD.
IS YOUR FAMILY GOOD?
YEAH, I HAD DINNER WITH MY MA...
MMH.
... MY BROTHERS ARE ALL AWAY, SO

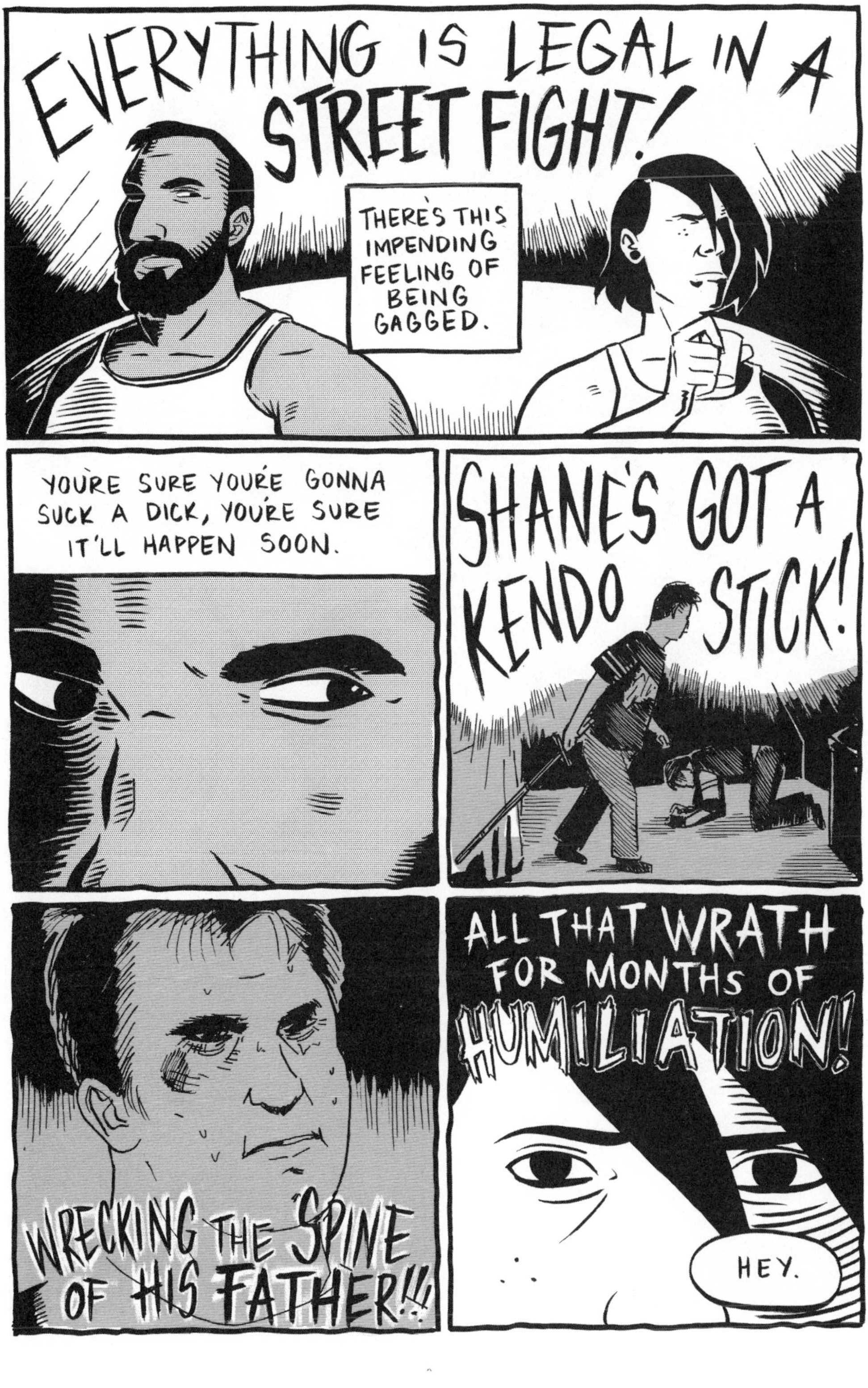
EVERYTHING IS LEGAL IN A STREET FIGHT!
THERE'S THIS IMPENDING FEELING OF BEING GAGGED.
YOU'RE SURE YOU'RE GONNA SUCK A DICK, YOU'RE SURE IT'LL HAPPEN SOON.
SHANE'S GOT A KENDO STICK!
WRECKING THE SPINE OF HIS FATHER!!!
ALL THAT WRATH FOR MONTHS OF HUMILIATION!
HEY.

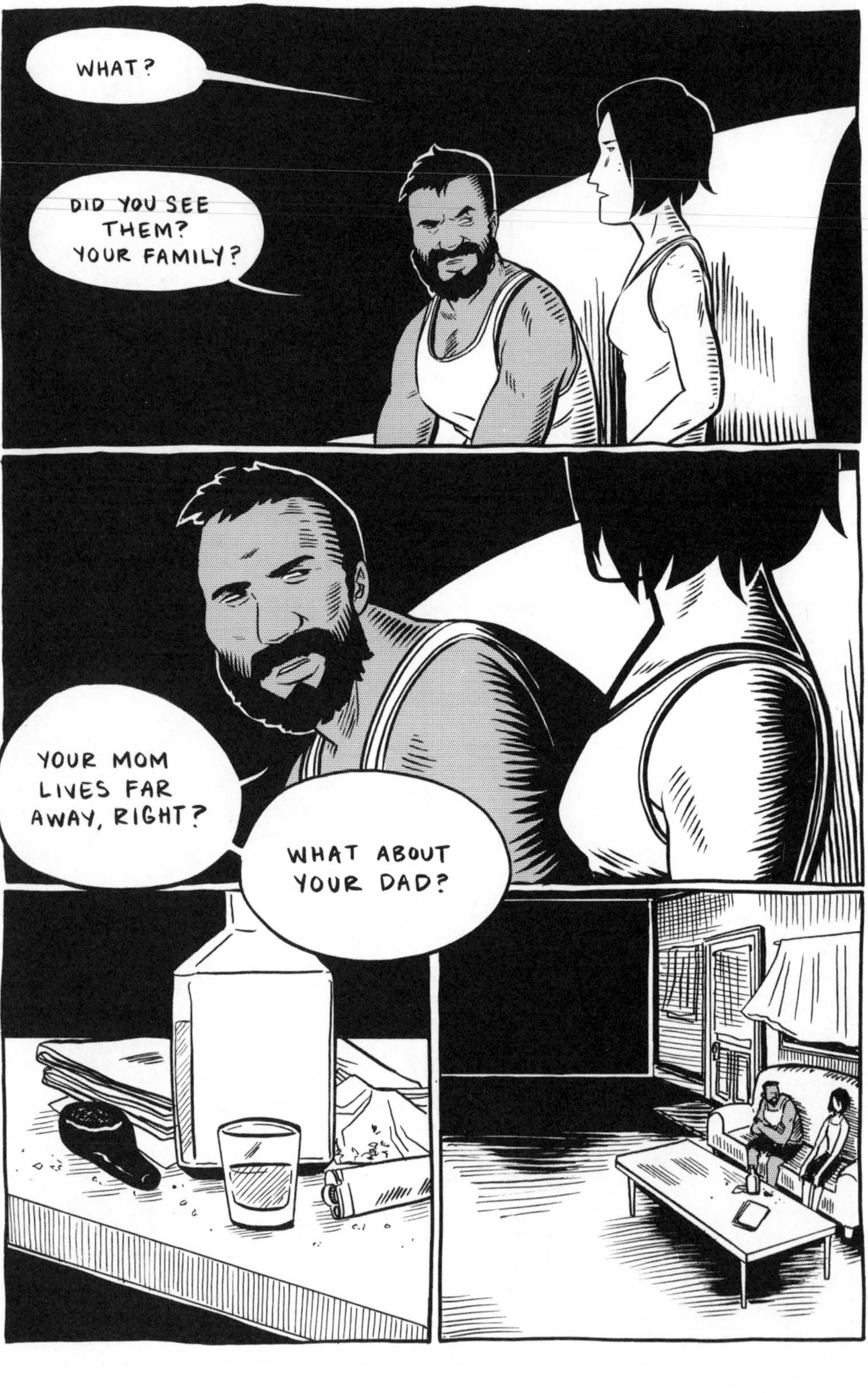
WHAT?
DID YOU SEE THEM? YOUR FAMILY?
YOUR MOM LIVES FAR AWAY, RIGHT?
WHAT ABOUT YOUR DAD?

DECEMBER
2008

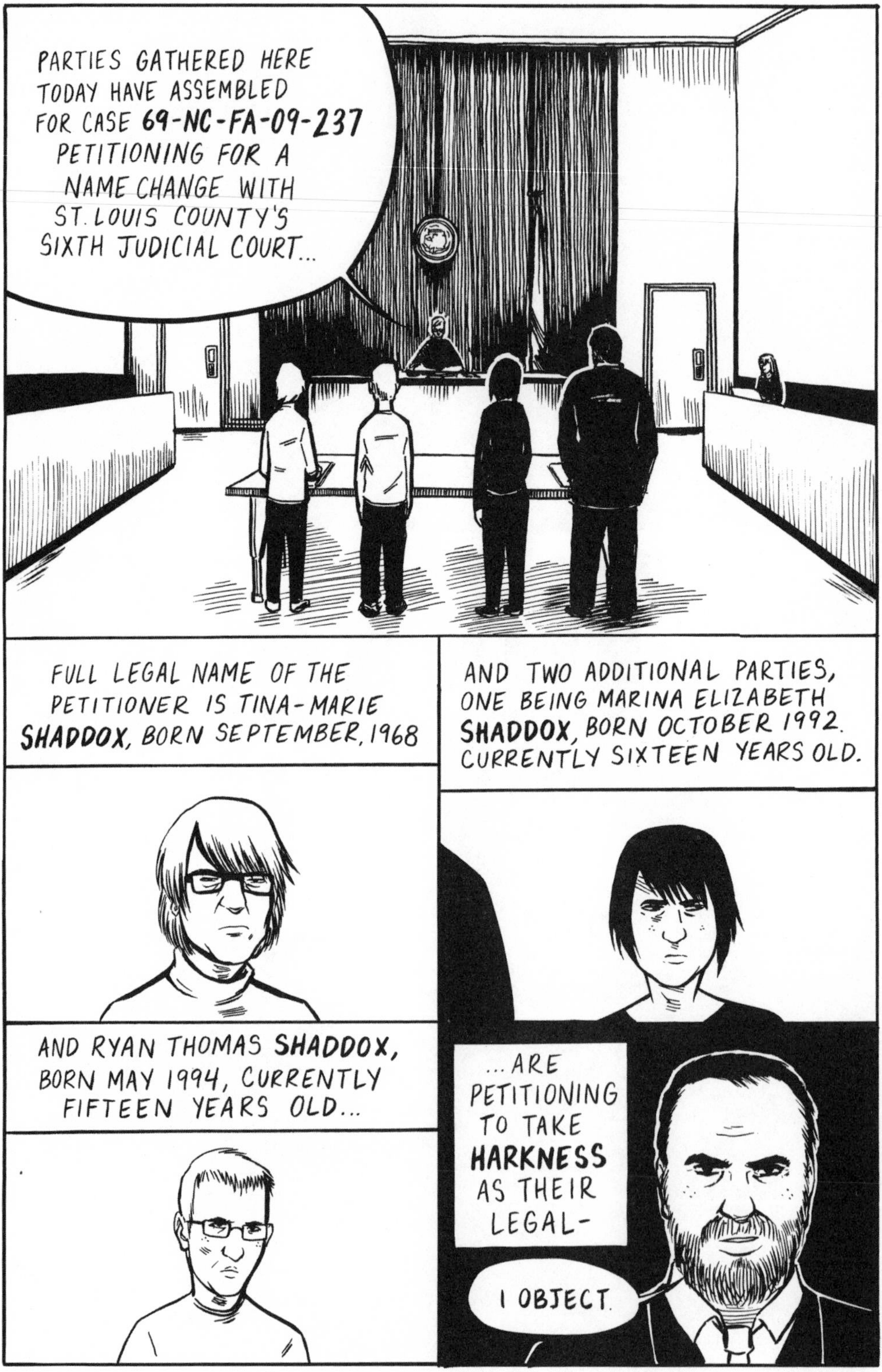
PARTIES GATHERED HERE TODAY HAVE ASSEMBLED FOR CASE 69-NC-FA-09-237 PETITIONING FOR A NAME CHANGE WITH ST. LOUIS COUNTY'S SIXTH JUDICIAL COURT...
FULL LEGAL NAME OF THE PETITIONER IS TINA-MARIE SHADDOX, BORN SEPTEMBER, 1968
AND TWO ADDITIONAL PARTIES, ONE BEING MARINA ELIZABETH SHADDOX, BORN OCTOBER 1992. CURRENTLY SIXTEEN YEARS OLD.
AND RYAN THOMAS SHADDOX, BORN MAY 1994, CURRENTLY FIFTEEN YEARS OLD...
...ARE PETITIONING TO TAKE HARKNESS AS THEIR LEGAL-
I OBJECT.

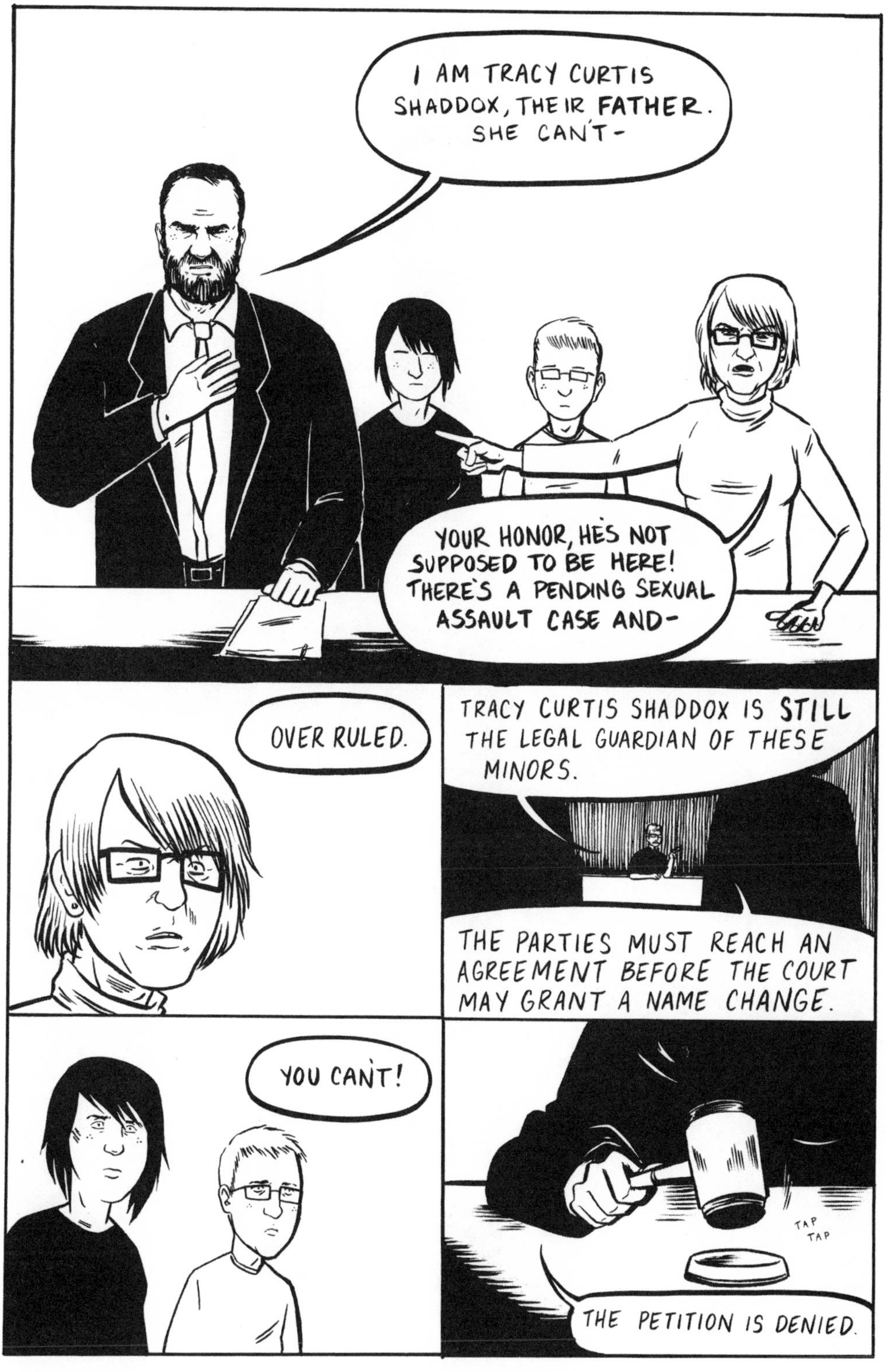
I AM TRACY CURTIS SHADDOX, THEIR FATHER. SHE CAN'T-
YOUR HONOR, HE'S NOT SUPPOSED TO BE HERE! THERE'S A PENDING SEXUAL ASSAULT CASE AND-
OVER RULED.
TRACY CURTIS SHADDOX IS STILL THE LEGAL GUARDIAN OF THESE MINORS.
THE PARTIES MUST REACH AN AGREEMENT BEFORE THE COURT MAY GRANT A NAME CHANGE.
YOU CAN'T!
TAP TAP
THE PETITION IS DENIED.

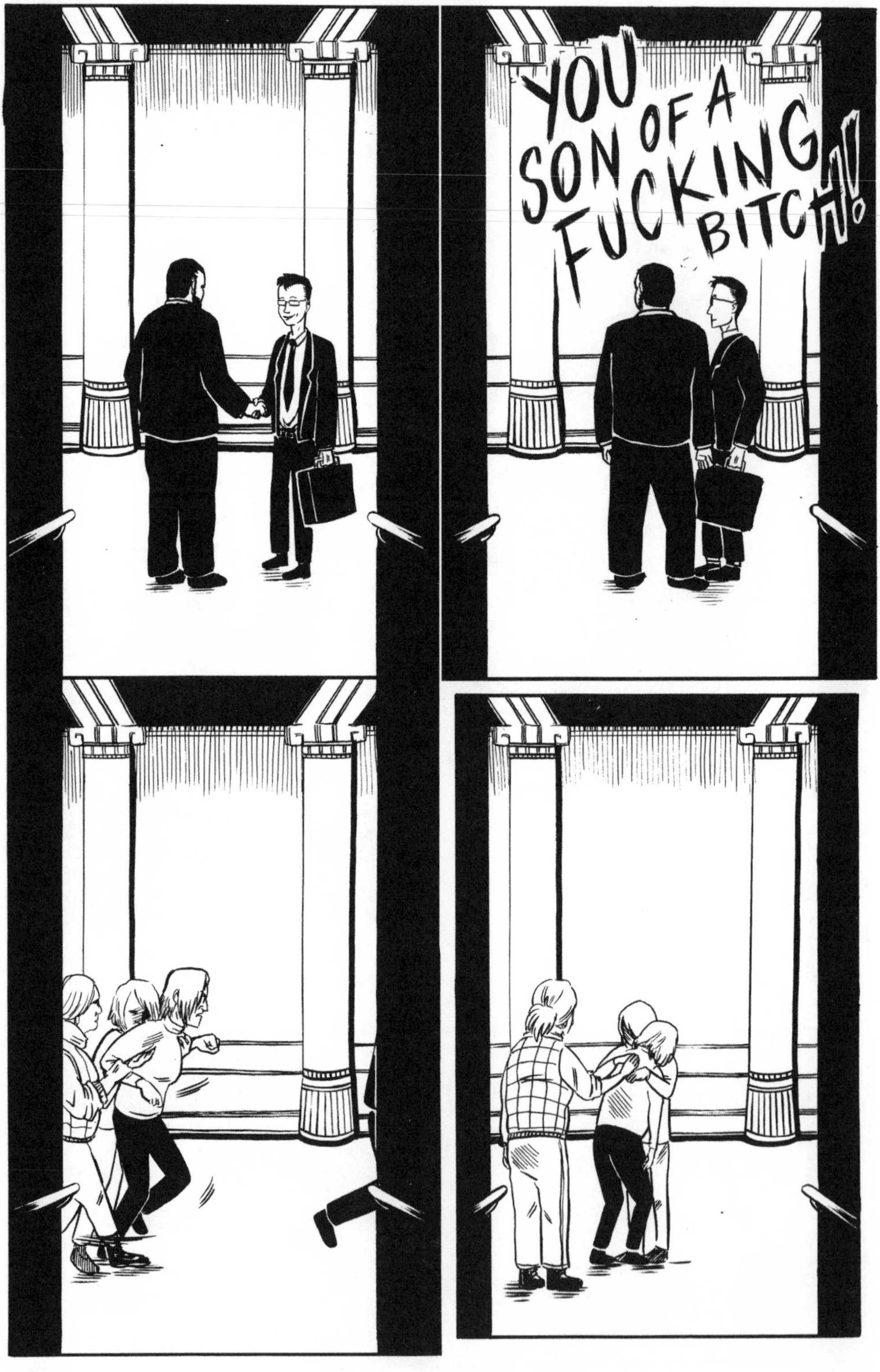
YOU SON OF A FUCKING BITCH!

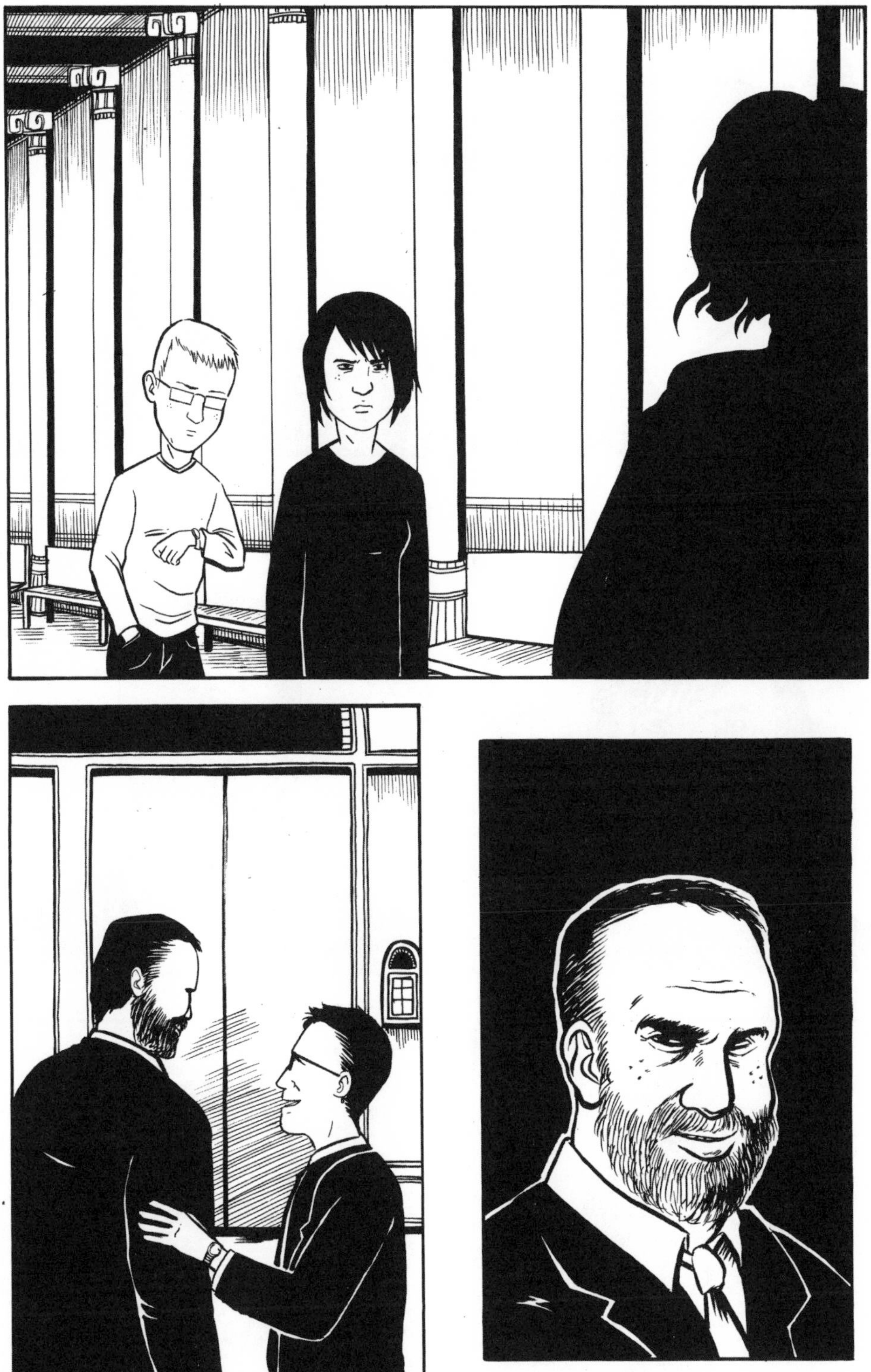

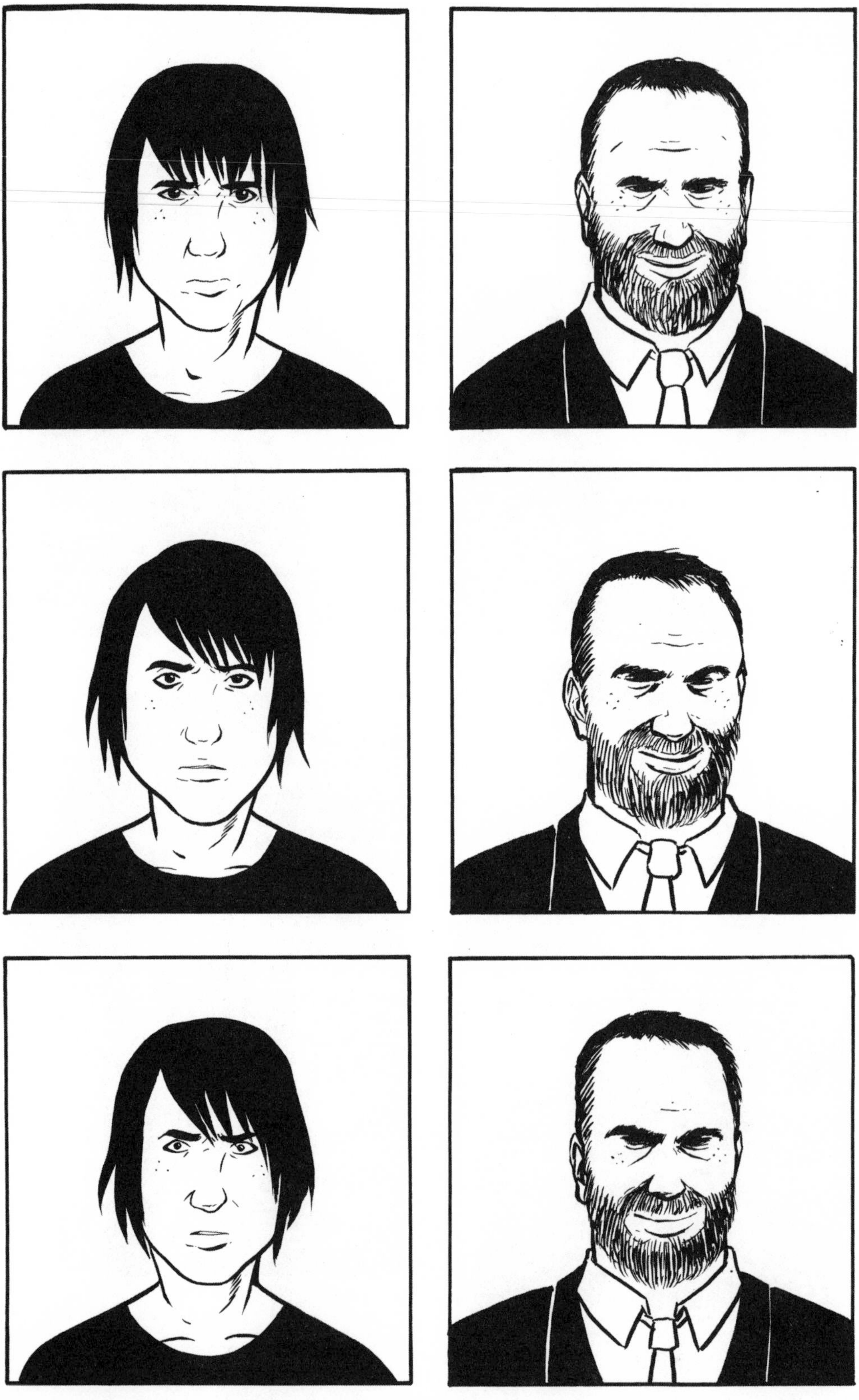

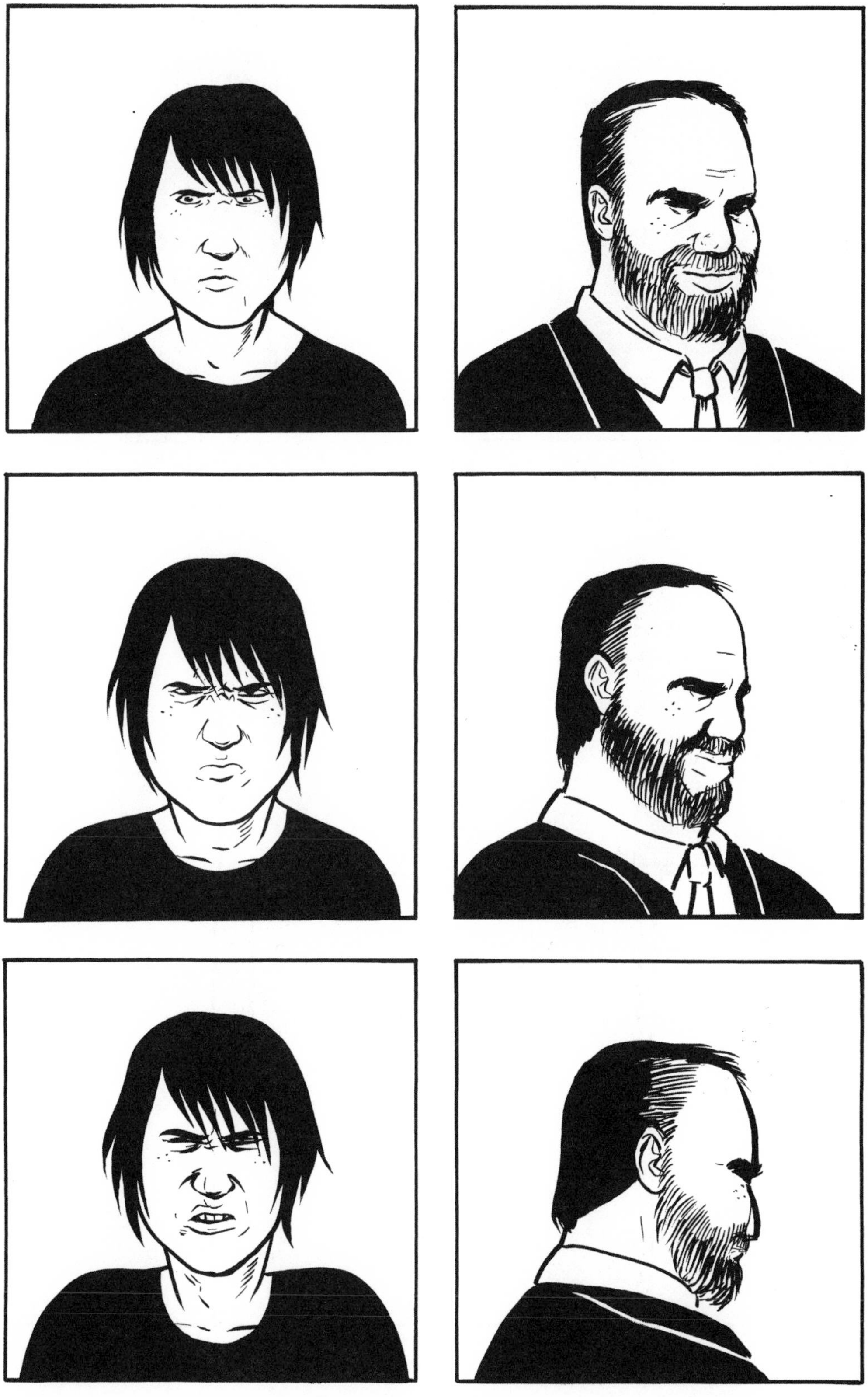

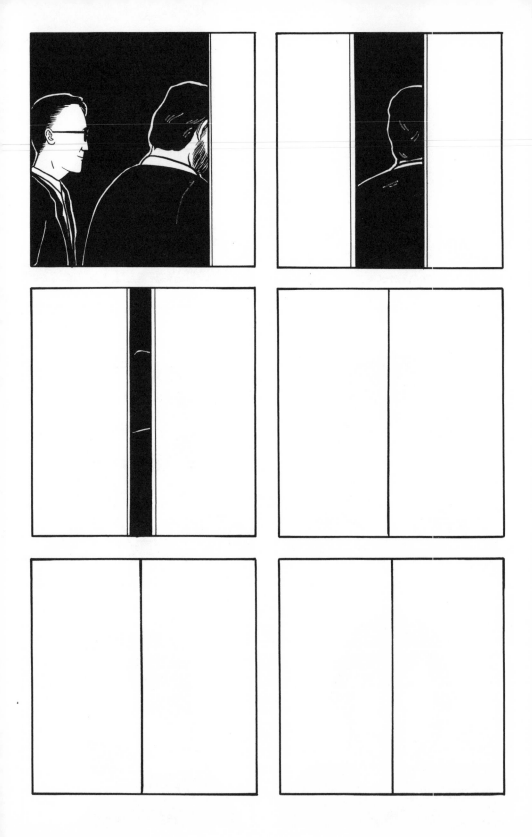

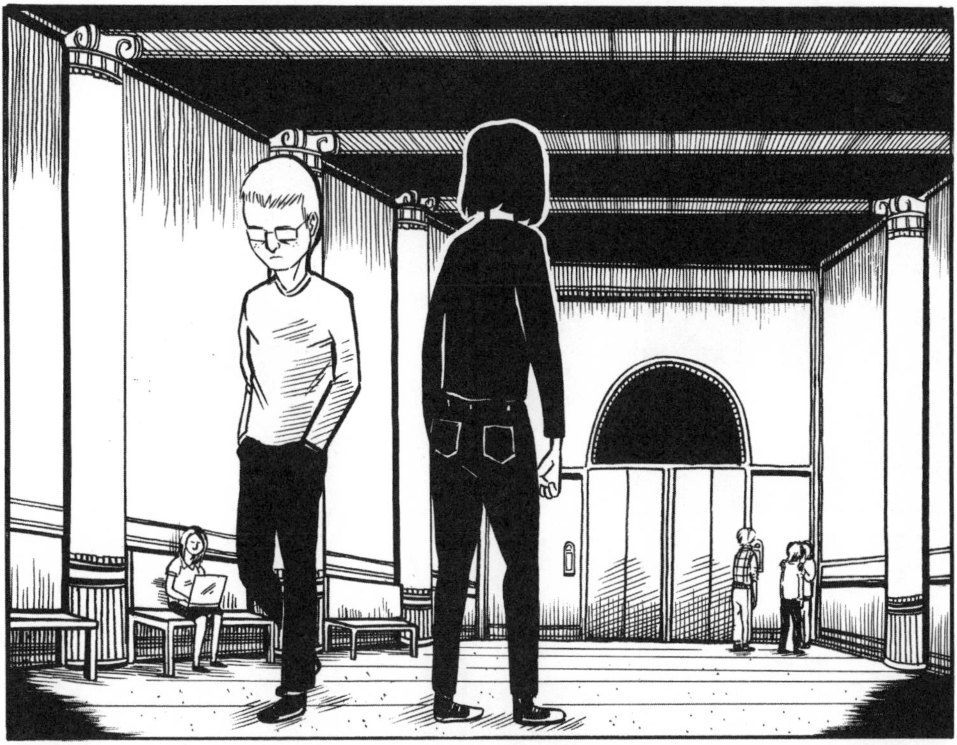

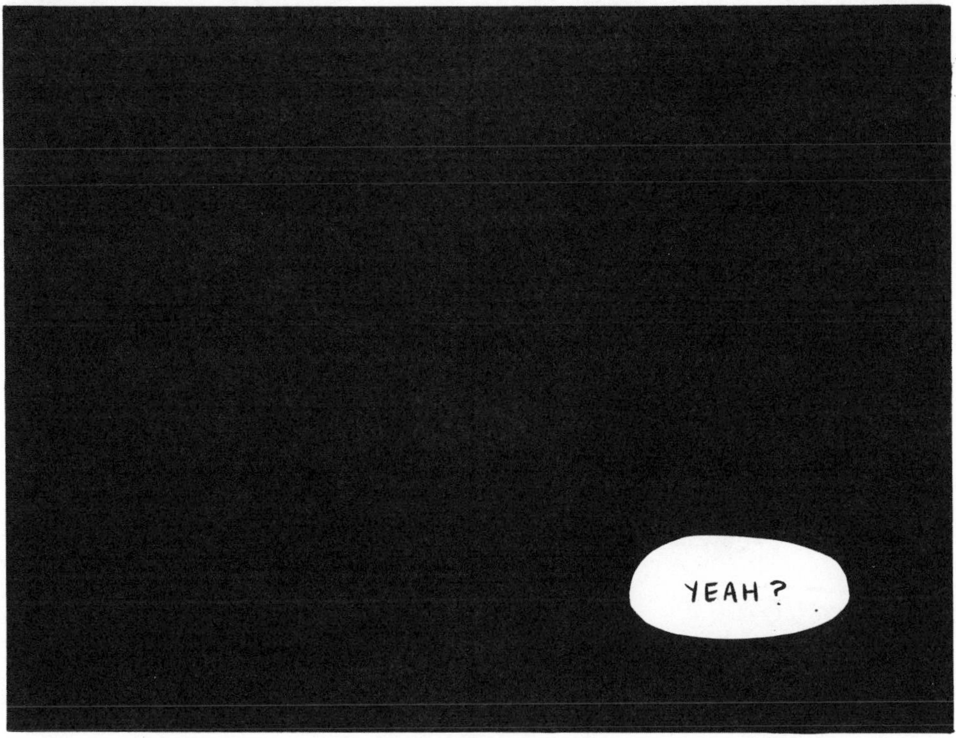
YEAH?

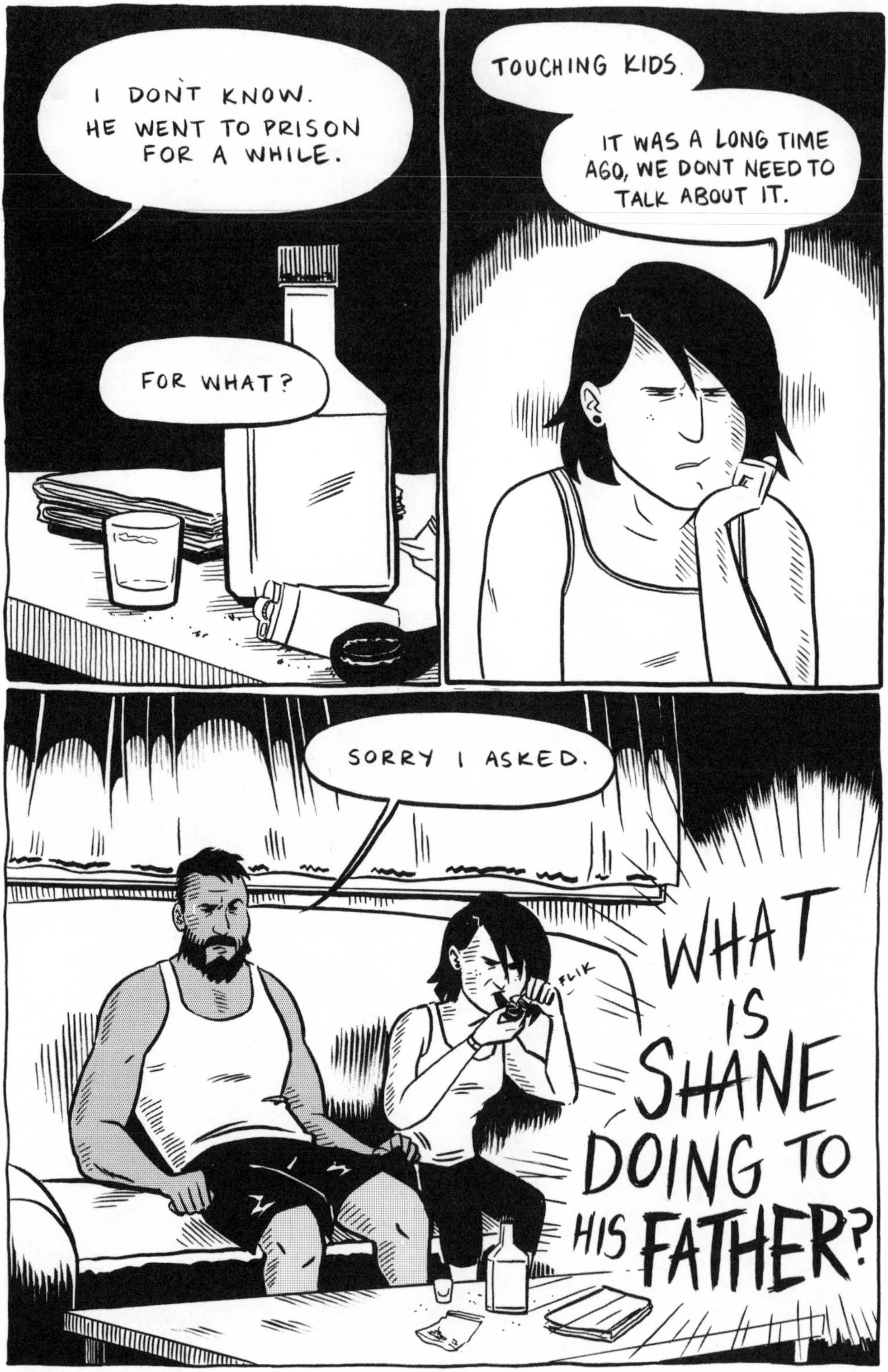
I DON'T KNOW.
HE WENT TO PRISON FOR A WHILE.
FOR WHAT?
TOUCHING KIDS.
IT WAS A LONG TIME AGO, WE DONT NEED TO TALK ABOUT IT.
SORRY I ASKED.
FLIK
WHAT IS SHANE DOING TO HIS FATHER?

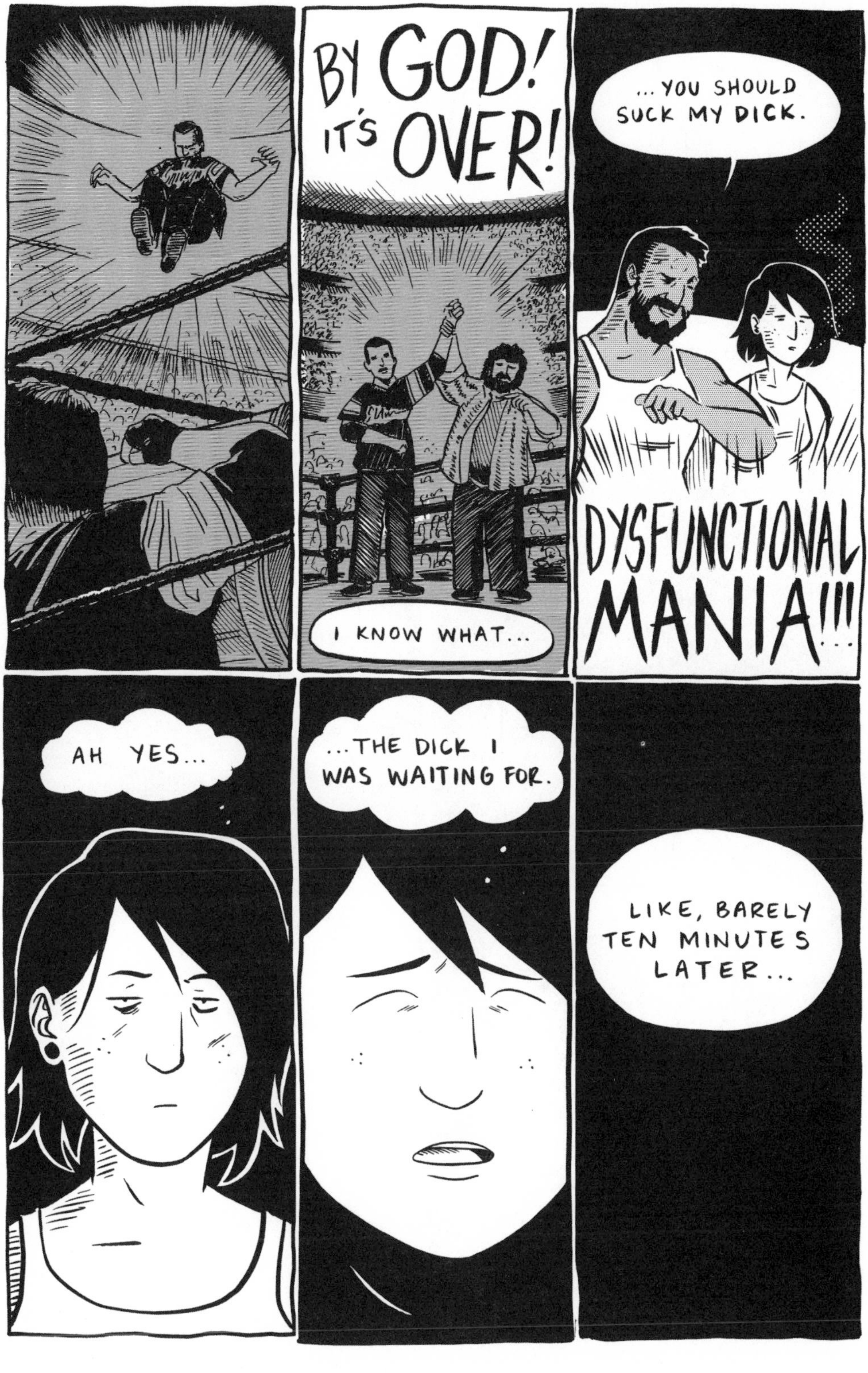
BY GOD! IT'S OVER!
I KNOW WHAT...
...YOU SHOULD SUCK MY DICK.
DYSFUNCTIONAL MANIA!!!...
AH YES...
...THE DICK I WAS WAITING FOR.
LIKE, BARELY TEN MINUTES LATER...

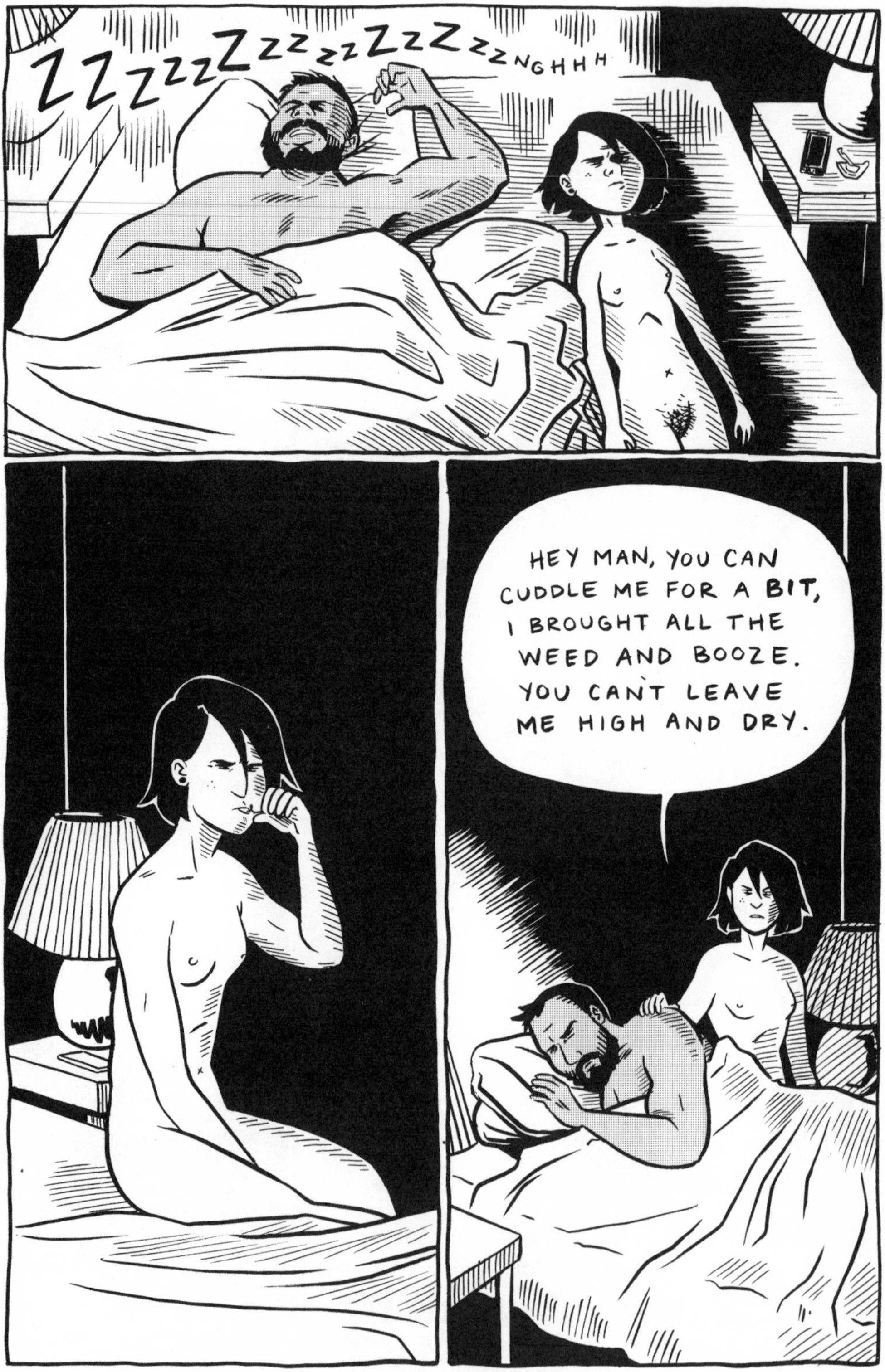
ZZZzzzZzzzzZzZzzzNGHHH
HEY MAN, YOU CAN CUDDLE ME FOR A BIT, I BROUGHT ALL THE WEED AND BOOZE. YOU CAN'T LEAVE ME HIGH AND DRY.

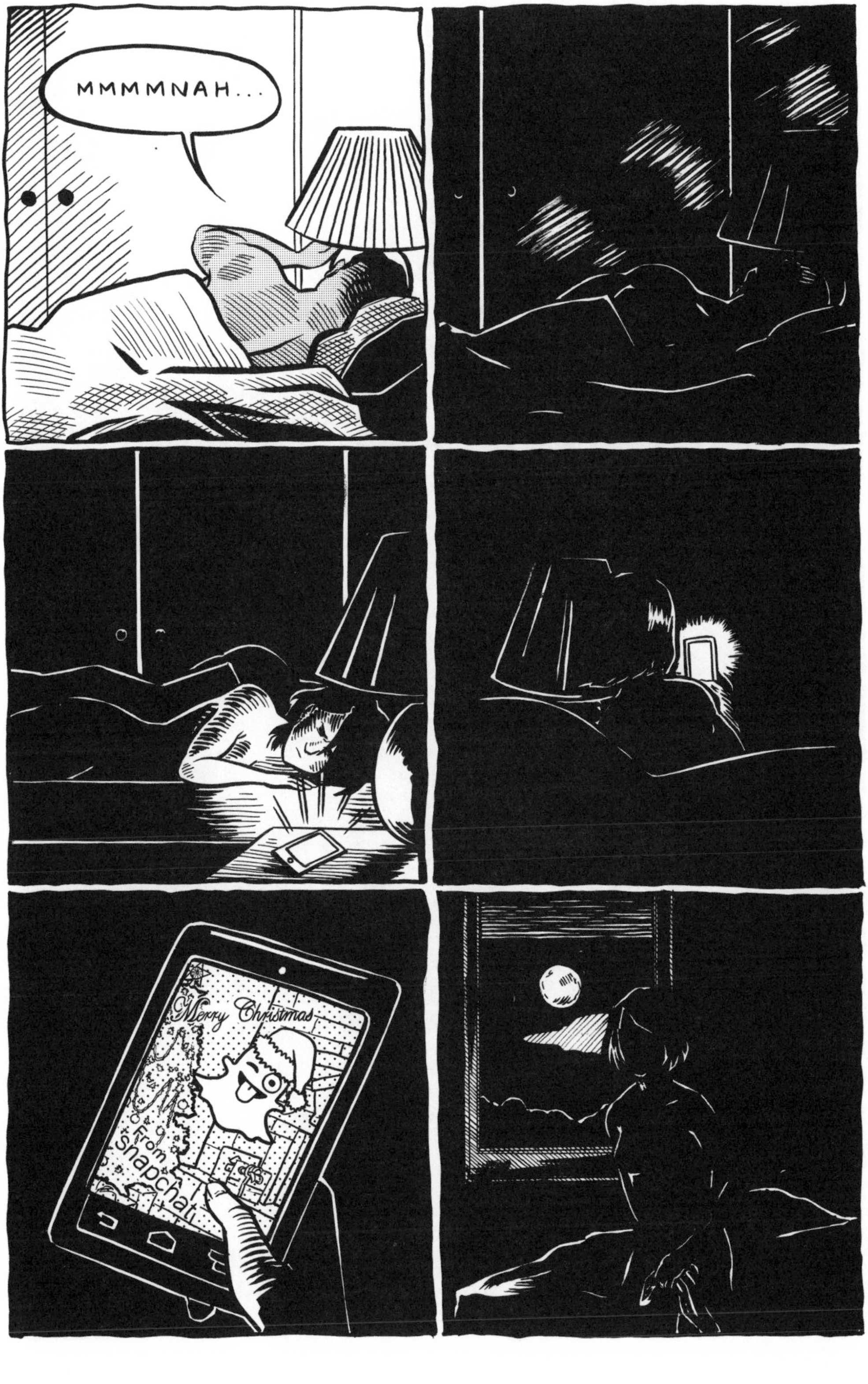
MMMMNAH...
Merry Christmas
From Snapchat

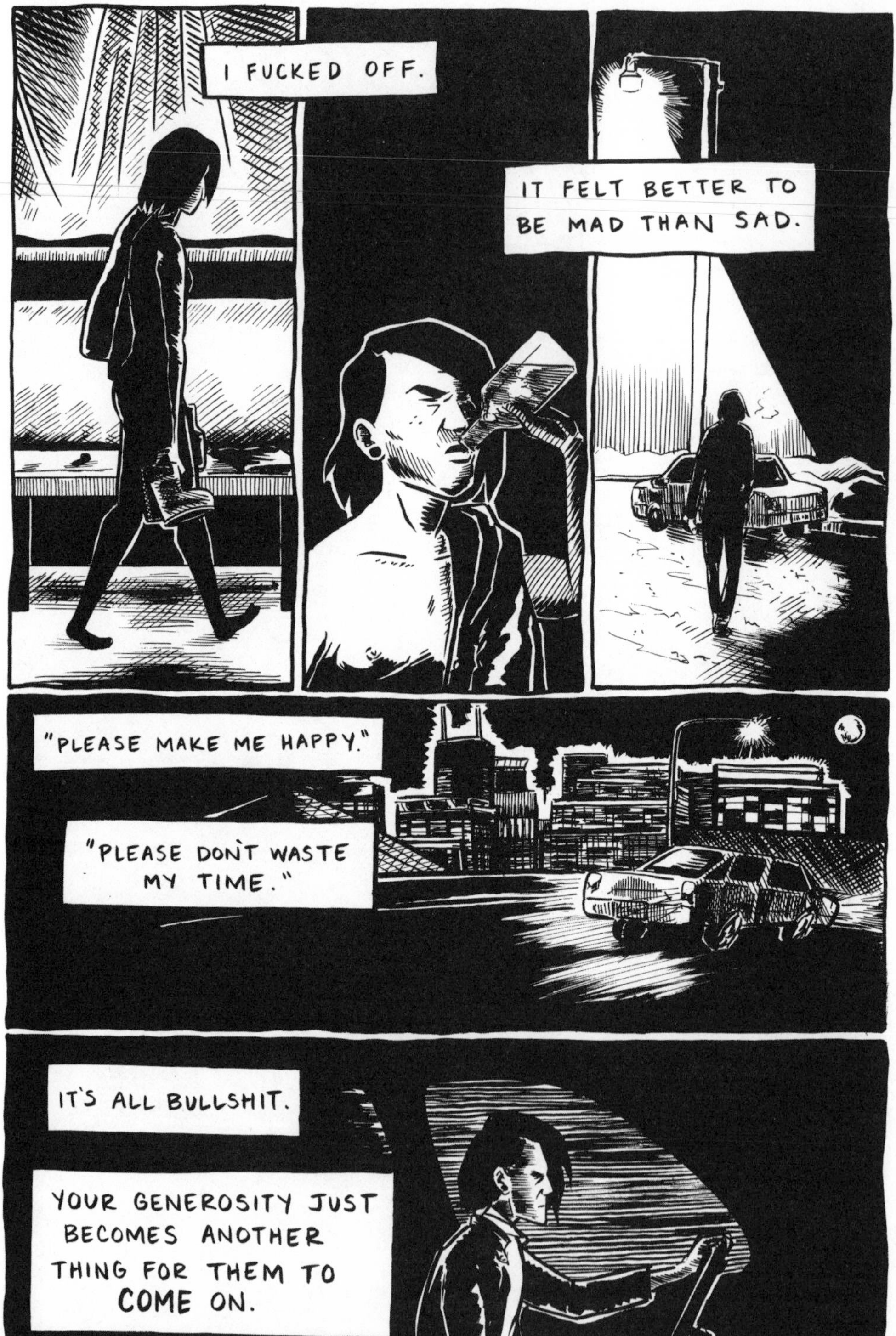
I FUCKED OFF.
IT FELT BETTER TO BE MAD THAN SAD.
"PLEASE MAKE ME HAPPY."
"PLEASE DON'T WASTE MY TIME."
IT'S ALL BULLSHIT.
YOUR GENEROSITY JUST BECOMES ANOTHER THING FOR THEM TO COME ON.

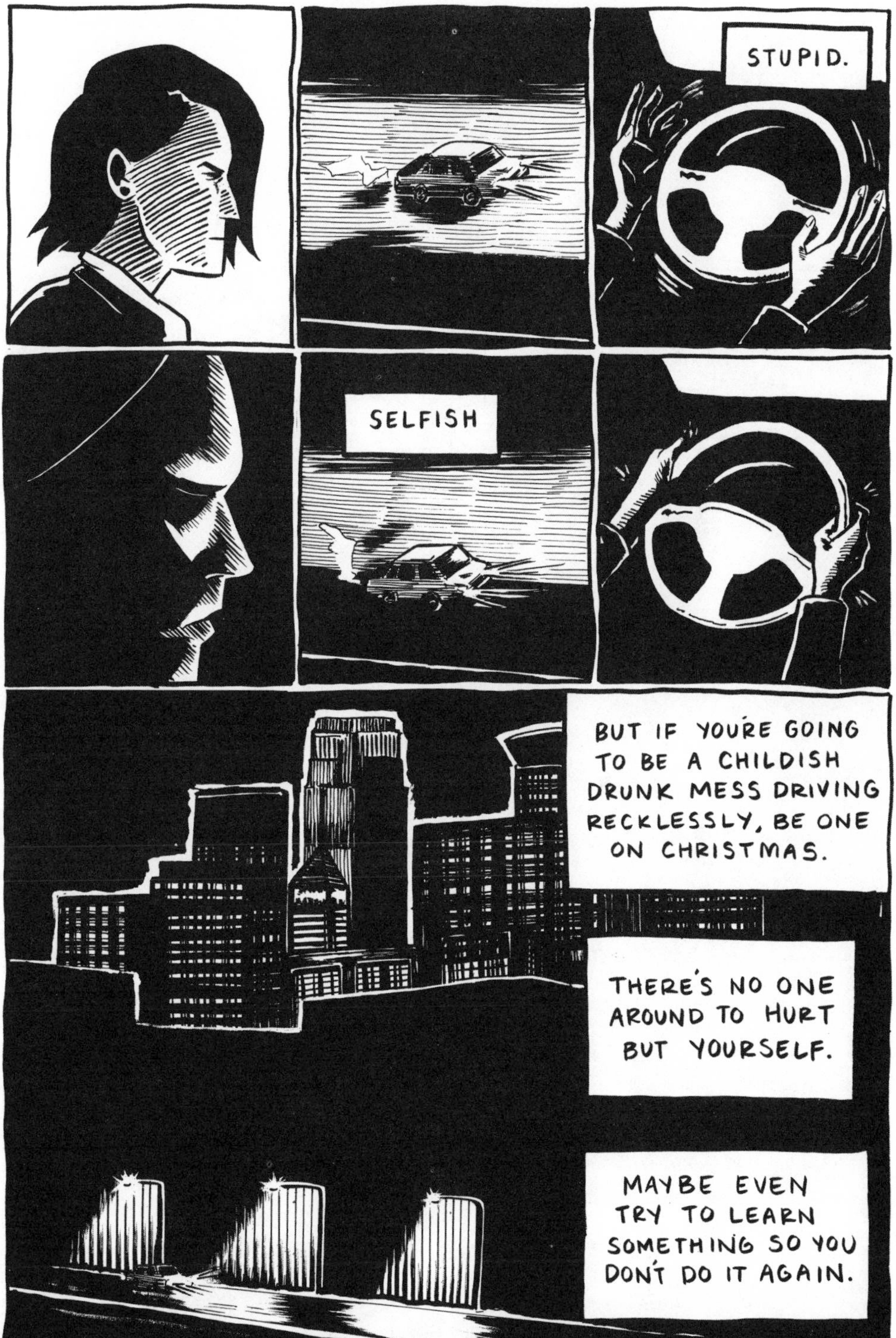
STUPID.
SELFISH
BUT IF YOU'RE GOING TO BE A CHILDISH DRUNK MESS DRIVING RECKLESSLY, BE ONE ON CHRISTMAS.
THERE'S NO ONE AROUND TO HURT BUT YOURSELF.
MAYBE EVEN TRY TO LEARN SOMETHING SO YOU DON'T DO IT AGAIN.

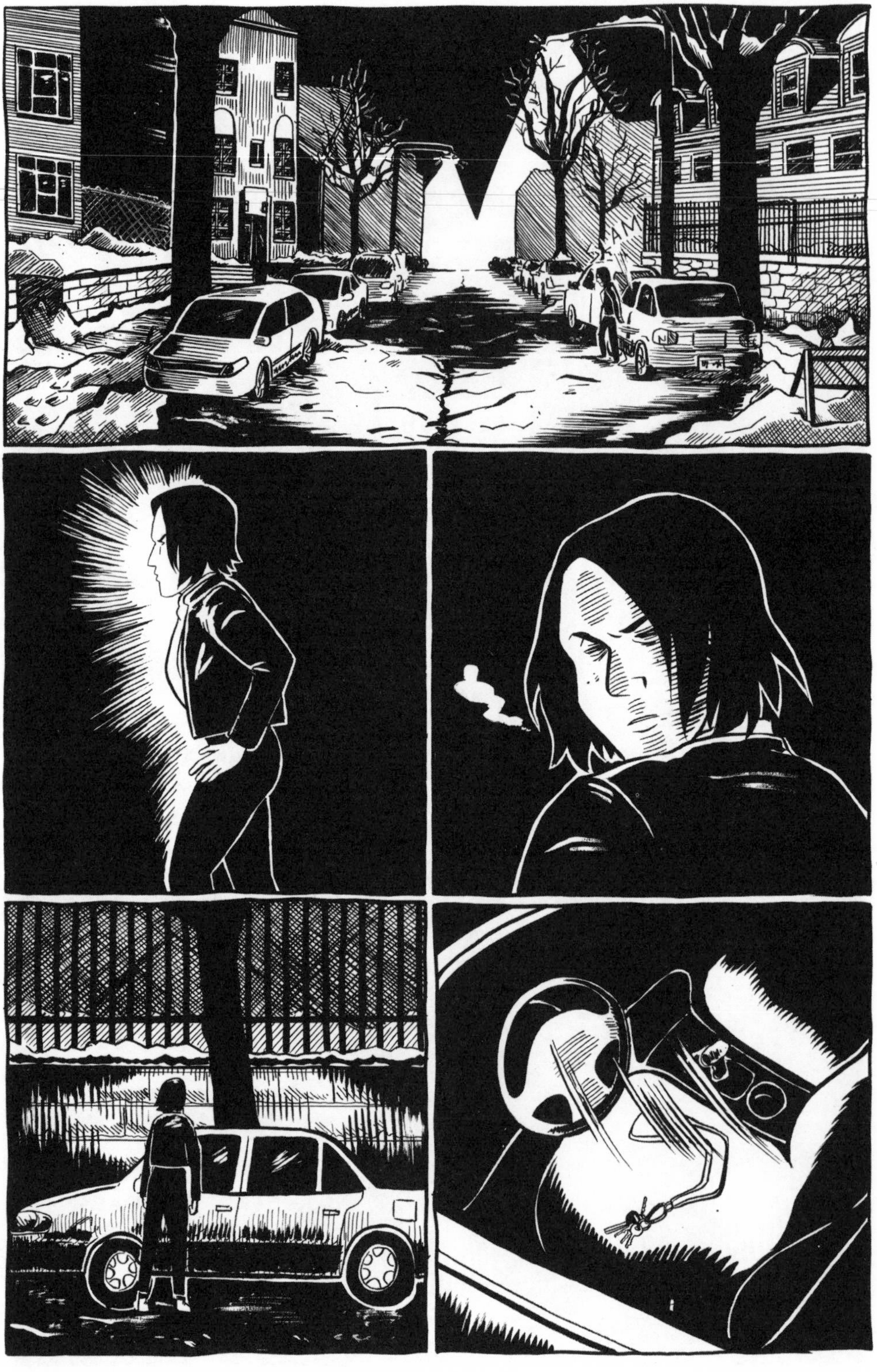

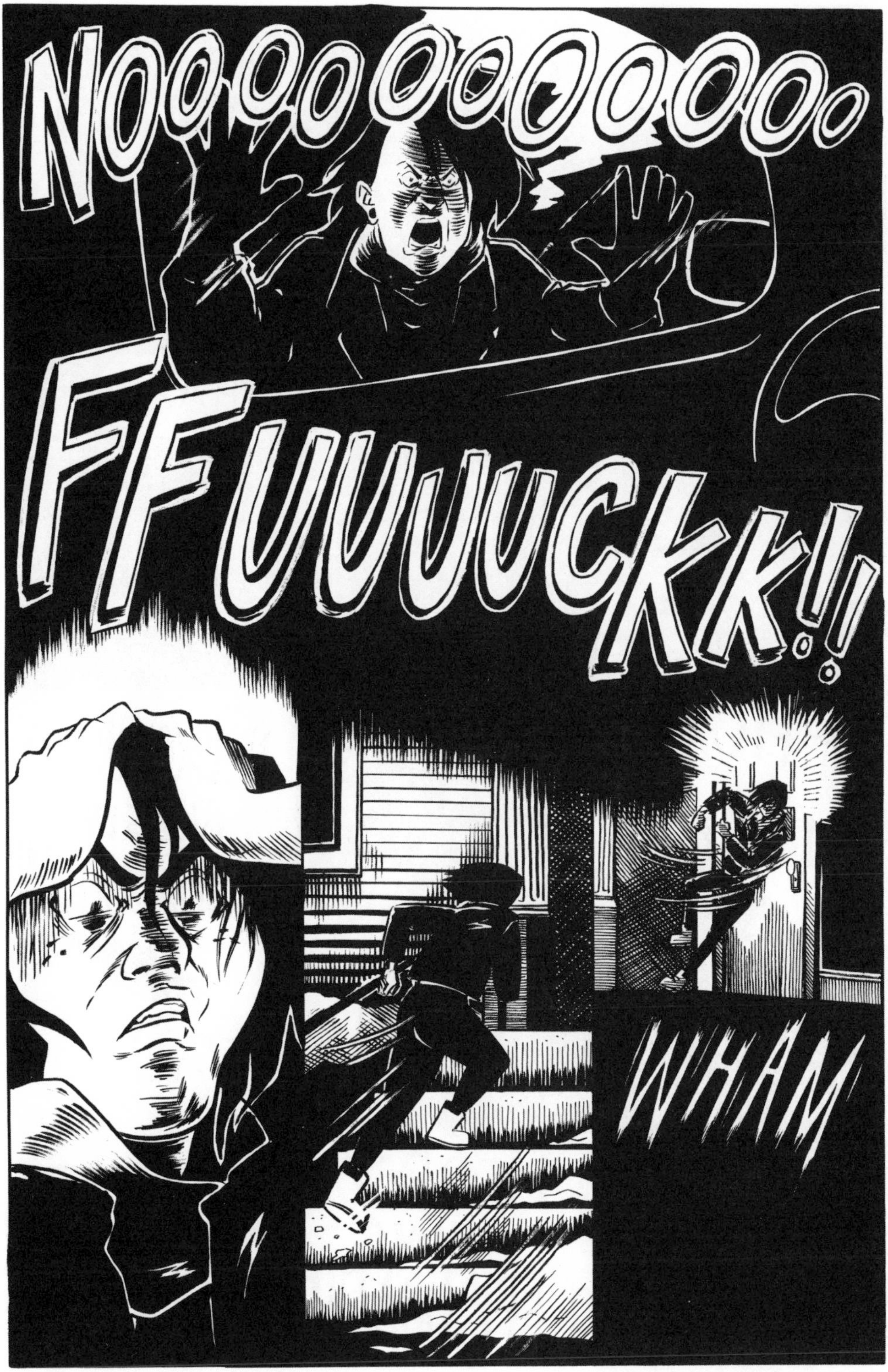
NOOOOOOOOOOOO
FFUUUUCKK!!
WHAM

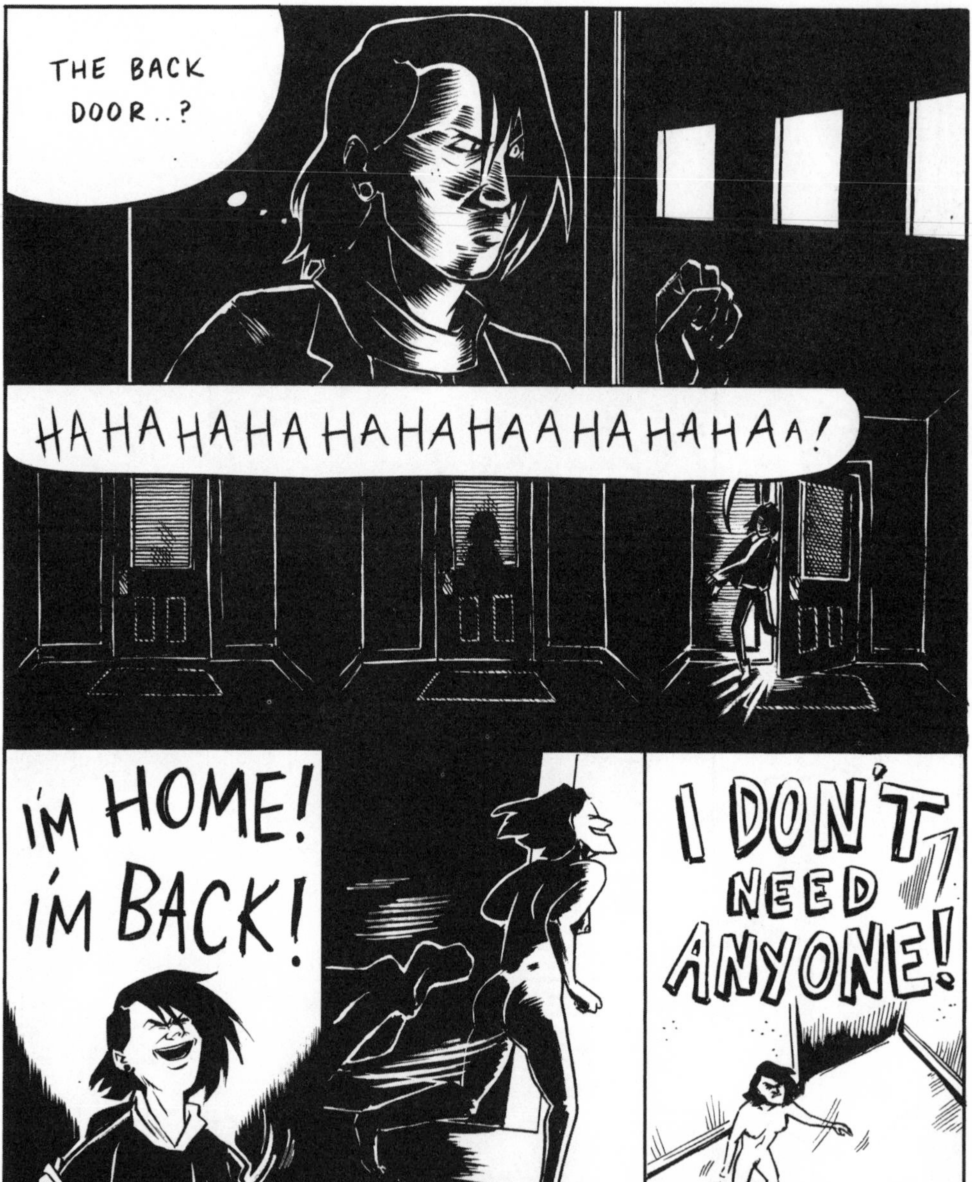
THE BACK DOOR..?
HAHAHAHAHAHAHAHAAHAHAHAHAA!
I'M HOME! I'M BACK!
MERRY FUCKING CHRISTMAS!!
I DON'T NEED ANYONE!
YOU HEAR ME??!

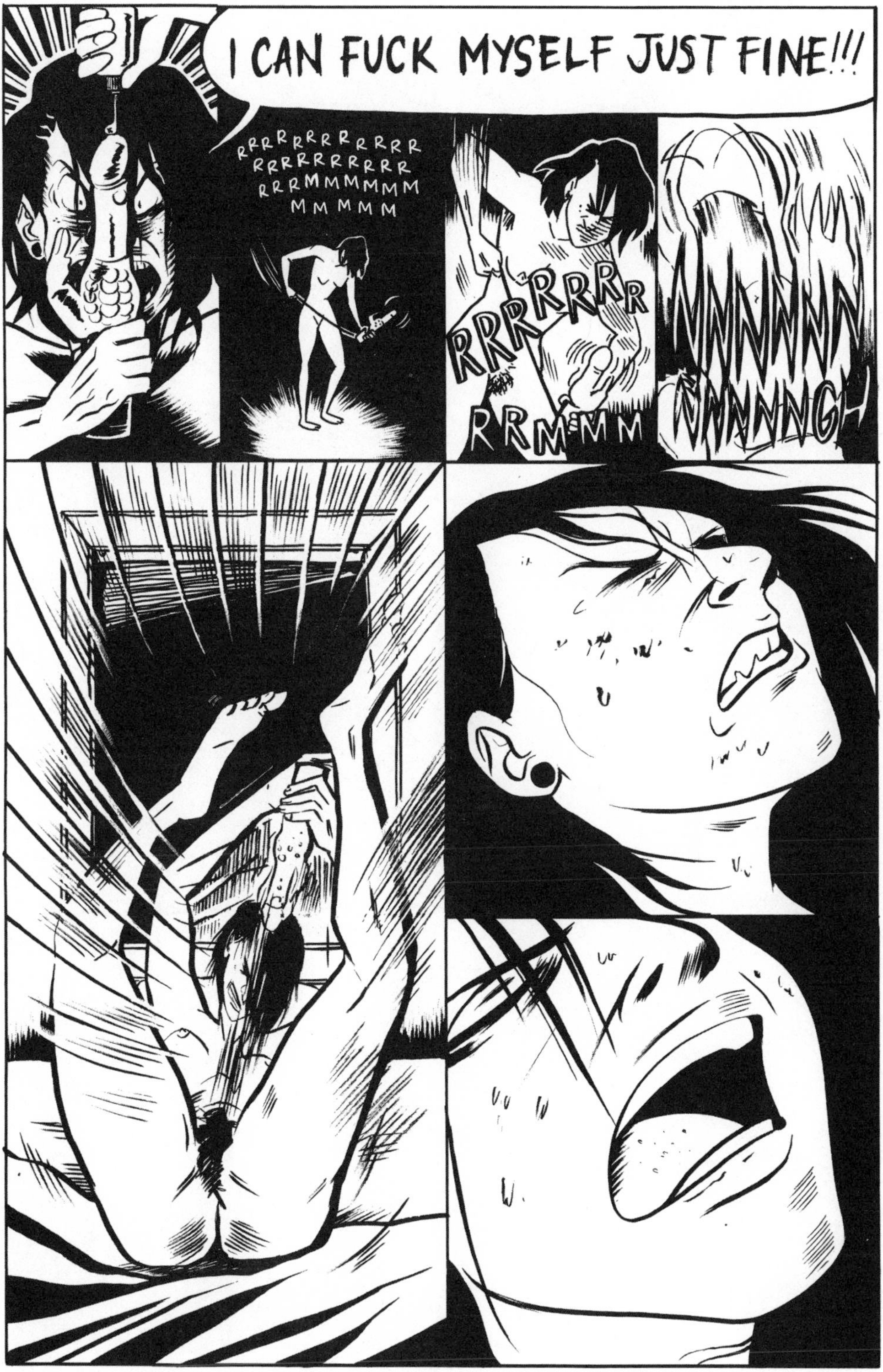
I CAN FUCK MYSELF JUST FINE!!!
RRRRRRRRRRRRR RRRRRRRRRRR RRRMMMMMMM MMMMM
RRRRRRRRR RRMMMM
NNNNNNNNNNNNGH

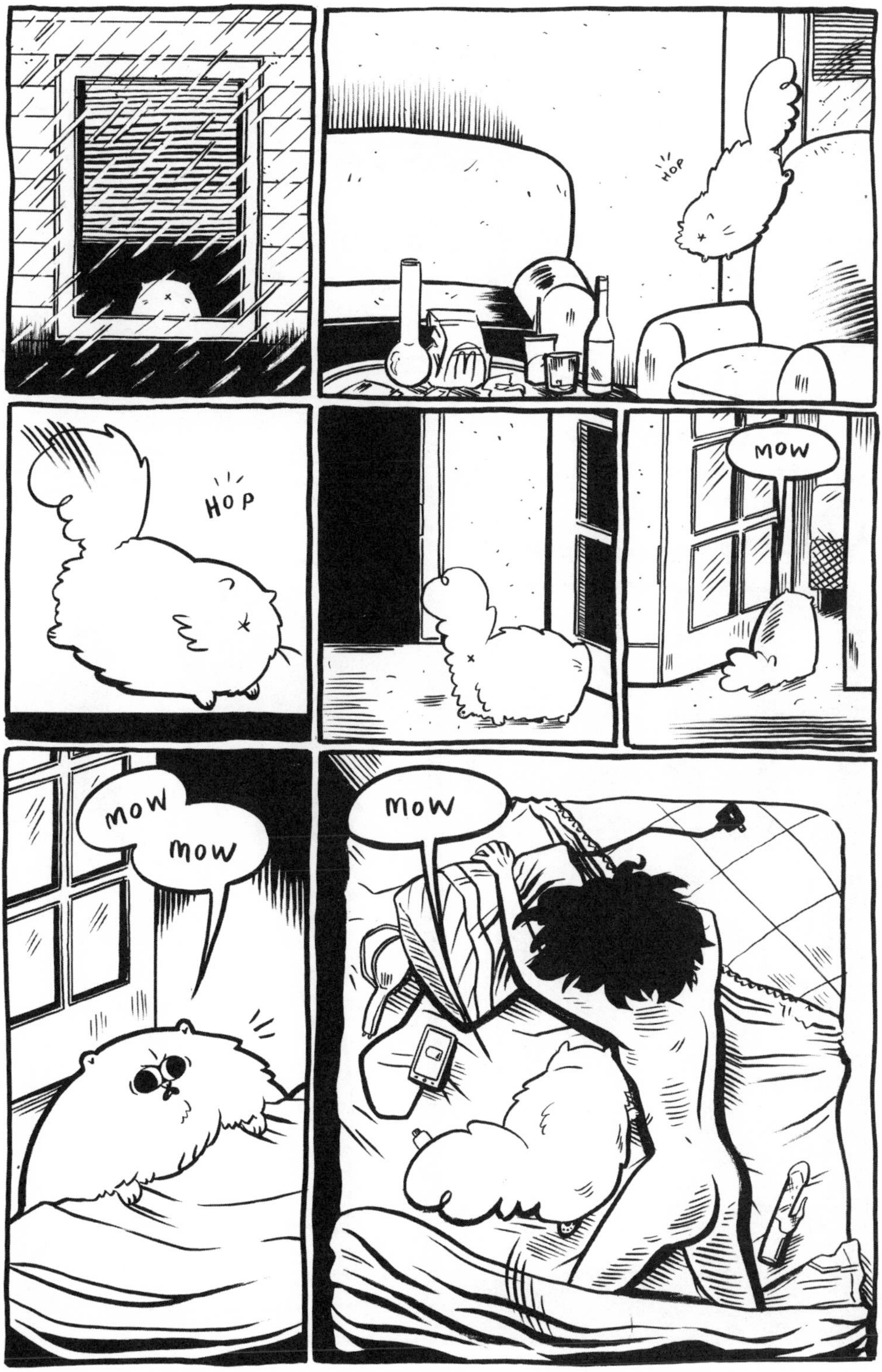
HOP
HOP
MOW
MOW
MOW
MOW

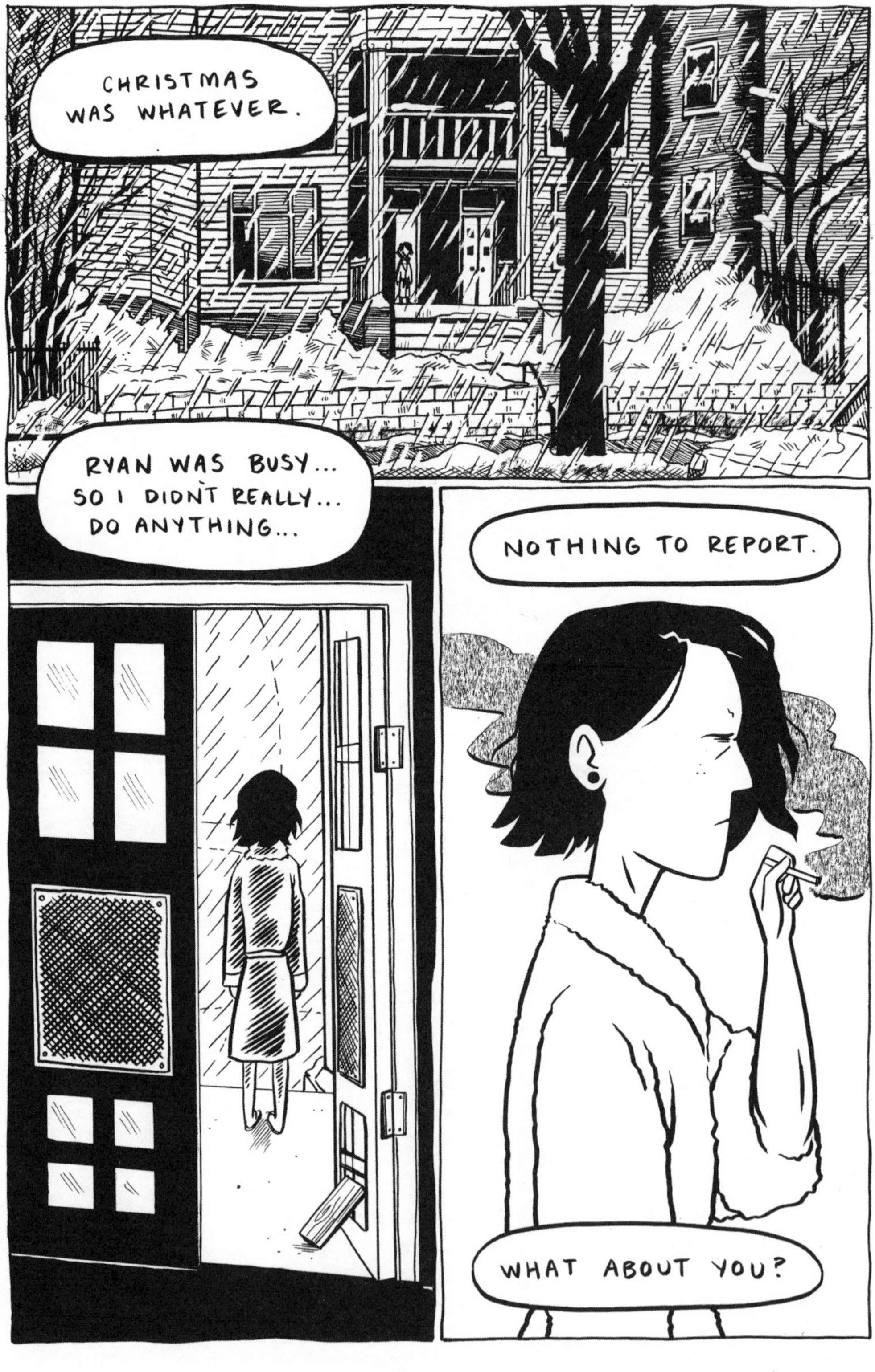

CHRISTMAS WAS WHATEVER.
RYAN WAS BUSY... SO I DIDN'T REALLY... DO ANYTHING...
NOTHING TO REPORT.
WHAT ABOUT YOU?

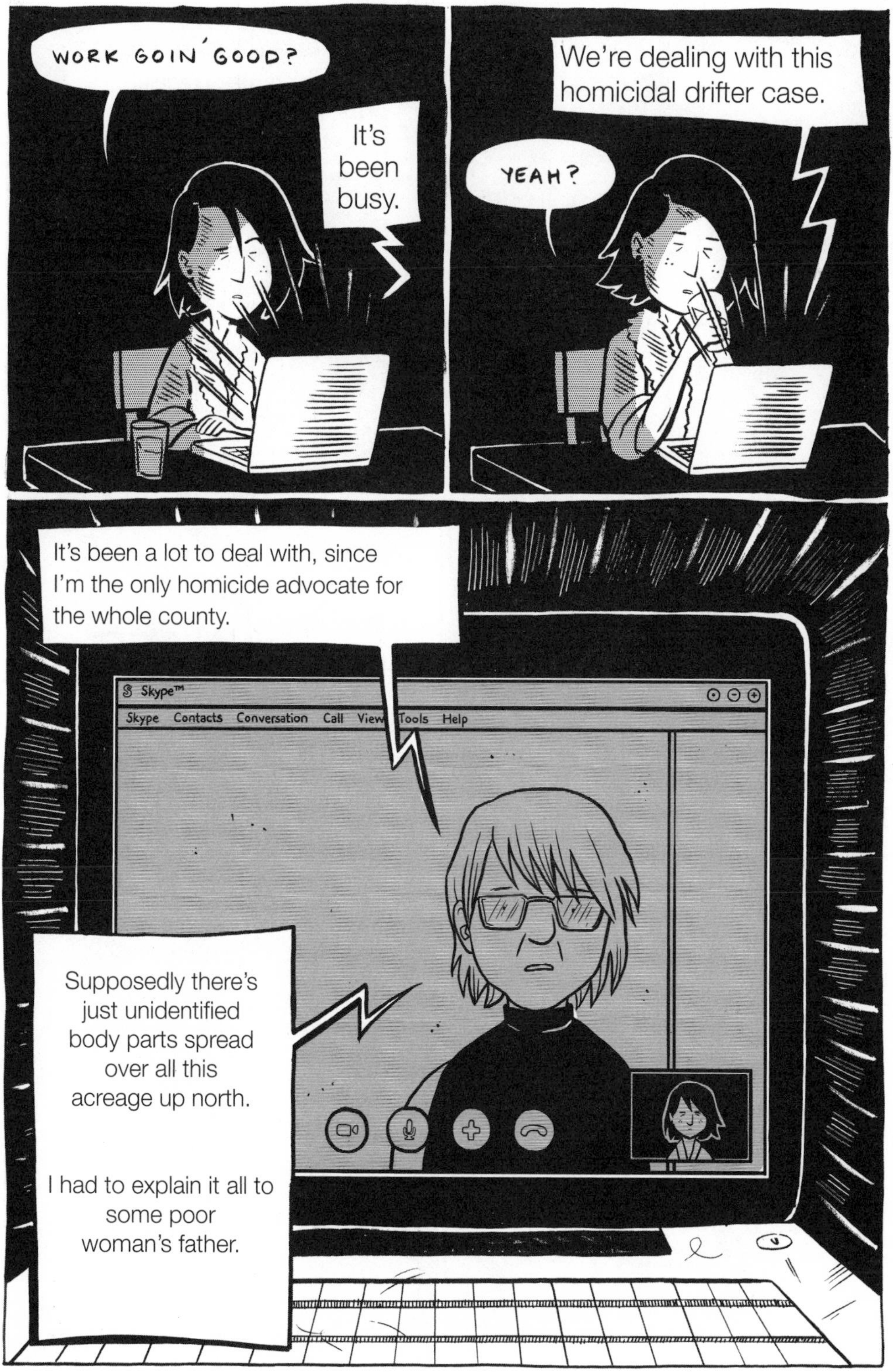
WORK GOIN' GOOD?
It's been busy.
We're dealing with this homicidal drifter case.
YEAH?
It's been a lot to deal with, since I'm the only homicide advocate for the whole county.
Skype™
Skype Contacts Conversation Call View Tools Help
Supposedly there's just unidentified body parts spread over all this acreage up north.
I had to explain it all to some poor woman's father.

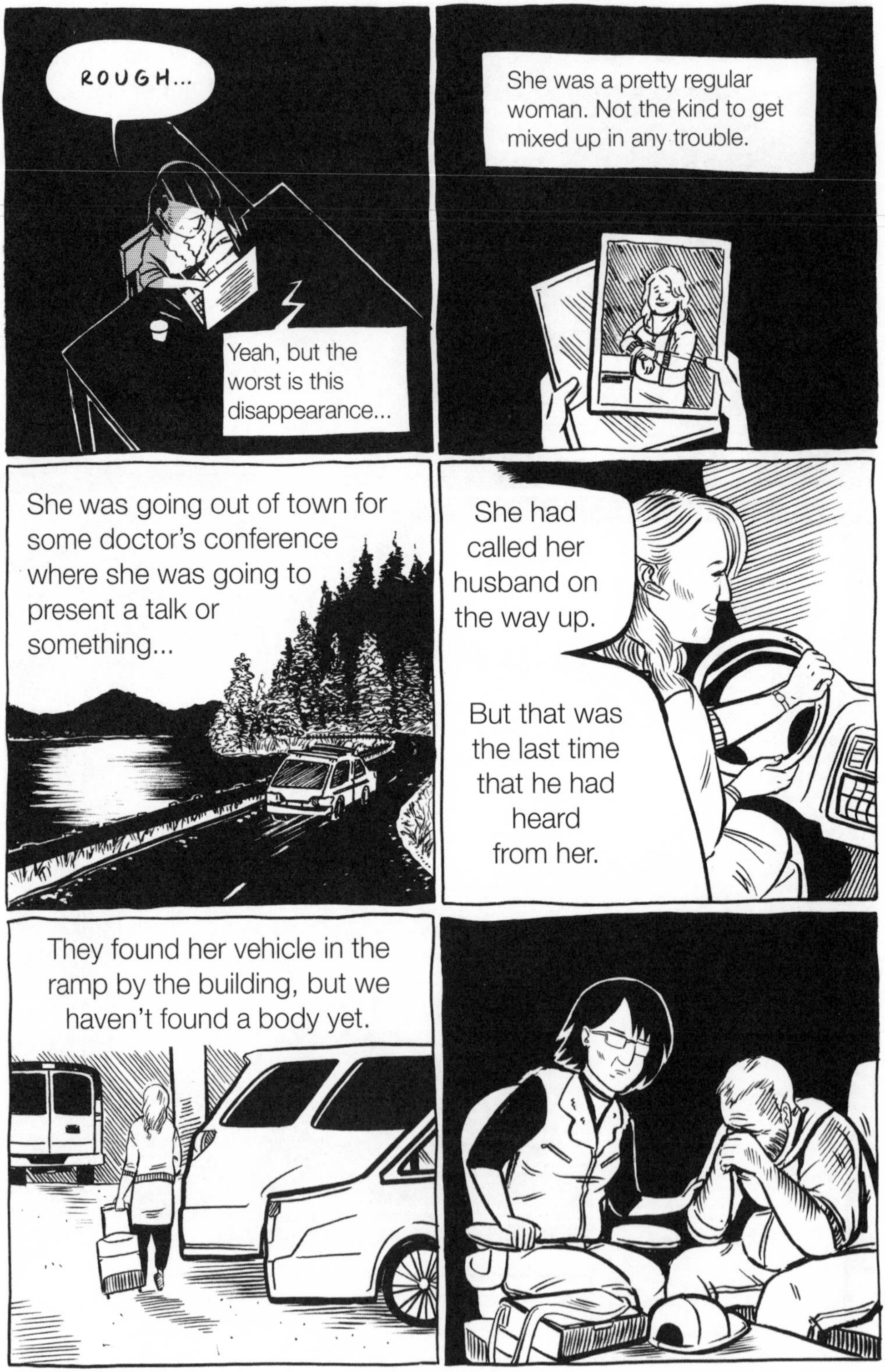
ROUGH...
Yeah, but the worst is this disappearance...
She was a pretty regular woman. Not the kind to get mixed up in any trouble.
She was going out of town for some doctor's conference where she was going to present a talk or something...
She had called her husband on the way up.
But that was the last time that he had heard from her.
They found her vehicle in the ramp by the building, but we haven't found a body yet.

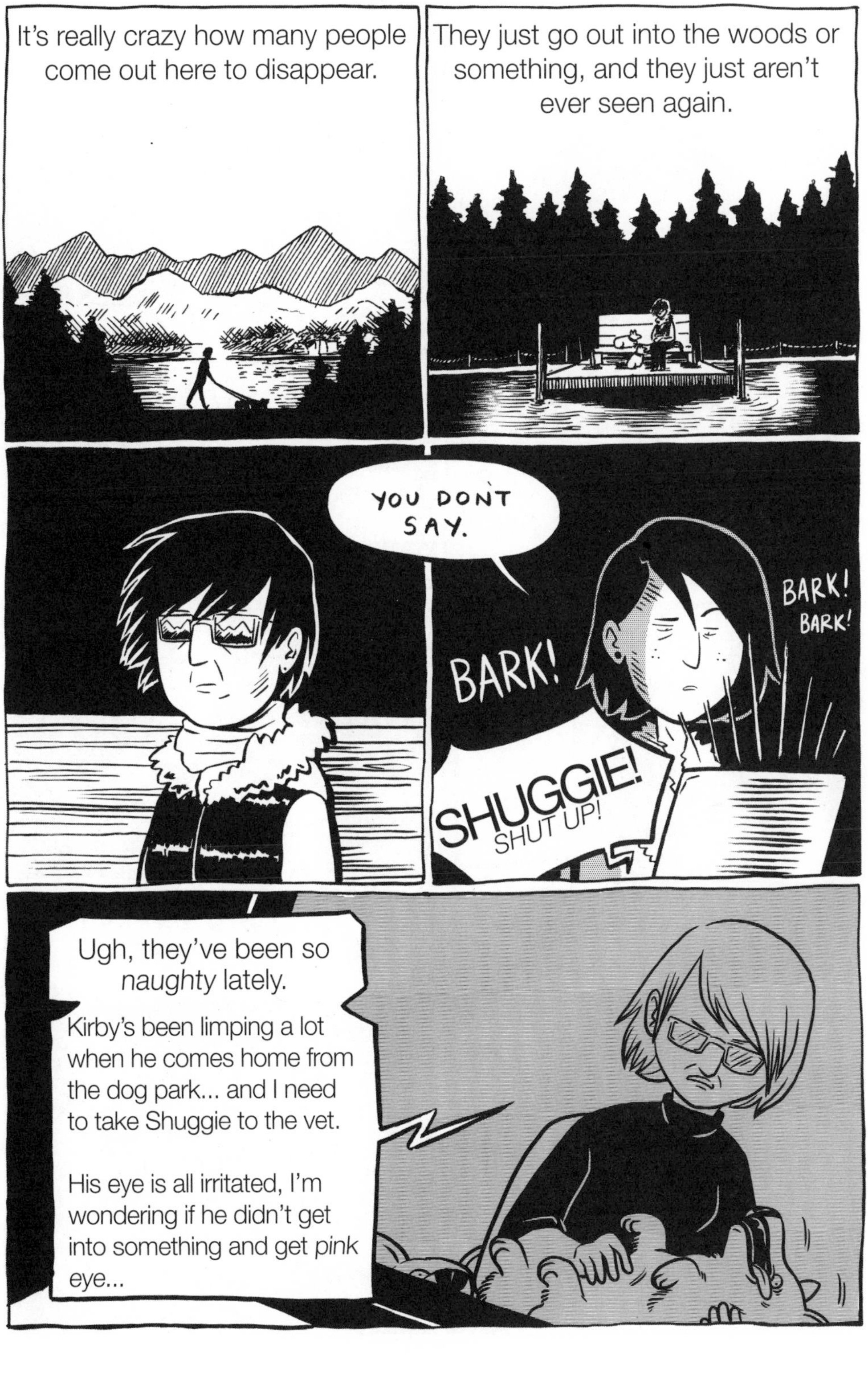
It's really crazy how many people come out here to disappear.
They just go out into the woods or something, and they just aren't ever seen again.
YOU DON'T SAY.
BARK! BARK!
BARK!
SHUGGIE! SHUT UP!
Ugh, they've been so *naughty* lately.
Kirby's been limping a lot when he comes home from the dog park... and I need to take Shuggie to the vet.
His eye is all irritated, I'm wondering if he didn't get into something and get *pink* eye...

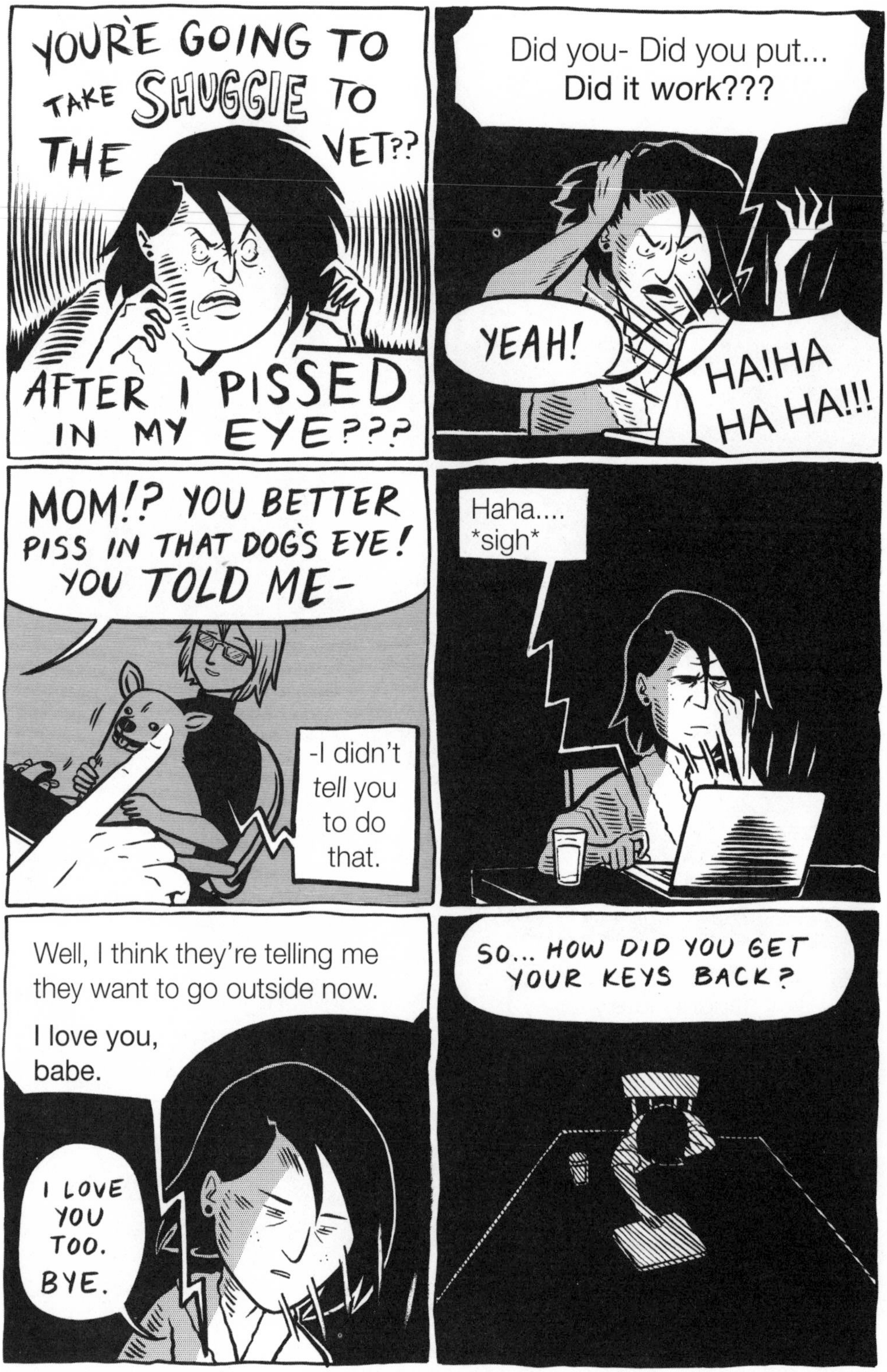
YOU'RE GOING TO TAKE SHUGGIE TO THE VET??
AFTER I PISSED IN MY EYE???
Did you- Did you put...
Did it work???
YEAH!
HA!HA HA HA!!!
MOM!? YOU BETTER PISS IN THAT DOG'S EYE! YOU TOLD ME-
-I didn't *tell* you to do that.
Haha....
sigh
Well, I think they're telling me they want to go outside now.
I love you, babe.
I LOVE YOU TOO. BYE.
SO... HOW DID YOU GET YOUR KEYS BACK?

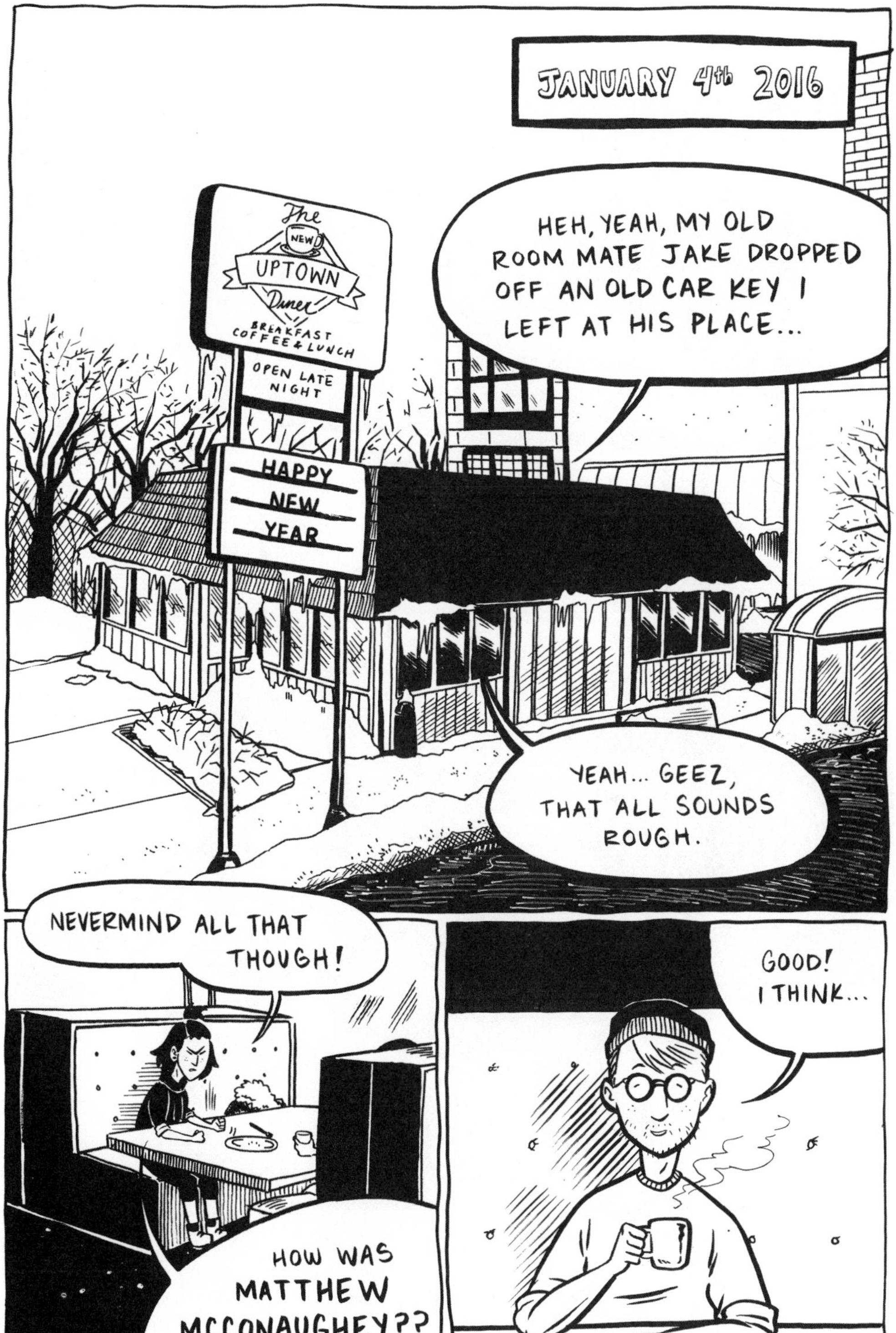
JANUARY 4th 2016
The NEW UPTOWN Diner
BREAKFAST COFFEE & LUNCH
OPEN LATE NIGHT
HAPPY NEW YEAR
HEH, YEAH, MY OLD ROOM MATE JAKE DROPPED OFF AN OLD CAR KEY I LEFT AT HIS PLACE...
YEAH... GEEZ, THAT ALL SOUNDS ROUGH.
NEVERMIND ALL THAT THOUGH!
HOW WAS MATTHEW MCCONAUGHEY??
GOOD! I THINK...

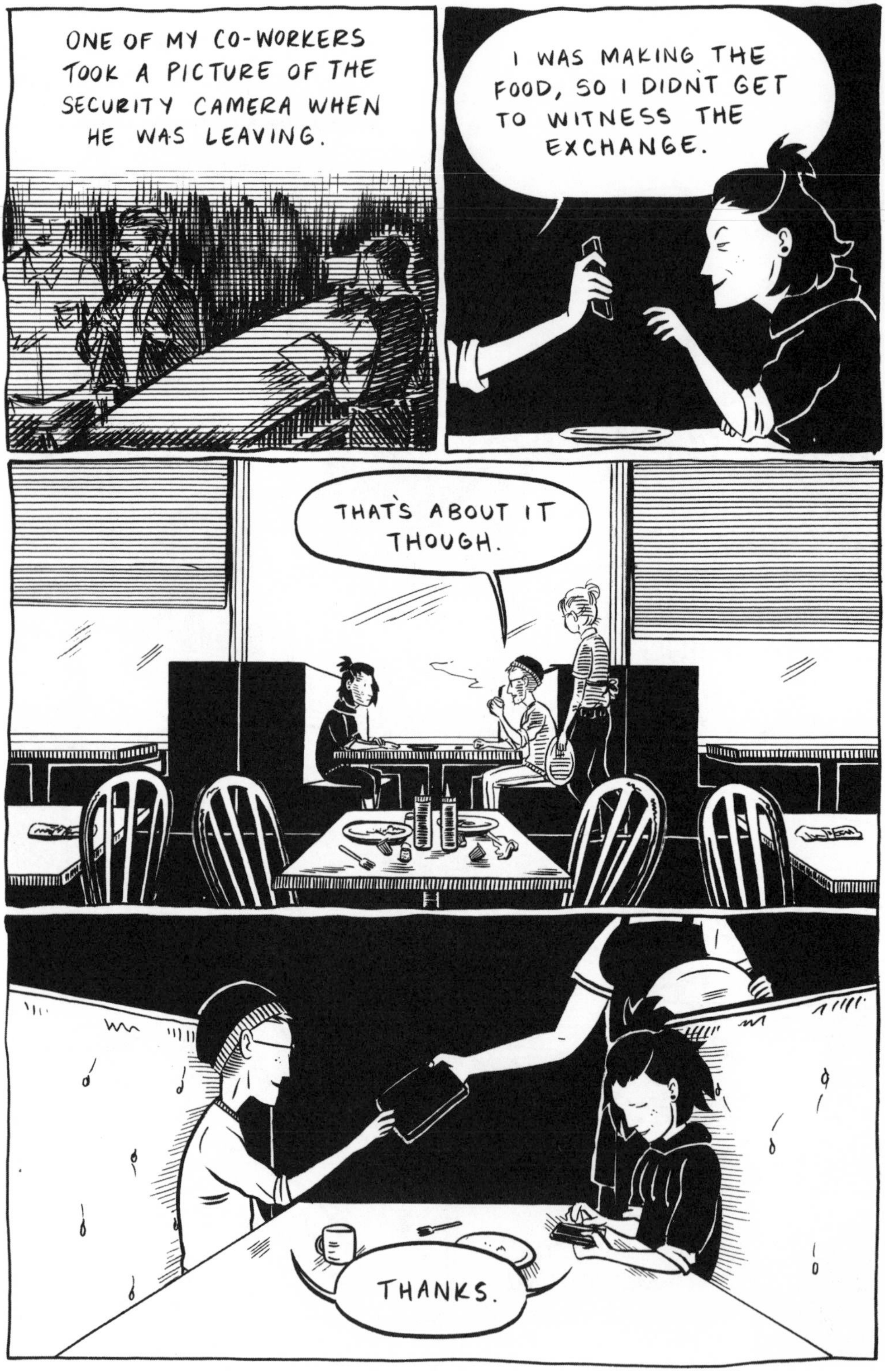
ONE OF MY CO-WORKERS TOOK A PICTURE OF THE SECURITY CAMERA WHEN HE WAS LEAVING.
I WAS MAKING THE FOOD, SO I DIDN'T GET TO WITNESS THE EXCHANGE.
THAT'S ABOUT IT THOUGH.
THANKS.

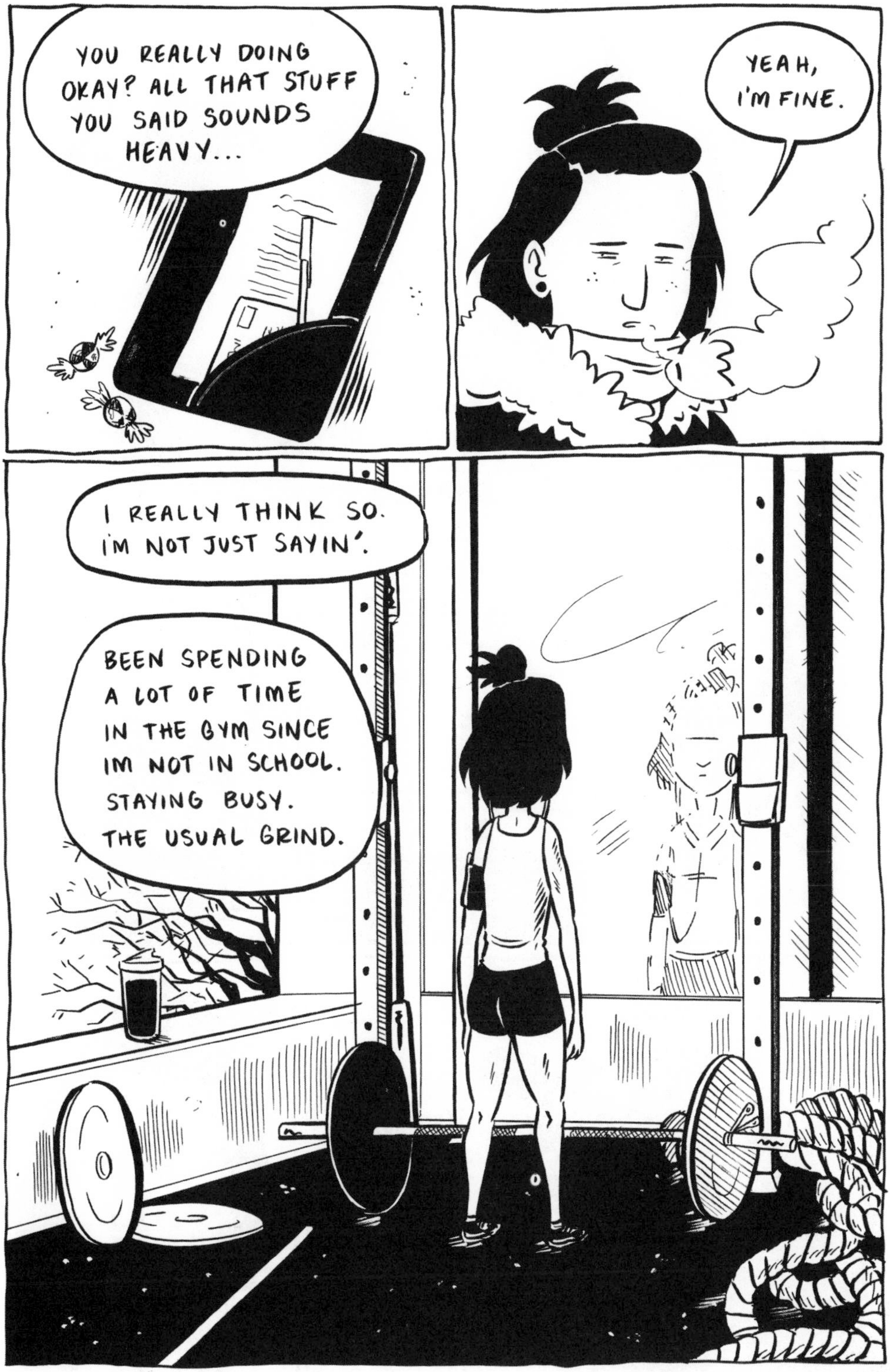
YOU REALLY DOING OKAY? ALL THAT STUFF YOU SAID SOUNDS HEAVY...
YEAH, I'M FINE.
I REALLY THINK SO. I'M NOT JUST SAYIN'.
BEEN SPENDING A LOT OF TIME IN THE GYM SINCE IM NOT IN SCHOOL. STAYING BUSY. THE USUAL GRIND.

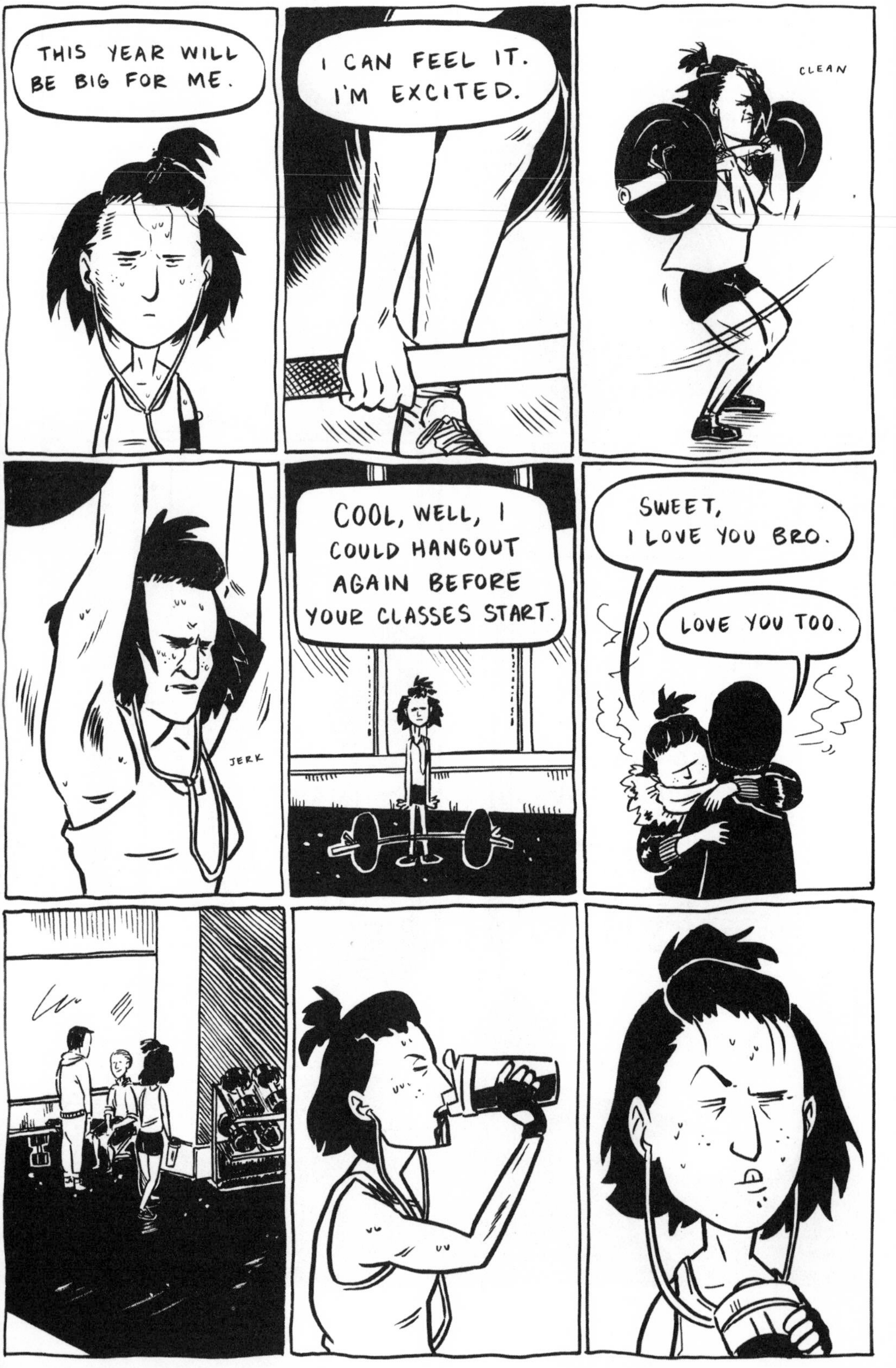

THIS YEAR WILL BE BIG FOR ME.
I CAN FEEL IT. I'M EXCITED.
CLEAN
JERK
COOL, WELL, I COULD HANGOUT AGAIN BEFORE YOUR CLASSES START.
SWEET, I LOVE YOU BRO.
LOVE YOU TOO.

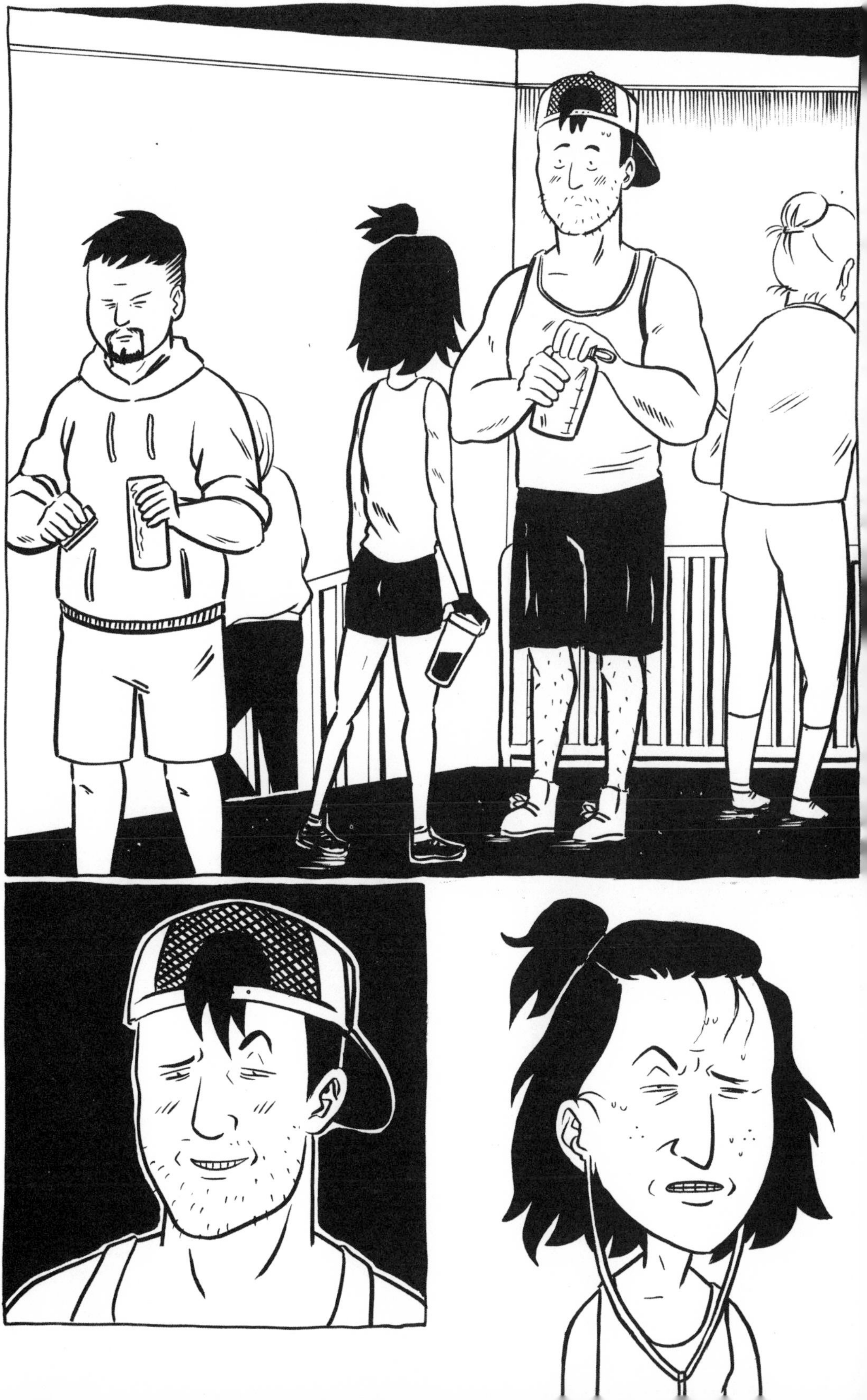

COMING FALL 2020!

PREVIEW OF *DESPERATE PLEASURES*
MS HARKNESS' FOLLOW-UP TO *TINDERELLA*

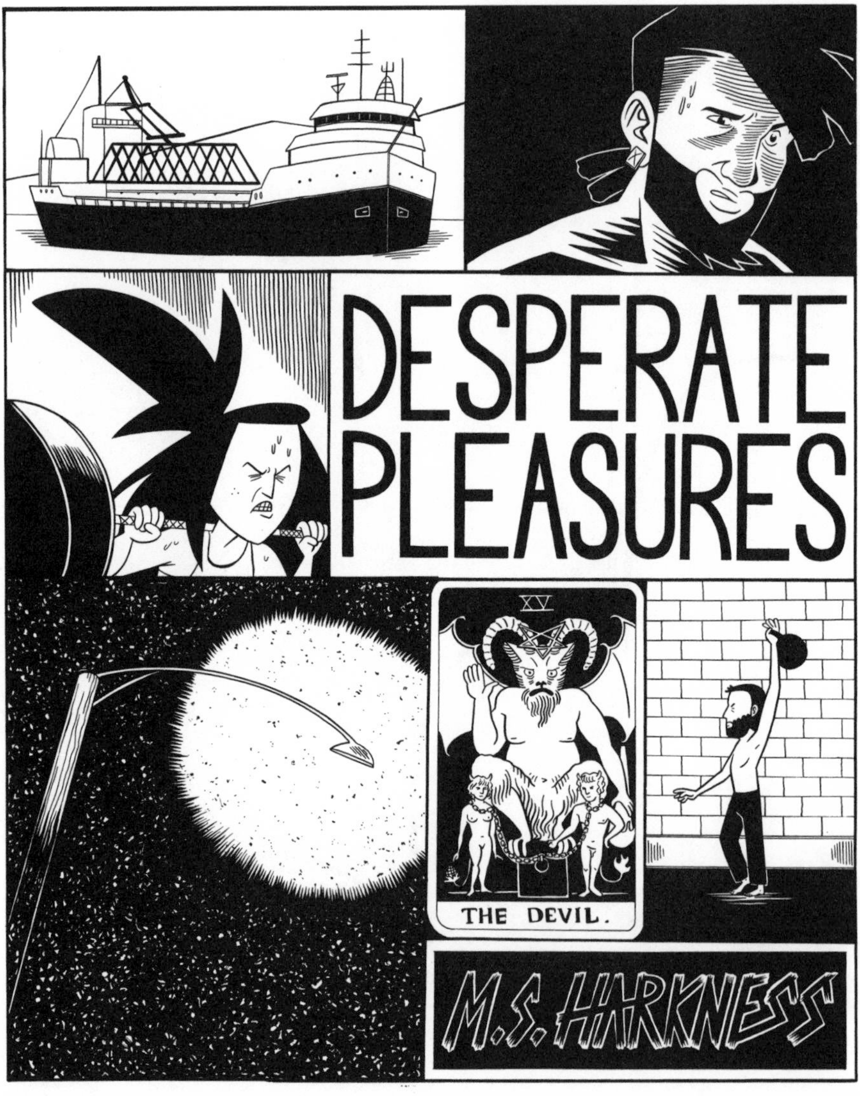
DESPERATE PLEASURES
XV
THE DEVIL.
M.S. HARKNESS

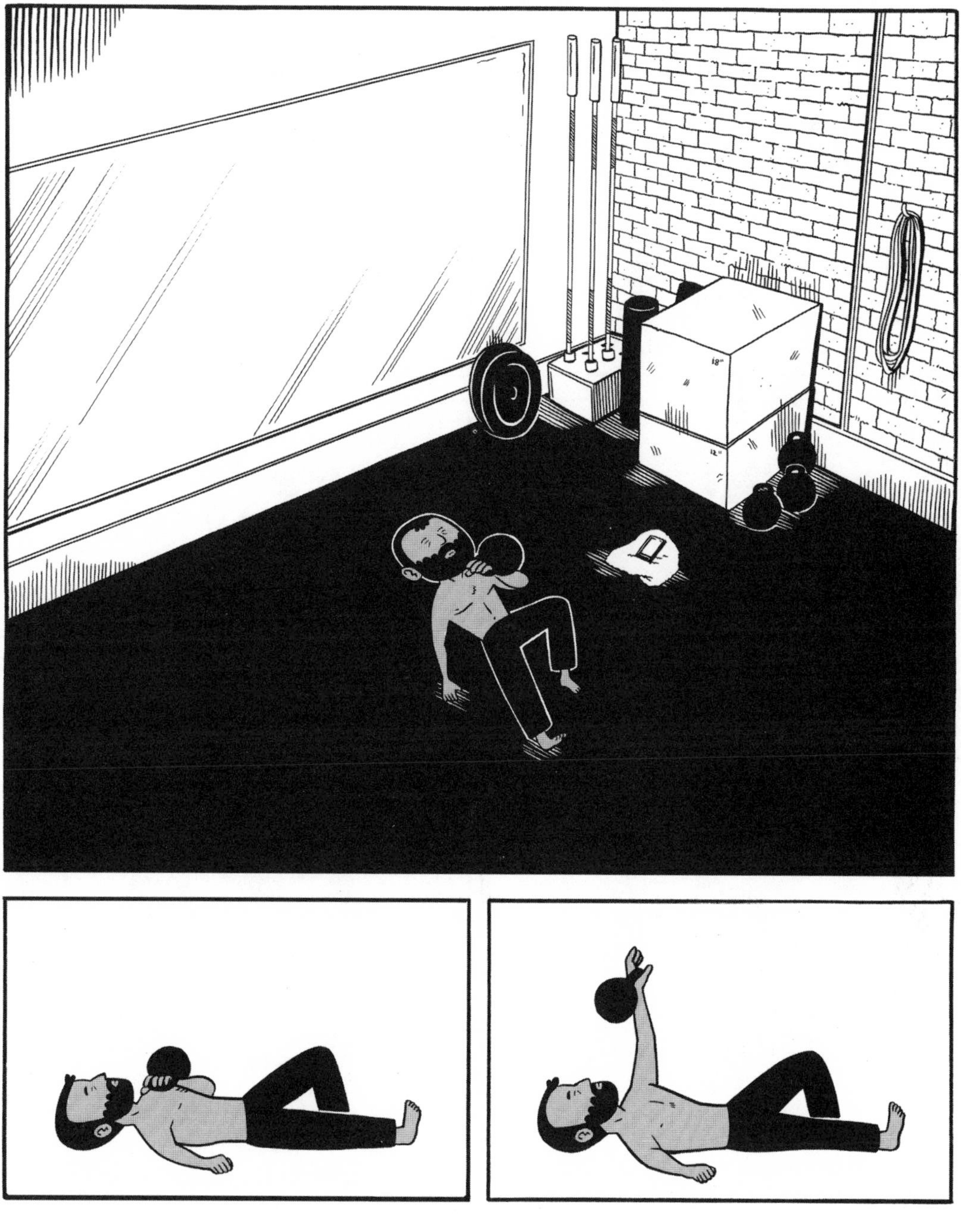
18"
12"

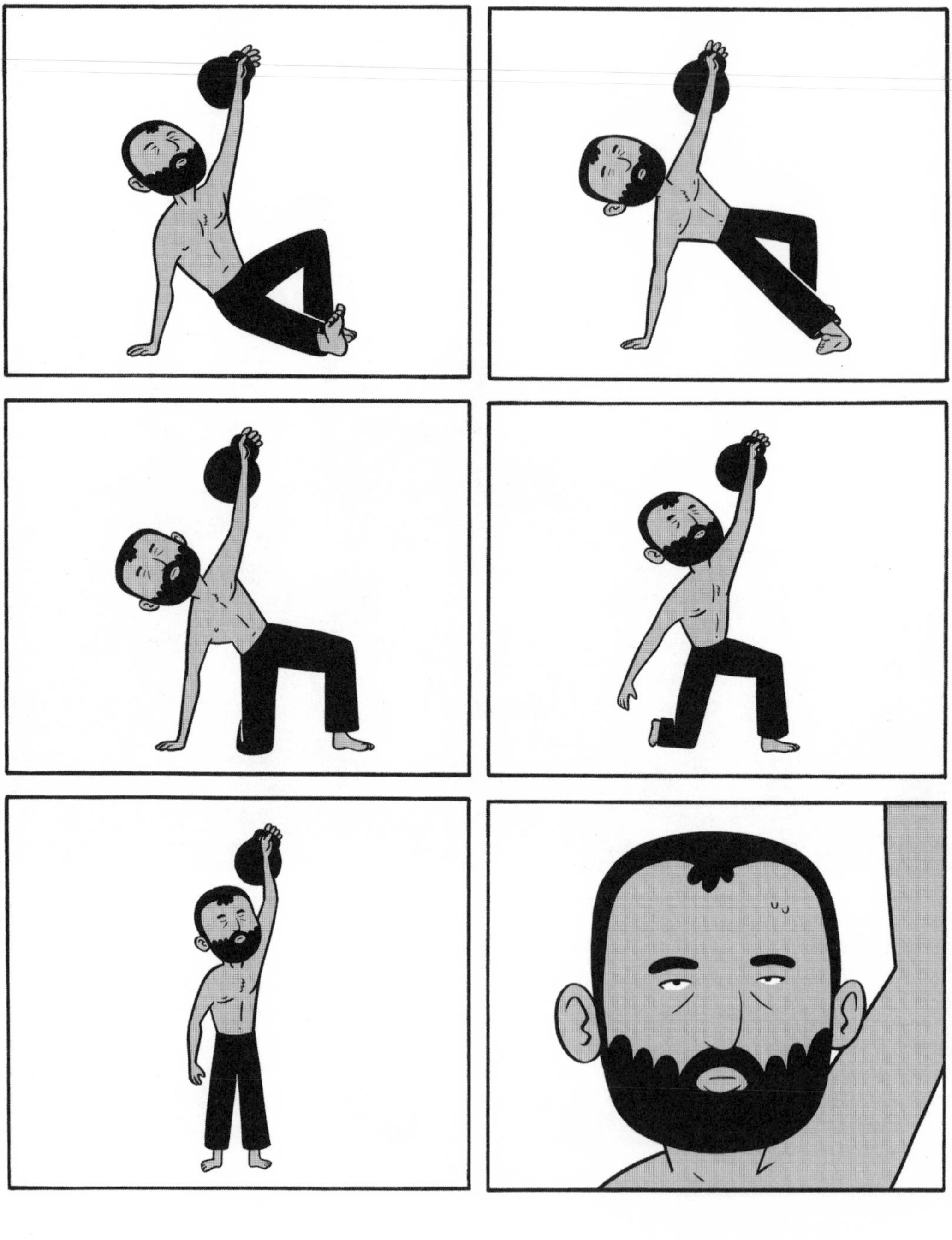

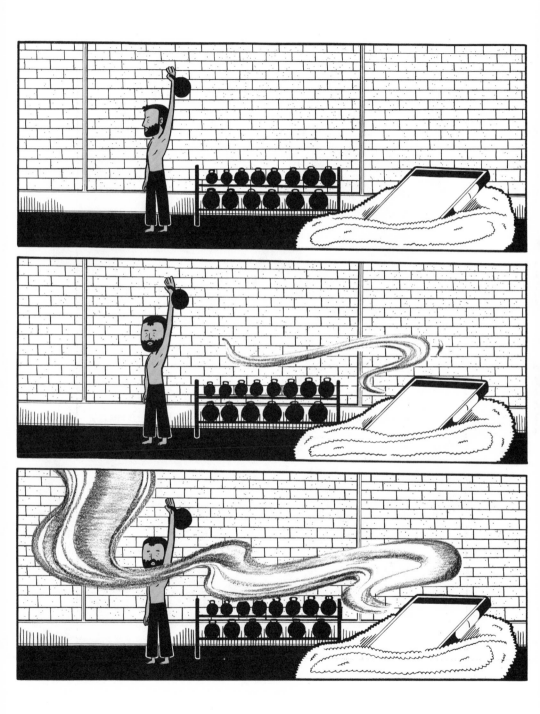

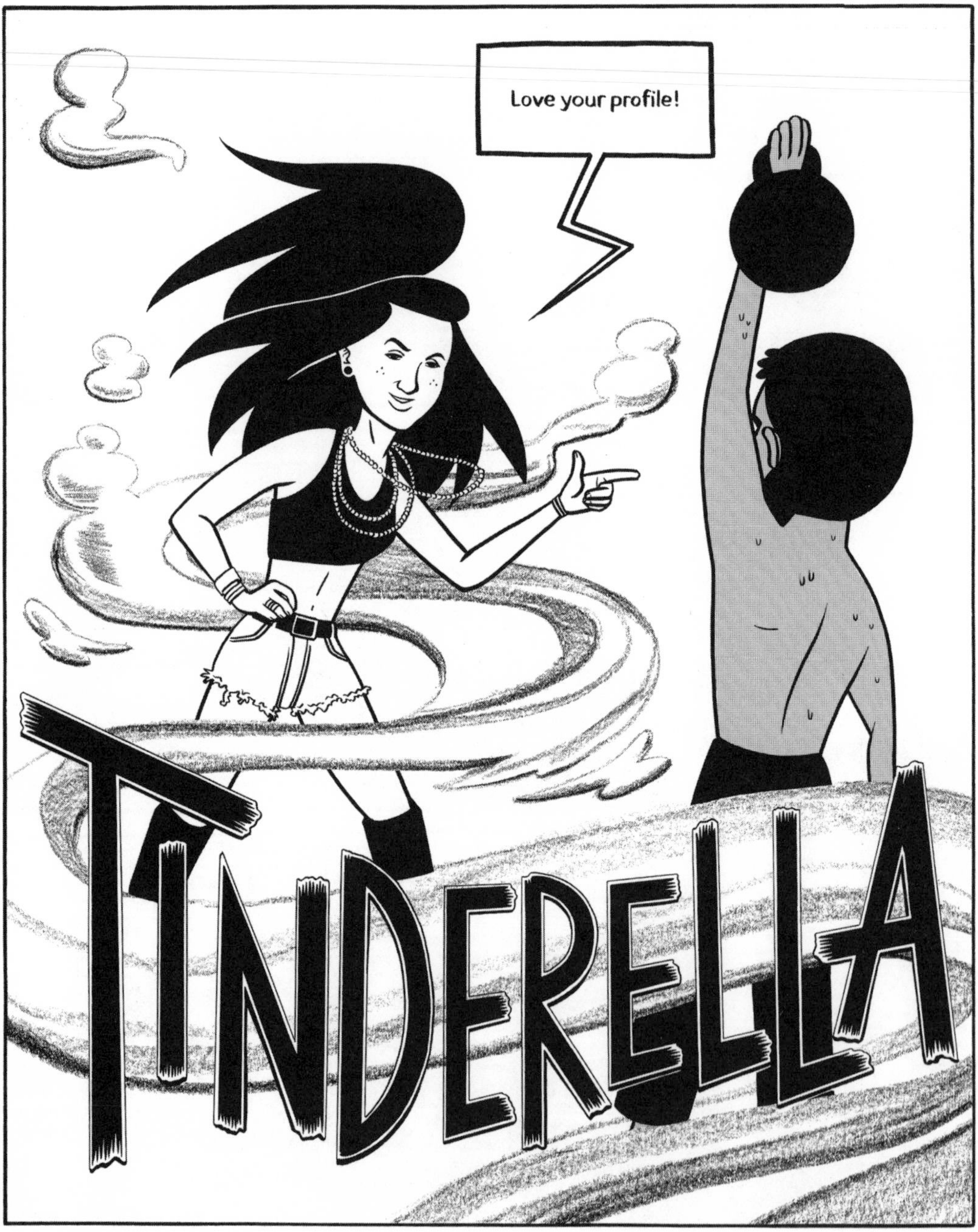
Love your profile!
TINDERELLA

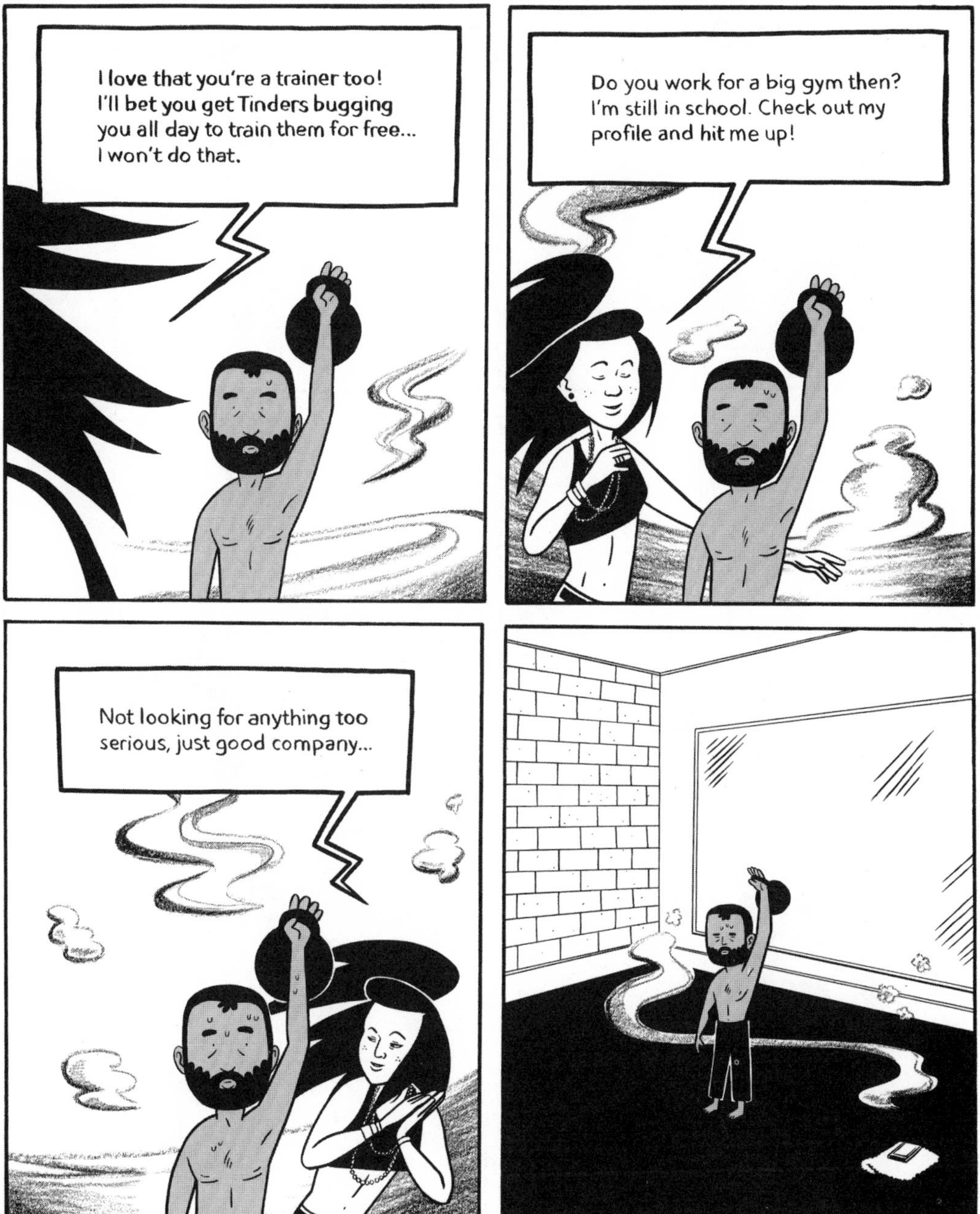
I love that you're a trainer too! I'll bet you get Tinders bugging you all day to train them for free... I won't do that.
Do you work for a big gym then? I'm still in school. Check out my profile and hit me up!
Not looking for anything too serious, just good company...

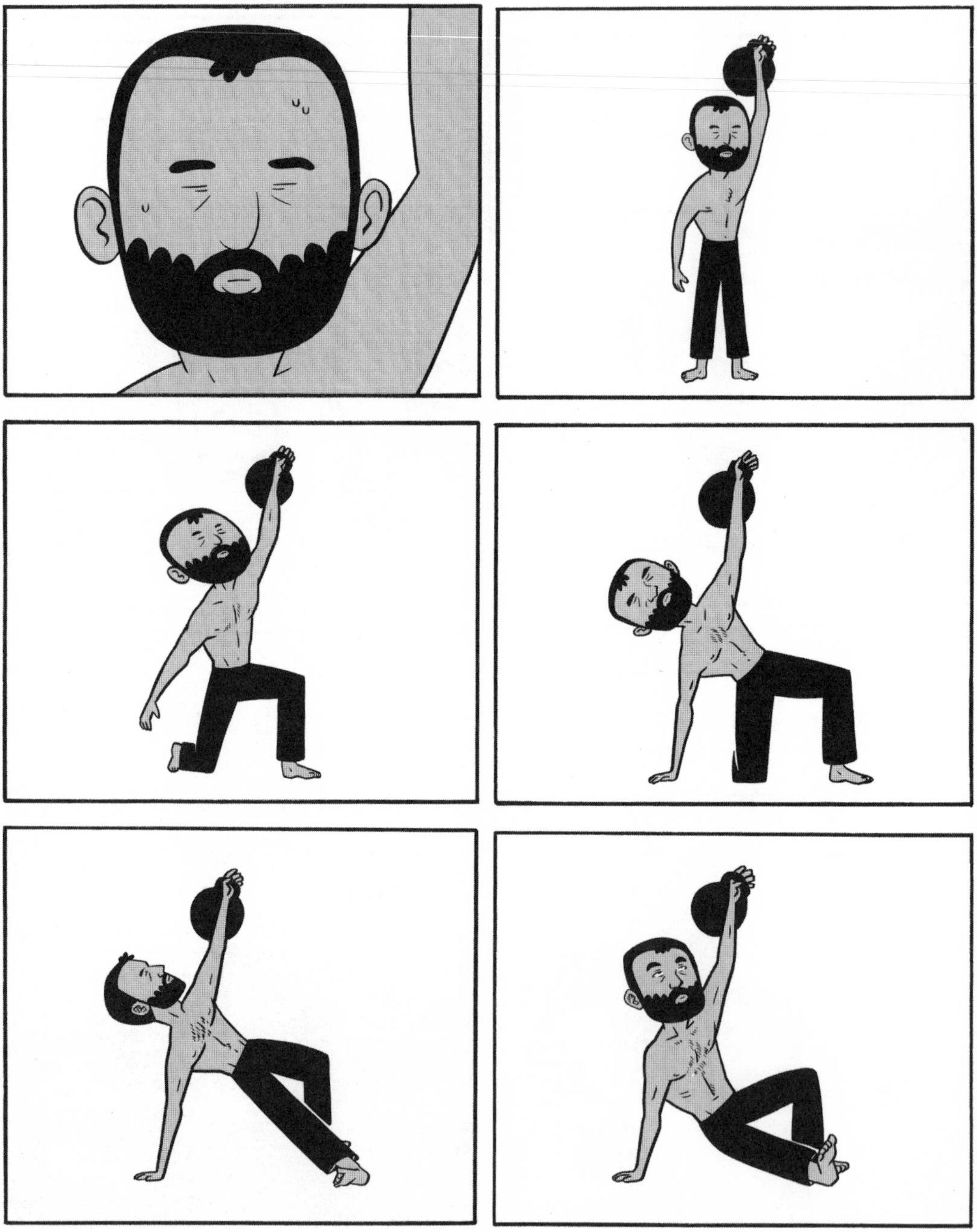

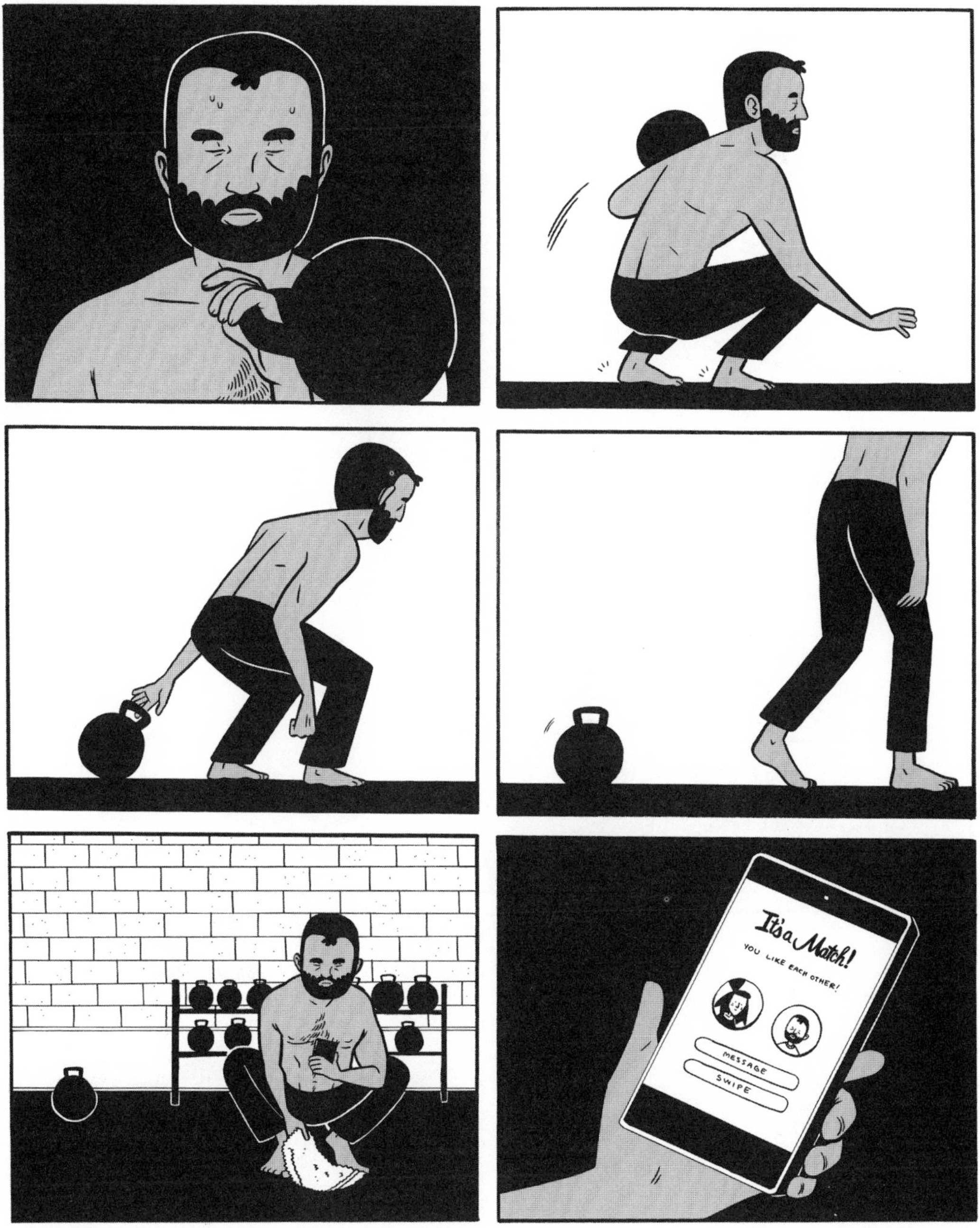
It's a Match!
YOU LIKE EACH OTHER!
MESSAGE
SWIPE

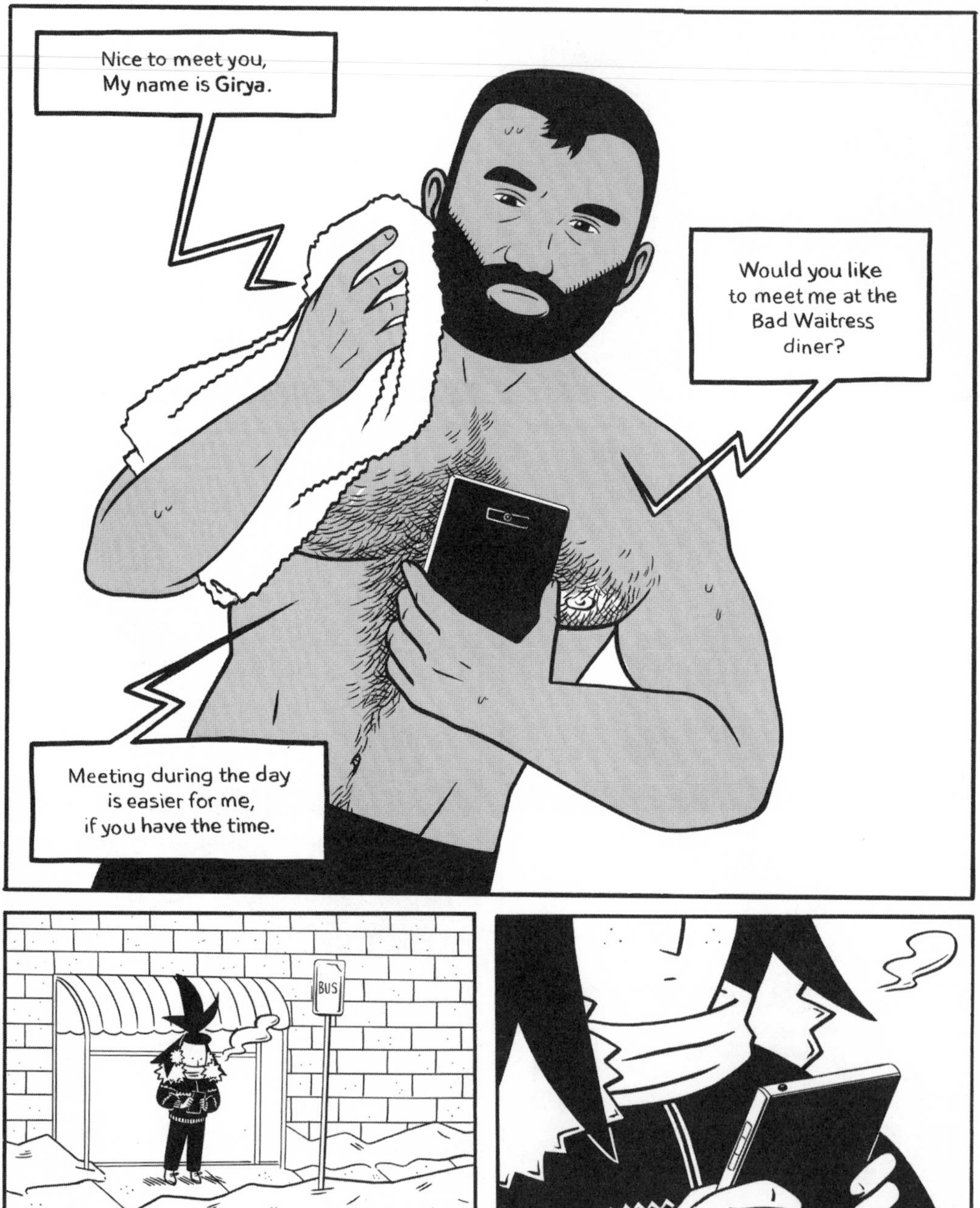
Nice to meet you,
My name is Girya.
Would you like to meet me at the Bad Waitress diner?
Meeting during the day is easier for me, if you have the time.
BUS

TO BE CONTINUED…

TO BE CONTINUED...

IN *DESPERATE PLEASURES*

M.S. Harkness weaves in and out of non-relationships, drug dealing, and sex work with the subtlety of a blunt axe. She's constantly searching for care and fulfillment, but never gets it quite right. *Desperate Pleasures* is a fearless autobiographical account of a young woman's difficult relationships caused by years of trauma and abuse. Uncomfortably intimate, filled with dark humor, *Desperate Pleasures* is unrelenting – and M.S. Harkness' best work to date.

October 6, 2020

ISBN: 978-1-941250-4-26

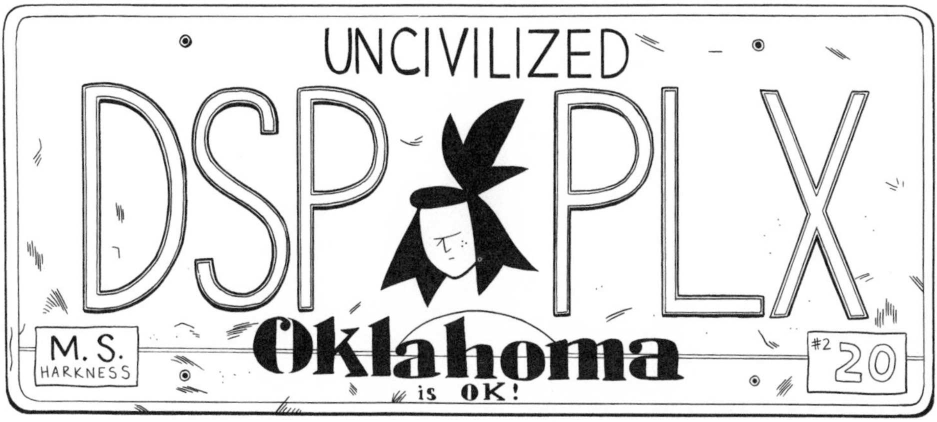
UNCIVILIZED
DSP PLX
M.S.
HARKNESS
Oklahoma
is OK!
#2
20

UNCIVILIZED BOOKS CATALOGUE

Holy Hannah by Will Dinski
Everything is Flammable by Gabrielle Bell
Cecil & Jordan in New York by Gabriele Bell
The Voyeurs by Gabrielle Bell
Truth is Fragmentary by Gabrielle Bell
Ginseng Roots by Craig Thompson
For Real #1 by James Romberger
Cannonball by Kelsey Wroten
A Book for Sad Pets by Kristin Tipping
Sweet Little Cunt: The Graphic Work of Julie Doucet by Anne Elizabeth Moore
Cartoon Dialectics by Tom Kaczynski
Incidents in the Night by David B.; Translated by Brian Evenson
An Iranian Metamorphosis by Mana Neyestani
War of Streets and Houses by Sophie Yanow
Amazing Facts & Beyond by Kevin Huizenga & Dan Zettwoch
Sammy The Mouse by Zak Sally
True Swamp by Jon Lewis
Eel Mansions by Derek Van Gieson
Over the Wall & Stonebreaker by Peter Wartman
Ed vs. Yummy Fur by Brian Evenson
One Dirty Tree by Noah Van Sciver
Pascin by Joann Sfar
Jacob Bladders and the State of the Art by Roman Muradov